That's Inter

But What's The Law In Pennsylvania?

Lee S. Weinberg
University of Pittsburgh

David M. Korman
University of Pittsburgh

KENDALL/HUNT PUBLISHING COMPANY
2460 Kerper Boulevard P.O. Box 539 Dubuque, Iowa 52004-0539

TABLE OF CONTENTS

Preface

The idea for this project grew out of our years of teaching undergraduates in an Introduction to Legal Studies course where curious students have pleaded with us hundreds of times, "That's interesting, but what's the law in Pennsylvania?" While a variety of good undergraduate casebooks are in use, we have yet to find one to help us in answering this omnipresent question. So despite the obvious market limitations of such a volume, we decided to give it a try in the hopes that other instructors in Pennsylvania will find it useful either as a companion to a larger text or as one of several smaller assigned books in introductory law courses. We have tried to find interesting (even entertaining) Pennsylvania cases which illustrate the current state of the law in Pennsylvania on a variety of issues raised in standard introductory courses in law and legal studies.

As lawyers, we hope you understand our uncontrollable urge to disclaim all potential liability. First, we hope that students are not too disappointed to learn that this book will not suffice as total preparation for the practice of law in Pennsylvania. Second, we have edited the cases and statutes included in the book and remind the reader that only the official documents should be relied on for accurate statements of the relevant principles of law. We have, for example, edited out many internal citations and footnotes, as well as entire sections of cases and statutes which we believe tangential to the specific issues we have chosen to address. Third, readers are reminded that the law can be tricky. Lawyers can often distinguish cases to the puzzlement of laypersons, just as jurists often distinguish cases to the puzzlement of lawyers - and the ecstasy of professors of law. Finally, remember that the law is constantly changing either by statute or case law. Inasmuch as we have attempted to include legal issues which are controverial and uncertain, we anticipate that some changes in the law will occur even before this volume is published. Thus, the prudent reader, who is seeking particular legal guidance should, of course, turn to an attorney for advice.

Finally, we would welcome the comments of students or instructors as to our choices of issues and cases. Future editions will endeavor to take into account what we are certain to be helpful suggestions. Please send your reactions to us c/o the Graduate School of Public and International Affairs, University of Pittsburgh, Pittsburgh, PA 15260 or via electronic mail (weinberg@vms.cis.pitt.edu or (roman2@vms.cis.pitt.edu).

LSW
DMK

Acknowledgments

We would like to thank Richard L. Rosenzweig, Esq. and Stephen Underwood for their assistance in the collection of the cases and statutes in this volume.

The Right To Die: Does a criminal committed to a mental hospital have the right to starve himself to death?

While the U.S. Supreme Court decision in *Cruzan v. Director, Missouri Department of Health*, 110 S.Ct. 2841 (1990), offered guidelines for when food and water may be withheld from a person in a persistent vegetative state, new issues surrounding the "right to die" arise on a regular basis. In 1990, the Commonwealth Court was faced with an unusual set of facts concerning an individual's "right to die." An inmate at the Farview State Hospital, a state institution for the mentally ill which includes a forensic unit for mentally ill persons who have been convicted of crimes and who require treatment, refused both medical treatment and food and water on the grounds that he wanted to "meet his maker." He argued in effect that while he may have been "committable," that he still was "competent" and that the state had no right to forcibly treat and feed him.

It is important to realize the differences in the tests used to establish whether a person is "competent" versus whether the person is "committable." In general, a person is "committable" under the Mental Health Procedures Act if he poses a clear and present danger to himself or others. The issue of "incompetency" however, centers on whether the person understands his situation. Does he understand that if he does not eat he will die? As the court notes, a competent adult generally has the right to refuse treatment and food. Should a person lose this right once they are convicted of a crime? Prison and hospital administrators agreed as to his competency, but argued that he had no right to starve himself to death even if he was competent.

Commonwealth of Pennsylvania v. Joseph Kallinger
134 Pa. Cmwlth. 415 (1990)

Judge Pellegrini delivered the opinion of the court.

The Commonwealth of Pennsylvania, Department of Public Welfare, (Department), Farview State Hospital (Farview), files this Request for Special Emergency Relief asking this Court for a Declaratory Judgment authorizing the involuntary administration of necessary nutrition and medical treatment in order to preserve the safety, health and life of Joseph Kallinger (Kallinger).

We are called upon to decide a sensitive matter which is without precedent in this Commonwealth. Joseph Kallinger wants to starve himself to death. The Department, who has custody, wants to force him to involuntarily receive food through a nasogastric tube and other medical treatment. We must decide if the Department has such right.

The current dilemma developed after Kallinger was recently readmitted to Farview on May 17, 1990, from the State Correctional Institution at Huntingdon (Huntingdon). On June 22, 1990, he stated, as a result of his vision of Christ in a toilet bowl telling him to join him, that he would refuse to eat or drink, and that he desires to "meet his maker." He has also refused treatment for an abscess on his foot. On June 30, 1990, Kallinger agreed to be transferred to Wayne Memorial Hospital in Wayne County, Pennsylvania, in order to have intravenous fluids, including antibiotics, administered to him. However, he continued in his refusal to accept nutrition and other medical treatment.

On July 3, 1990, the Department filed an action for Declaratory Relief in the Court of Common Pleas of Wayne County, seeking authority to provide necessary treatment, nutrition and hydration to Kallinger. On that day, the trial court entered a preliminary order permitting the Department to do so. However, on July 10, 1990, after holding a hearing on the matter, the trial court dissolved its preliminary order and determined that Kallinger was competent and could reject nutrition and hydration necessary to preserve his health, safety and life.

The Department filed a Petition For Review seeking Special Emergency Relief pursuant to the original jurisdiction of this Court, and seeking review of the trial court's Order pursuant to our appellate jurisdiction. Sections 761 and 762 of the Judicial Code, 42 Pa.C.S. § 761, 762.

On July 13, 1990, this Court granted the Department's request for a preliminary injunction, ordering that Kallinger may be involuntarily administered medical treatment, nutrition and hydration, pending further adjudication. On July 18, 1990, following a hearing, a second Order was issued continuing the involuntary medication and feeding of Kallinger pending final adjudication of this matter.

The Department offered testimony and evidence that if Kallinger is allowed to starve to death, this would have major negative repercussions on the prison and mental health systems; that Kallinger's death would have adverse effects on other patients, their families and the staff of the mental hospital; and other patients may also "copy-cat" Kallinger's actions.

Kallinger contends that despite such adverse repercussions to the Commonwealth, he should be allowed to die if he so chooses. He argues that his right to privacy overrides any interests of the Commonwealth because the use of a nasogastric tube to feed him is an overly intrusive procedure which could last a number of years. We note at the outset that Kallinger is committed to Farview, a mental hospital for the criminally insane. He suffers from a serious mental illness, diagnosed by Mokarram Jafri, M.D., as a Borderline Personality Disorder. However, he is competent in the sense that he fully understands his decision and realizes that death will result if he continues to refuse nutrition and medical treatment.

We also recognize that Kallinger, through this action, may be attempting to manipulate the system in order to stay at Farview rather than return to Huntingdon. His authorization of his attorneys to enter appearances on his behalf -- one to say that he has the right to die, the other to say the state had an obligation to make him stay alive -- is certainly part of that manipulation. Although Kallinger has in the past and is now manipulating the system in which he finds himself, if the Department is not allowed to involuntarily provide him with nutrition and medical care, we assume that Kallinger will indeed starve himself to death.

While Kallinger is sufficiently competent to make a decision to starve himself to death, this is not a "right to die" case in the usual sense. There has been much public debate and court activity over whether such a right exists and in what circumstances it exists, and these cases involve decisions made by enfranchised citizens or someone acting on their behalf, that their substantial rights of privacy allows them to make that decision. What this case concerns is whether the Commonwealth's interest in an orderly administration of the prison system is paramount over any residual right of privacy that Kallinger has which would make it an invasion of privacy on the part of the Commonwealth to force feed him.

The narrow issue then presented to us is whether the Commonwealth has a right to force a competent prisoner within the Commonwealth's penal system to receive involuntary medical treatment and nutrition and hydration through a nasogastric feeding tube. To decide this issue, a balancing test is employed, balancing the Commonwealth's interests against the prisoner's remaining right to privacy. *Matthews v. Eldridge*, 424 U.S. 319, 96 S.Ct. 893, 47 L.Ed.2d 18 (1976).

Kallinger argues that his right to privacy is superior to the interests of the Commonwealth, no matter what effect it may have on the prison system. He argues that as a prisoner, he did not give up his right to starve himself, citing the Supreme Court of Georgia decision in *Zant v. Prevatte*, 248 Ga. 832, 286 S.E.2d 715 (1982). In that case, the Georgia court held that a competent prisoner had a right to starve himself to death.

The court, in ruling that the state does not have the right to force medical treatment and food on a competent prisoner, stated: A prisoner does not relinquish his constitutional right to privacy because of his status as a prisoner. The state has no power to monitor this man's physical condition against his will; neither does it have the right to feed him to prevent his death from starvation if that is his wish . . . . The state can incarcerate one who has violated the law and, in certain circumstances, even take his life. But it has no right to destroy a person's will by frustrating his attempt to die if necessary to make a point. *Zant*, 248 Ga. at 833-834, 286 S.E.2d at 716-717.

Kallinger further argues that the procedure for forcing nutrition and hydration into him is overly intrusive. The procedure which the Department has been and wishes to continue using is a nasogastric tube which is inserted through the nose into the stomach. This tube will remain in his body and will have to be frequently removed and replaced. Kallinger correctly points out that there are several risks involved in this procedure, including internal bleeding and possibly even death.

While admitting that there are risks to Kallinger as a result of his forced feeding, the Commonwealth argues that its interest in prison security and discipline, the morale of medical and custodial staff, as well as the law of this Commonwealth, far outweigh any right of privacy that Kallinger may have. We agree.

The Commonwealth has an overwhelming interest in maintaining prison security, order and discipline. The Supreme Court has stated that "maintaining institutional security and preserving internal order and discipline are essential goals that may require limitation or retraction of the detained constitutional rights of . . . convicted prisoners." *Bell v. Wolfish*, 441 U.S. at 546, 99 S.Ct. at 1878. This lack of a reasonable expectation of privacy deprives the convicts of Fourth Amendment rights in their prison cells.

Prison officials are given a wide range of discretion in the promulgation and enforcement of rules to govern the prison community in order to maintain security, order and discipline. Individual freedoms may be curtailed whenever prison officials, in exercise of their informed discretion, reasonably conclude that their exercise possesses the likelihood of disrupting prison order or stability or otherwise interfering with the legitimate penological objectives of the prison environment.

Other jurisdictions confronted with the same situation have held that compelled nutrition and medical treatment is proper because of the strong state interest in orderly prison administration outweighs any convict's residual rights. In *Von Holden v. Chapman*, 87 A.D.2d 66, 450 N.Y.S.2d 623 (1982), Mark David Chapman, serving a twenty year to life term for the murder of former Beatle John Lennon, attempted to starve himself to death while in a mental institution. The Supreme Court of New York, Appellate Division, in allowing involuntary feeding through a nasogastric tube, found that the legitimate interest in prison security and administration clearly included the right to prevent a prisoner's suicide.

In *Commissioner of Correction v. Myers*, 379 Mass. 255, 399 N.E.2d 452 (1979), the Massachusetts Supreme Court allowed forced hemodialysis to a prisoner suffering a kidney condition on the basis of maintaining prison order. The court stated that imprisonment imposed severe limitations on the prisoner's right to privacy and bodily integrity.

In the present case, the uncontradicted testimony shows that if Kallinger would be permitted to die, other patients at Farview would almost certainly copy the same tactic, manipulating the system to get a change of conditions, possibly resulting in their death. Allowing a prisoner to die will cause other patients to become angry and lose faith in the system and make treatment more difficult; it may even spawn rioting at Farview or from prisoners at Huntingdon or other state institutions. It is clear that allowing a prisoner to starve to death while in state custody would have an unpredictable negative effect on the security and order within the prison system.

Besides preserving order with the prison system, the Commonwealth has a strong interest in maintaining the health of prisoners in its custody. The obligation of the Commonwealth to provide for the health and safety of the inmates in their custody is derived from two very important interests: the preservation of human life and the prevention of suicide. The preservation of human life is of great interest to the state. . . .

The Commonwealth has a duty under the Eighth Amendment to protect the health and welfare of those persons in its custody, and may be cast in civil damages for its failure to observe such duty, Furthermore, the Commonwealth has a duty to "provid[e] appropriate medical treatment to reduce the danger that an inmate suffering from a serious mental disorder represents to himself or others." *Washington v. Harper*, 110 S.Ct. 1028, 1030, 108 L.Ed.2d 178 (1990).

The United States Supreme Court in *Washington v. Harper* allowed the forced administration of antipsychotic drugs to a prisoner on the basis that the state's interest in providing appropriate medical treatment outweighed the inmate's liberty interest. The Supreme Court found that the state has not only an interest, but an "obligation to provide prisoners with medical treatment consistent not only with their own medical interests, but also with the needs of the institution.". . .

The second related state interest is the Commonwealth's duty to prevent suicide. "American law has always accorded the State the power to prevent, by force if necessary, suicide -- including suicide by refusing to take appropriate measures necessary to preserve one's life." *Cruzan v. Director, Missouri Department of Health*, 110 S.Ct. at 2859, 111 L.Ed.2d 224 (1990).

Pennsylvania public policy strongly opposes the commission of suicide. Pennsylvania law makes it a crime to aid or solicit another person to commit suicide. Crimes Code, 18 Pa.C.S. § 2505. A police officer also has the right to use force to prevent a suicide from occurring. 18 Pa.C.S. § 508(d)(1). By asking the Commonwealth to stand by and watch him die while it has custody and control over him, Kallinger is asking it to aid and abet his suicide.

The leading case in support of a state's duty to prevent suicide is *Von Holden v. Chapman*. The Supreme Court of New York, Appellate Division, in rejecting Chapman's right to privacy claim, held that "it is self-evident that the right of privacy does not include the right to commit suicide . . . . To characterize a person's self-destructive acts as entitled to Constitutional protection would be ludicrous."

Since Kallinger is a patient at Farview, the Commonwealth's interest in maintaining the integrity of the medical and psychiatric professions is also of great importance. Several courts have held that the integrity of the medical profession is an interest which should be balanced against a person's privacy right to refuse medical treatment or nutrition.

If Kallinger is allowed to starve himself to death, repercussions would be felt throughout the medical and psychiatric professions. Dr. Jafri, Chief of Psychiatric Services at Farview, stated that Kallinger's death would "have a negative impact upon the staff [in] that we could not carry out a moral and ethical obligation of keeping a patient alive." Jack Wolford, M.D., Psychiatric Director for the Department, testified that "it would be devastating to the staff and the staff morale if they had to allow someone to cease living, virtually by their own hand, while under our care."

Furthermore, if he is allowed to die, other patients and their families would have serious doubts about whether the psychiatric staff is providing their patients with proper psychiatric treatment and medical care. Dr. Jafri testified that his death "will not encourage the confidence of their patients in our ability to manage and take care their needs, as [well as] the moral confidence of the public." Dr. Wolford stated that the patients "would lose trust in the system of care."

The Commonwealth of Pennsylvania has an overwhelming interest in the orderly administration of its prison system. The Commonwealth must maintain prison security, order and discipline. It must also fulfill its duty to provide proper medical care to the inmates, thus preserving life and preventing suicide. These vital interests, along with the need to preserve the integrity of the physicians and psychiatrists working within the penal system, clearly outweigh any diminished right to privacy held by Kallinger.

Accordingly, we order that Farview can and must continue to provide appropriate nutrition through a nasogastric tube and appropriate medical care to Joseph Kallinger so long as he continues to refuse nutrition and medical treatment. Kallinger shall remain committed to Farview until such time as the medical and psychiatric staff feel it's appropriate for him to return to a State Correctional Institution.

The Living Will: How can a person retain control over his medical care when he is unable to communicate his desires?

As the U.S. Supreme Court indicated in *Cruzan v. Director, Missouri Department of Health*, 110 S. Ct. 2841 (1990), a competent person's desires concerning his (or her) medical care (and its termination) will generally be honored if effectively communicated. The Supreme Court reasoned in that case that while a state has a legitimate interest in preserving life, such an interest is outweighed by a "clear and convincing" statement of a competent individual's wishes.

In 1991, the Pennsylvania legislature passed "Living Will" legislation allowing a person to so designate in an Advance Medical Directive his (or her) choices) of medical care should he (or she) become terminal or in a state of permanent unconsciousness. The statute provides specific language and procedures for how to execute an such a document.

Another means in Pennsylvania for dealing with this very difficult situations is through the use of a "Durable Power of Attorney." This document appoints a surrogate -- or agent -- to make decisions for the donor of the power, should the donor be unable to communicate. A sample of such an instrument follows the statute. The benefit of this instrument is that there are a myriad of medical conditions from which a person may suffer, and (assuming you have confidence in your surrogate) it may be better to have the surrogate make the decision based on the best available evidence at the time, rather than to try to prospectively "cover all the bases" with an Advanced Medical Directive as provided for in the statute.

Many Pennsylvania residents are opting for the consistent and congruent use of both instruments as the most effective means of assuring that their wishes will be given full legal effect.

AN ACT

Establishing a procedure whereby a person may execute in advance a written declaration indicating to a physician the person's desire for a physician to initiate, continue, withhold or withdraw certain life-sustaining medical treatment in the event the person is incompetent and is determined to be in a terminal condition or to be permanently unconscious; and providing penalties.

TABLE OF CONTENTS

Section 1. Short title.

This act shall be known and may be cited as the Advance Directive for Health Care Act.

Section 2. Legislative findings and intent.

(a) Findings. The General Assembly finds that all competent adults have a qualified right to control decisions relating to their own medical care. This right is subject to certain interests of society, such as the maintenance of ethical standards in the medical profession and the preservation and protection of human life. Modern medical technological procedures make possible the prolongation of human life beyond natural limits. The application of some procedures to an individual suffering a difficult and uncomfortable process of dying may cause loss of patient dignity and secure only continuation of a precarious and burdensome prolongation of life.

(b) Intent. Nothing in this act is intended to condone, authorize or approve mercy killing, or to permit any affirmative or deliberate act or omission to end life other than as defined in this act. Furthermore, this act shall create no presumption concerning the intent of any person who has not executed a declaration to consent to the use or withholding of life-sustaining procedures in the event of a terminal condition or a state of permanent unconsciousness.

Section 3. Definitions.

The following words and phrases when used in this act shall have the meanings given to them in this section unless the context clearly indicates otherwise:

"Attending physician." The physician who has primary responsibility for the treatment and care of the declarant.

"Declarant." A person who makes a declaration in accordance with this act.

"Declaration." A written document, voluntarily executed by the declarant in accordance with this act.

"Health care provider." A person who is licensed by the laws of this Commonwealth to administer health care in the ordinary course of business or practice of a profession.

"Incompetent." The lack of sufficient capacity for a person to make or communicate decisions concerning himself.

"Life-sustaining treatment." Any medical procedure or intervention that, when administered to a qualified patient, will serve only to prolong the process of dying or to maintain the patient in a state of permanent unconsciousness. Life-sustaining treatment shall include nutrition and hydration administered by gastric tube or intravenously or any other artificial or invasive means if the declaration of the qualified patient so specifically provides.

"Permanently unconscious." A medical condition that has been diagnosed in accordance with currently accepted medical standards and with reasonable medical certainty as total and irreversible loss of consciousness and capacity for interaction with the environment. The term includes without limitation a persistent vegetative state or irreversible coma.

"Person." An individual, corporation, partnership, association, or Federal, State or local government or governmental agency.

"Qualified patient." A person who has executed a declaration and who has been determined to be in a terminal condition or to be permanently unconscious.

"Terminal condition." An incurable and irreversible medical condition caused by injury, disease or physical illness which will, in the opinion of the attending physician, to a reasonable degree of medical certainty, result in death regardless of the continued application of life-sustaining treatment.

Section 4. Declaration.

(a) Execution. An individual of sound mind who is 18 years of age or older or who is otherwise authorized to give medical consent on his behalf pursuant to the act of February 13, 1970 (P.L.19, No.10), entitled "An act enabling certain minors to consent to medical, dental and health services, declaring consent unnecessary under certain circumstances," may execute at any time a declaration governing the initiation, continuation, withholding or withdrawal of life-sustaining treatment. The declaration must be signed by the declarant, or by another on behalf of and at the direction of the declarant, and must be witnessed by two individuals each of whom is 18 years of age or older. A witness shall not be the person who signed the declaration on behalf of and at the direction of the declarant.

(b) Form. A declaration may but need not be in the following form and may include other specific directions including, but not limited to, designation of another person to make the treatment decision for the declarant if the declarant is incompetent and is determined to be in a terminal condition or to be permanently unconscious.

DECLARATION

I, being of sound mind, willfully and voluntarily make this declaration to be followed if I become incompetent. This declaration reflects my firm and settled commitment to refuse life-sustaining treatment under the circumstances indicated below.

I direct my attending physician to withhold or withdraw life-sustaining treatment that serves only to prolong the process of my dying, if I should be in a terminal condition or in a state of permanent unconsciousness.

I direct that treatment be limited to measures to keep me comfortable and to relieve pain, including any pain that might occur by withholding or withdrawing life-sustaining treatment.

In addition, if I am in the condition described above, I feel especially strong about the following forms of treatment:

I ( ) do ( ) do not want cardiac resuscitation.

I ( ) do ( ) do not want mechanical respiration.

I ( ) do ( ) do not want tube feeding or any other artificial or invasive form of nutrition (food) or hydration (water).

I ( ) do ( ) do not want blood or blood products.

I ( ) do ( ) do not want any form of surgery or invasive diagnostic tests.

I ( ) do ( ) do not want kidney dialysis.

I ( ) do ( ) do not want antibiotics.

I realize that if I do not specifically indicate my preference regarding any of the forms of treatment listed above, I may receive that form of treatment.

Other instructions:

I ( ) do ( ) do not want to designate another person as my surrogate to make medical treatment decisions for me if I should be incompetent and in a terminal condition or in a state of permanent unconsciousness. Name and address of surrogate (if applicable): Name and address of substitute surrogate (if surrogate designated above is unable to serve):

I made this declaration on the   day of   (month, year).

Declarant's signature:

Declarant's address:

The declarant or the person on behalf of and at the direction of the declarant knowingly and voluntarily signed this writing by signature or mark in my presence.

Witness's signature:

Witness's address:

Witness's signature:

Witness's address:

(c) Invalidity of specific direction.--Should any specific direction in the declaration be held to be invalid, the invalidity shall not offset other directions of the declaration which can be effected without the invalid direction.

(d) Medical record.--A physician or other health care provider who is furnished a copy of the declaration shall make it a part of the declarant's medical record and, if unwilling to comply with the declaration, promptly so advise the declarant.

Section 5. When declaration becomes operative.

A declaration becomes operative when:

(1) a copy is provided to the attending physician; and

(2) the declarant is determined by the attending physician to be incompetent and in a terminal condition or in a state of permanent unconsciousness.

When the declaration becomes operative, the attending physician and other health care providers shall act in accordance with its provisions or comply with the transfer provisions of section 9.

Section 6. Revocation.

(a) General rule.--A declaration may be revoked all. any time and in any manner by the declarant, without regard to the declarant's mental or physical condition. A revocation is effective upon communication to the attending physician or other health care provider by the declarant or a witness to the revocation.

(b) Medical record.--The attending physician or other health care provider shall make the revocation a part of the declarant's medical record.

Section 7. Liability.

(a) General rule. No physician or other health care provider who, consistent with this act, causes or participates in the initiating, continuing, withholding or withdrawal of life-sustaining treatment from a qualified patient who is incompetent shall, as a result thereof, be subject to criminal or civil liability, or be found to have committed an act of unprofessional conduct, if the attending physician has followed the declarant's wishes as expressed earlier by the declarant in the form of a declaration executed pursuant to this act.

(b) Absence of declaration.--The absence of a declaration by a patient shall not gave rise to any presumption as to the intent of the patient to consent to or to refuse the initiation, continuation or termination of life-sustaining treatment.

Section 8. Duty of physician to confirm terminal condition.

For purposes of section 5, an attending physician shall, without delay after the diagnosis that the declarant is in a terminal condition or in a state of permanent unconsciousness, certify in writing that the declarant is in a terminal condition or in a state of permanent unconsciousness and arrange for the physical examination and confirmation of the terminal condition or state of permanent unconsciousness of the declarant by a second physician.

Section 9. Transfer of declarant.

An attending physician or other health care provider who is unwilling to comply with this act shall, as promptly as practical, take all reasonable steps to transfer care of the declarant to another physician or health care provider.

Section 10. Effect on suicide and life insurance.

(a) Criminal effect. The withholding or withdrawal of life- sustaining treatment from a qualified patient in accordance with the provisions of this act shall not, for any purpose, constitute suicide or homicide.

(b) Life insurance. The making of, or failure to make, a declaration in accordance with this act shall not affect in any manner the sale, procurement or issuance of any policy of life insurance, nor shall it be deemed to modify the terms of an existing policy of life insurance. No policy of life insurance shall be legally impaired or invalidated in any manner by the withholding or withdrawal of life-sustaining treatment from an insured patient, notwithstanding any term of the policy to the contrary.

Section 11. Declaration optional.

No physician or other health care provider, and no health care service plan, health maintenance organization, insurer issuing disability insurance, self-insured employee welfare benefit plan, nonprofit hospital plan or Federal, State or local government-sponsored or operated program shall:

(1) require any person to execute a declaration as a condition for being insured for, or receiving, health care services; or

(2) charge any person a different rate or fee whether or not the person executes or has executed a declaration.

Section 12. Preservation of existing rights.

The provisions of this act are cumulative with existing law regarding the right of an individual to consent or refuse to consent to life-sustaining treatment and shall not impair or supersede any existing rights or responsibilities which a health care provider, a patient, including a minor or incompetent patient, or the family of a patient may have in regard to the withholding or withdrawal of life-sustaining treatment under the laws of this Commonwealth.

Section 13. Power of attorney.

Nothing in this act shall limit a power of attorney executed under 20 Pa.C.S. Ch. 56 (relating to powers of attorney).

Section 14. Penalties.

Any person who willfully conceals, cancels, defaces, obliterates or damages the declaration of another without the consent of the declarant commits a felony of the third degree. Any person who falsifies or forges the declaration of another, or willfully conceals or withholds personal knowledge of a revocation as provided in section 6, with the intent to cause a withholding or withdrawal of life-sustaining treatment contrary to the wishes of the declarant and, because of such an act, directly causes life-sustaining treatment to be withheld or withdrawn and death to be hastened, shall be subject to prosecution for criminal homicide as provided in 18 Pa.C.S. Ch. 25 (relating to criminal homicide). Any person who willfully, by Undue influence, fraud or duress, causes a person to execute a declaration pursuant to this act commits a felony of the third degree.

Section 15. Effective date.

This act shall take effect immediately.

MEDICAL AND GENERAL DURABLE POWER OF ATTORNEY

KNOW ALL BY THESE PRESENTS THAT I, John Doe (henceforth "Donor"), do make constitute and appoint Mary Doe (henceforth "Agent") as my true and lawful attorney for me and in my name and on my behalf GENERALLY TO DO AND PERFORM ALL MATTERS AND THINGS, transact all business, make, execute and acknowledge all contracts, orders, deeds, writings, checks, assurances and instruments which may be requisite or proper to effect any matter or thing, appertaining, or belonging to me, with the same powers, and to all intents and purposes with the same validity as I could, if personally present; hereby ratifying and confirming whatsoever said attorney shall and may do, by virtue hereof.

FURTHER, I give to said Agent the power to authorize my admission to a medical, nursing, residential or similar facility and to enter into agreements for my care, including the power to authorize medical and surgical procedures. This power is to be construed and implemented in accordance with the provisions of Chapter 56 of Title 20, Consolidated Pennsylvania Statutes, (and especially 20 Pa. C.S. 5603 (h)) in effect on the date of execution of this Durable Power of Attorney.

If the situation should arise in which there is no reasonable expectation of my recovery from physical or mental disability, I request that I be allowed to die and not be kept alive by artificial means or heroic measures. I do not fear death itself as much as the indignities of deterioration, dependency and hopeless pain, I, therefore, ask that medication be mercifully administered to me to alleviate suffering even though this may hasten the moment of my death.

This request is made after careful consideration. I hope that said Agent will feel morally bound to follow its mandate. I recognize that this appears to place a heavy responsibility upon said Agent but it is with the intention of relieving said Agent of such responsibility and of placing it upon myself in accordance with my strong convictions, that I have made this statement. (If these provisions are unacceptable, they should be crossed-out and the Donor should initial here _____).

I do further nominate the said Agent as the guardian of my estate and person should I be adjudicated incompetent. This nomination is pursuant to 20 Pa. C.S. Section 5604, or any similar law.

I do further direct said Agent to charge me, and/or my estate, a reasonable fee (based on time expenditure) and reimbursement for reasonable costs arising from said Agent acting in my behalf pursuant to this Power of

Attorney.

I further authorize the said Agent to so pay or reimburse himself/herself from any and all my assets subject to this Power of Attorney.

This instrument may be recorded in the appropriate offices necessary to effectuate the rights and duties above described.

I provide further that should be unwilling or unable to serve as my attorney in fact, then I appoint as my attorney in fact, with all the powers and authority afore described.

_____

A photocopy of this Power of Attorney shall be as effective as an original.

> or

A photocopy of this Power of Attorney shall be as effective as an original, PROVIDED THAT THE ORIGINAL WITH RAISED NOTARIAL SEAL IS PRODUCED FOR INSPECTION AND COMPARISON. (one of the above provisions MUST be crossed-out and the Donor MUST initial here _____).

_____

This power of attorney shall not be affected by any subsequent disability or incapacity, whether physical or mental, from which I may suffer.

> or

This power of attorney shall take effect upon my becoming disabled or incapacitated, whether physically or mentally, and shall remain in effect for the duration of such disability or incapacity.
(one of the above provisions MUST be crossed-out and the Donor MUST initial here _____).

_____

IN WITNESS WHEREOF, and intending to be legally bound hereby, I have hereunto set my signature this ___ day of _____ , 19__.

John Doe

(Standard Acknowledgment Form)

Corporal Punishment: May teachers use physical force to discipline students?

In *Goss v. Lopez*, 419 U.S. 565 (1975), the U.S. Supreme Court ruled that students suspended from public schools have the right to some degree of due process. The Court concluded in that case that the more severe the possible penalty, the more due process must be afforded the student.

The question arises, therefore, whether the imposition of a physical penalty (corporal punishment) by a teacher triggers any due process rights for the student. The U.S. Supreme Court has held in *Ingraham v. Wright*, 430 U.S. 651 (1977), that such punishment does not, per se, violate the Eighth Amendment's prohibition against "cruel and unusual punishment."

However, if the physical punishment is excessive or is designed to cause injury, it may lead to tort liability for such injuries. In the *Metzger* case that follows, an injured student brought a federal Civil Rights action against a teacher who caused him to sustain a broken nose, fractured teeth and other injuries.

Parents of school children continue to express concern about possible abuse of this controversial disciplinary tactic. Their concern is reflected in the following regulations promulgated by the Pennsylvania Department of Education. Though some school districts prohibit corporal punishment, the regulations contained in Title 22 of the Pennsylvania Code, specify the conditions under which such punishment may legally be imposed.

Of particular interest is the "buy-out provision" in sub-section (d). This led the younger of the two authors (the one young enough to have small children) to write the following note at the beginning of the school year:

Dear Teacher:

Please be advised that I prohibit the use of corporal punishment in the disciplining of my child. Eric is very bright. If he misbehaves, simply hit the child next to him. Eric will get the message.

Metzger v. Osbeck
847 F. 2d 518 (Third Circuit, 1988)

Judge Greenberg delivered the opinion of the court.

This civil rights action, filed pursuant to 42 U.S.C. § 1983, arises from a poolside disciplinary encounter between teacher Richard Osbeck and student Charles Metzger at Log College Junior High School in Bucks County, Pennsylvania, from which Metzger emerged with a broken nose and other injuries requiring hospitalization. The district court granted a motion for summary judgment in which Osbeck, principal Harry L. Clark, supervisor Ronald Y. White, the Centennial School

District, the Centennial School Board, and its members all joined and from which Metzger and his parents appeal. Upon plenary review of defendants' motion, we find that there is a genuine issue of material fact regarding Osbeck's intentions when disciplining Metzger. Accordingly, we will reverse the district court's order of June 26, 1987 entered on the motion to the extent that it dismissed the Metzgers' substantive due process claim and pendent state claims against Osbeck. We will, however, otherwise affirm the order.

In reviewing a grant of summary judgment, we apply the same test used by the district court and thus unless we find that no genuine issue as to any material fact remains for trial and that the moving parties are entitled to summary judgment as a matter of law, we must reverse. At the summary judgment stage, the judge's role "is not himself to weigh the evidence and determine the truth of the matter," but to determine whether the evidence creates a genuine issue of material fact which,"because [it] may reasonably be resolved in favor of either party," "properly can be resolved only by a finder of fact." In determining whether a factual dispute exists, the judge must view the evidence in the light most favorable to the nonmoving party. If from this perspective the judge discerns a "genuine" dispute over a "material" fact, the motion must be denied.

We agree with the district judge's statement in his memorandum opinion granting defendants' motion for summary judgment that a reasonable jury could find the following facts:

Metzger was enrolled in a swimming class taught by defendant Richard Osbeck ('Osbeck'), the chairman of the school's physical education department. Metzger was failing swimming for failure to participate in class, but had not been a source of disciplinary problems for Osbeck. January 28, 1983 was the last day of the marking period, so Osbeck used class time for a recreational swim. Metzger had a written excuse from class that day: he recalls that he was suffering from the flu and had a swollen leg. During class, Metzger traded baseball cards with several fellow students on the pool deck.

Several feet away, Osbeck stood talking to a student teacher. Osbeck overheard Metzger using inappropriate language in the course of a conversation with a female student about baseball cards. He walked to where Metzger was standing, and, standing behind him, placed his arms around Metzger's neck and shoulder area. Holding Metzger in that position, Osbeck quietly asked him, 'Was that you using foul language?,' and, when there was no response, said 'That kind of language is unacceptable in this class. Do you understand me?' In the course of the questioning, Osbeck's arm moved slightly upward, from Metzger's Adam's apple to under his chin; at some point, Metzger felt pressure on the underneath portion of the chin and had to stand up on his toes. Osbeck then released Metzger, intending to turn him around. Instead, Metzger, who had lost consciousness at some point, fell face down onto the pool deck. As a consequence of his fall, Metzger suffered lacerations to his lower lip, a broken nose, fractured teeth and other injuries requiring hospitalization.

The district judge granted Osbeck summary judgment as he concluded that Metzger had suffered no due process violations because a jury in the circumstances of the case could not infer that Osbeck intended to injure him or acted in reckless disregard of a risk of which he should have been aware. The other defendants were granted summary judgment as there was no school policy authorizing the conduct of which plaintiffs complained, there was no legal or factual basis for vicarious liability of the supervisors, and there was no showing that Osbeck had received inadequate training.

We have concluded that we cannot agree with the district judge to the extent he found that the restraint employed by Osbeck "in the circumstances in which it was employed, does not permit the inference that Osbeck intended to injure Metzger or recklessly disregarded a risk of injury of which he should reasonably have been aware." A decision to discipline a student, if accomplished through excessive force and appreciable physical pain, may constitute an invasion of the child's Fifth Amendment liberty interest in his personal security and a violation of substantive due process prohibited by the Fourteenth Amendment. The district court observed that the most commonly cited framework for evaluating the constitutional import of allegations of excessive force is that employed by Judge Friendly in *Johnson v. Glick*, 481 F.2d 1028, 1033 (2d Cir.), cert. denied, 414 U.S. 1033, 94 S.Ct. 462 (1973):

In determining whether the constitutional line has been crossed, a court must look to such factors as the need for the application of force, the relationship between the need and the amount of force that was used, the extent of injury inflicted, and whether force was applied in a good faith effort to maintain or restore discipline or maliciously and sadistically for the very purpose of causing harm.

Even if physical reinforcement of a teacher's verbal admonitions is pedagogically appropriate and condoned by school disciplinary policy, we believe a reasonable jury could find that the restraints employed by Osbeck, if responsible for the student's loss of consciousness, exceeded the degree of force needed to correct Metzger's alleged breach of discipline and that the substantial injuries sustained by Metzger served no legitimate disciplinary purpose. If the jury is persuaded that Osbeck employed those restraints with the intent to cause harm, Osbeck will be subject to liability for crossing the "constitutional line" separating a common law tort from a deprivation of a substantive due process.

In reaching this conclusion we note that it is undisputed that Osbeck intentionally placed his arms around Metzger's neck and shoulders. While we recognize that Osbeck disclaims any ill-will toward Metzger and that the circumstances of the encounter suggest he was motivated by a legitimate disciplinary desire to admonish, not injure, the student, we cannot say that a reasonable jury could not believe that Osbeck intended the consequences of his act or believed them to be a substantially certain result of it. Thus we cannot deprive plaintiffs of an opportunity to

20

have a jury resolve the issue of Osbeck's intent in their favor. In this regard we observe that a jury might reasonably conclude that in view of Osbeck's position as a physical education instructor and wrestling coach, he was aware of the inherent risks of restraining Metzger. If it did, it could discredit Osbeck's disclaimer of punitive intent and could find that he intended to cause Metzger harm or believed harm was substantially certain to attend his actions. In short, we cannot permit a summary judgment to be granted to a defendant who, by an intentional act, may have caused serious harm simply because he says he did not intend the harm. Thus, the evidence at this stage of the proceedings is not so one-sided that Osbeck must prevail as a matter of law. Our result is consistent with the general approach that a court should be reluctant to grant a motion for summary judgment when resolution of the dispositive issue requires a determination of state of mind, for in such cases "much depends upon the credibility of witnesses testifying as to their own states of mind, and assessing credibility is a delicate matter best left to the fact finder." *Watts v. University of Delaware*, 622 F.2d 47, 52 (3d Cir. 1980).

In view of the aforesaid, we will reverse the dismissal of the Metzgers' substantive due process claim and pendent state claims against Osbeck and remand the matter for further proceedings consistent with this opinion. We will, however, affirm the dismissal of all other constitutionally based claims against Osbeck and all claims against the other defendants for the reasons set forth in the district court's opinion.

Judge Weis concurring in part and dissenting in part:

Plaintiff alleges an infringement of rights under the substantive due process requirements of the Fourteenth Amendment. He has, however, not produced enough evidence to demonstrate a constitutional violation.

Evidence giving rise to a common law tort will not necessarily establish a claim under section 1983. The mere fact that a state official has committed a tort will not suffice to support a cause of action for constitutional harm. "Our Constitution deals with the large concerns of the governors and the governed, but it does not purport to supplant traditional tort law in laying down rules of conduct to regulate liability for injuries that attend living together in society." *Daniels v. Williams*, 474 U.S. 327, 332 (1986). The incident here was a disciplinary encounter between a teacher and a pupil. The majority posits that, in this context, a constitutional violation occurs if the teacher uses excessive force and causes appreciable physical pain. The court's analysis recognizes that the teacher constitutionally was permitted to utilize physical contact in disciplining the student. Only if the force employed was excessive will a section 1983 claim be established.

A teacher's constitutional liability is not determined by what is "pedagogically appropriate and condoned by school disciplinary policy," as the majority implies. Those considerations may be relevant to the state tort action but not to the substantive due process claim. Constitutional standards do not vary from school district to school district nor do they depend on the educational philosophy of each individual school administration.

I begin with the proposition that there is a substantive due process entitlement to personal integrity which the state may infringe only in limited circumstances. *Youngberg v. Romeo*, 457 U.S. 307, 315 (1982). That right of bodily security protects students from excessive physical force when school authorities mete out discipline. *Hall v. Tawney*, 621 F.2d 607 (4th Cir. 1980). In positive terms, corporal punishment does not per se violate a public school child's constitutional rights.

The majority here apparently adopts the test set out in *Hall*. There, the court proposed the following inquiry: whether the force applied caused injury so severe, was so disproportionate to the need presented, was so inspired by malice or sadism rather than a merely careless or unwise excess of zeal that the punishment amounted to a brutal and inhumane abuse of official power literally shocking to the conscience. Plaintiff advances the theory that the extent of his injuries, which he contends are serious, provides proof of liability. If the injury were less substantial, I suspect the majority would affirm the summary judgment here.

In my view, however, it is the intent to use excessive force -- not the extent of injury -- which is dispositive of the constitutional claim. The extent of injury at times may reflect the amount of force used or even suggest malice on the part of the state official. A savage beating, for example, may result in injuries that directly relate to the number and force of the blows. No such correlation exists here.

Nor is the intent to cause physical contact a controlling element. A teacher who slaps an unruly child to enforce obedience in a classroom obviously commits a volitional act with intent to inflict pain. Those facts, however, do not establish a constitutional violation; they do not demonstrate the use of excessive force -- the hallmark of abuse of governmental position.

On the other hand, if the teacher hits a small child so hard as to knock her down a flight of steps with resulting serious injury, the intent to strike the pupil again is present. The evidence of intent to use excessive force could be perceived by the predictably serious injury resulting from the blow and the child's position atop the staircase.

Other examples demonstrate the nuances of the problem. A teacher aims a light slap at a student's shoulder, but the pupil moves suddenly, deflecting the teacher's hand. As a consequence, the teacher's ring strikes the child's eye, resulting in a tragic injury. Or perhaps the teacher does no more than gently shove a disobedient child with a hidden impairment and causes an unforeseeable serious injury.

These contrasting situations illustrate the principle this court expounded in *Rhodes v. Robinson*, 612 F.2d 766 (3d Cir. 1979). In *Rhodes*, an inmate sought recovery for an emotional injury stemming from prison guards' illegal conduct. We said that the critical element was "not the nature of the plaintiff's injury but the manner of the infliction of that injury." Id. at 772. The Due Process Clause "extends to protection from an official's abusive exercise of his powers to inflict grossly undue harm." Acknowledging that emotional injury could be compensable, we concluded that "where a person suffers injury as an incidental and unintended consequence of official actions, the abuse of power contemplated in the due process and eighth amendment cases does not arise." Id.

The focus on abuse of power is a prime distinction between constitutional violations and routine torts. That concern counsels caution in relying on extent of injury to determine when conduct rises to the level of a constitutional violation. It is true that tortfeasors must take a victim as they find him. And it is also true that it is no defense against unintended damages that the act would not have caused as serious an injury to the average person. But these concepts affect the amount of damages, not liability.

By contrast, it must be conceded in this case that the teacher could use physical force, and therefore the initial physical conduct was lawful. The defendant's act of pushing the pupil's chin upward, alone, is not likely to cause injury or even pain. At most one would expect momentary discomfort, which in itself would not present an unconstitutional method of emphasizing the correctional message to a student deserving of a strong admonition. Nothing in the record, as the district judge and I read it, would allow a reasonable jury to conclude that the defendant's actions were meant to cause any injury, let alone one of the type that occurred. The injuries were unexpected and unintended. Plaintiff has failed to produce evidence which would justify any inference to the contrary.

This case is nothing but a routine tort matter which properly should be decided by a state court. In devoting time and effort to litigation of this nature, federal courts deprive parties with cases raising federal questions of the attention they deserve. In my view, this case has gone far enough. I would affirm the entry of summary judgment in favor of Osbeck as well as the other defendants.

I also must disagree with the majority's footnote that this case can be sent to the jury on a theory of "gross negligence." In cases of this nature, the use of "gross" as opposed to "simple" negligence will not serve to overcome the distinction between an ordinary tort and a constitutional violation. As Chief Judge Gibbons pointed out in his dissent in *Davidson v. O'Lone*, 752 F.2d 817 (3d Cir. 1984), aff'd sub nom. *Davidson v. Cannon*, 474 U.S. 344 (1986): "The prevailing view is that there are no 'degrees' of care or negligence, as a matter of law; there are only different amounts of care as a matter of fact; and 'gross negligence' is merely the same thing as ordinary negligence, 'with the addition,' as Baron Rolfe once put it, 'of a vituperative epithet.'" See id. at 853 (quoting W. Prosser, *Handbook of the Law of Torts* 182 (4th ed. 1971)).

Nor would an instruction on gross negligence be consistent with the charge given in the school discipline trial in *Hall* and repeated in *Justice v. Dennis*, 834 F.2d 380 (4th Cir. 1987), an arrestee case. In the latter decision, the court of appeals approved a charge that "directs the jury to consider whether the force 'shocks the conscience' and appears to have been applied 'maliciously and sadistically' for the purpose of causing harm." Id. at 383.

I suggest that the term "gross negligence" only multiplies the complexities of distinguishing between common law tort and constitutional violation. Although the Supreme Court reserved deciding whether "something less than intentional conduct, such as recklessness or 'gross negligence' will trigger the substantive protections of the Due Process Clause," I find no persuasive reason for further muddling the blurred line between state law torts and actions under section 1983.

I dissent.

STUDENT RIGHTS AND RESPONSIBILITIES
22 Pa. Code § 12.5

§ 12.5. Corporal punishment.

(a) Corporal punishment, namely physically punishing a student for an offense, may be administered by teachers and school officials to discipline students when authorized by, and in accordance with policies and guidelines established by, the board of school directors.

(b) Reasonable force may be used but under no circumstances shall a student be punished in such a manner as to cause bodily injury.

(c) Where corporal punishment is authorized, school authorities shall notify all parents of this policy. Corporal punishment may not be administered to a child whose parents have notified school authorities that such disciplinary method is prohibited.

(d) In situations where a parent or school board prohibits corporal punishment, reasonable force may still be used by teachers and school authorities under the following circumstances:

(1) To quell a disturbance.
(2) To obtain possession of weapons or other dangerous objects.
(3) For the purpose of self-defense.
(4) For the protection of persons or property.

(e) Corporal punishment should never be administered in the heat of anger. It should be recognized that corporal punishment always contains the danger of excessiveness. No disciplinary action should exceed in degree the seriousness of the offense. Students shall not be required to remove clothing when being punished.

Defending Your Home: When can you shoot an intruder?

The Pennsylvania legislature has enacted a statute addressing the issue of how much force may used to defend one's property, the issue raised in the famous case of *Katko v. Briney*, 183 N.W. 2d 657 (1971). Although the decision in *Katko* is initially upsetting to many, it reaffirms the respect for life which is so essential in American jurisprudence. The use of deadly force is prohibited except under certain very restricted circumstances.

What follows is Section 507 of the Crimes Code which deals with the use of force in defense of property. It is extremely important to note that the Pennsylvania Crimes Code specifically defines "deadly force" as "force which, under the circumstances in which it is used, is readily capable of causing death or serious bodily injury." 18 Pa.C.S. Sec. 501. Only sub-sections (C) (4i) and (C) (4ii) of Section 507 pertain to the use of deadly force for protection of property. Thus, the use of a firearm, or other deadly force, is still very restricted to the circumstances specified in said sub-sections. Lastly, to understand the statute it must be understood that the word "believes" is defined at Section 501 of the act as "reasonably believes." This means that the actor must not only subjectively believe that he (or she) is in danger, but this belief must be objectively "reasonable." In short, the utilization of deadly force is a matter of last resort.

The Pennsylvania statute departs from the common law somewhat in that it expands the rights of individuals in their homes to use deadly force to repel intruders.

18 Pa.C.S. § 507

§ 507. Use of force for the protection of property

(A) USE OF FORCE JUSTIFIABLE FOR PROTECTION OF PROPERTY. The use of force upon or toward the person of another is justifiable when the actor believes that such force is immediately necessary:

(1) to prevent or terminate an unlawful entry or other trespass upon land or a trespass against or the unlawful carrying away of tangible movable property, if such land or movable property is, or is believed by the actor to be, in his possession or in the possession of another person for whose protection he acts; or

(2) to effect an entry or reentry upon land or to retake tangible movable property, if:

(i) the actor believes that he or the person by whose authority he acts or a person from whom he or such other person derives title was unlawfully dispossessed of such land or movable property and is entitled to possession; and

(ii)(A) the force is used immediately or on fresh pursuit after such dispossession; or

(B) the actor believes that the person against whom he uses force has no claim of right to the possession of the property and, in the case of land, the circumstances, as the actor believes them to be, are of such urgency that it would be an exceptional hardship to postpone the entry or reentry until a court order is obtained.

(B) MEANING OF POSSESSION. For the purpose of subsection (a) of this section:

(1) A person who has parted with the custody of property to another who refuses to restore it to him is no longer in possession, unless the property is movable and was and still is located on land in his possession.

(2) A person who has been dispossessed of land does not regain possession thereof merely by setting foot thereon.

(3) A person who has a license to use or occupy real property is deemed to be in possession thereof except against the licensor acting under claim of right.

(C) LIMITATIONS ON JUSTIFIABLE USE OF FORCE.

(1) The use of force is justifiable under this section only if the actor first requests the person against whom such force is used to desist from his interference with the property, unless the actor believes that:

(i) such request would be useless;

(ii) it would be dangerous to himself or another person to make the request; or

(iii) substantial harm will be done to the physical condition of the property which is sought to be protected before the request can effectively be made.

(2) The use of force to prevent or terminate a trespass is not justifiable under this section if the actor knows that the exclusion of the trespasser will expose him to substantial danger

of serious bodily injury.

(3) The use of force to prevent an entry or reentry upon land or the recaption of movable property is not justifiable under this section, although the actor believes that such reentry or caption is unlawful, if:

    (i) the reentry or recaption is made by or on behalf of a person who was actually dispossessed of the property; and

    (ii) it is otherwise justifiable under subsection (a)(2).

(4i) The use of deadly force is justifiable under this section if:

    (A) there has been an entry into the actor's dwelling;

    (B) the actor neither believes nor has reason to believe that the entry is lawful; and

    (C) the actor neither believes nor has reason to believe that force less than deadly force would be adequate to terminate the entry.

(4ii) If the conditions of justification provided in subparagraph (i) have not been met, the use of deadly force is not justifiable under this section unless the actor believes that:

    (A) the person against whom the force is used is attempting to dispossess him of his dwelling otherwise than under a claim of right to its possession; or

    (B) such force is necessary to prevent the commission of a felony in the dwelling. . . .

Invasion of Privacy: What constitutes invasion of privacy in Pennsylvania?

While the exact scope of the right is not clear, Pennsylvania courts have long recognized the tort of invasion of privacy. Like other states, Pennsylvania adopted the definition of this tort as it appears in the *Restatement (Second) of Torts* § 652 B - 652 E. In the following case, the court applied these definitions to a situation in which *Sports Illustrated* had published a photograph of the plaintiff -- a jubilant and inebrieated Pittsburgh Steeler fan at Three Rivers Stadium -- with his fly open. While somewhat sympathetic, the court ruled that "A factually accurate public disclosure is not tortious when connected with a newsworthy event even though offensive to ordinary sensibilities."

Neff v. Time, Inc.
406 F.Supp. 858 (1976)

Judge Marsh wrote the opinion for the court.

This diversity action was removed from the Court of Common Pleas of Allegheny County, Pennsylvania, where a complaint had been filed by John W. Neff, the plaintiff, against Time, Inc., the defendant. The complaint was verified by Neff and alleged that the defendant is the owner of a magazine known as Sports Illustrated sold weekly throughout Pennsylvania; that Neff is a private citizen employed in education; that in its issue of August 5, 1974, the defendant's magazine used Neff's picture without his prior knowledge and consent to illustrate an article entitled 'A Strange Kind of Love;' that the photograph shows Neff with the front zipper of his trousers completely opened implying that he is a 'crazy, drunken slob,' and combined with the title of the article, 'a sexual deviate.' Neff alleges that the unauthorized publication and circulation of his picture to illustrate the article invaded his right of privacy and subjected him to public ridicule and contempt, injured his personal esteem and the esteem of his profession, reflected on his character, diminished his high standing reputation among his family, friends, neighbors and business associates, destroyed his peace of mind and caused him severe mental and emotional distress to his damage in excess of $5,000, amended to aver in excess of $10,000.

The defendant filed a motion for summary judgment and attached eight affidavits in which the defendant admitted that an authorized employee took Neff's photograph and five others selected it for publication. No counter -

affidavits were filed by Neff. There is only one disputed issue of fact: Neff alleges that defendant has used his picture without his prior knowledge and consent; the defendant asserts that his picture was taken for and published in Sports Illustrated with his full knowledge and consent.

The undenied facts contained in affidavits filed by defendant establish beyond peradventure that the picture was taken with Neff's knowledge and with his encouragement; that he knew he was being photographed by a photographer for Sports Illustrated and thereby impliedly consented to its publication. Since Neff did not respond by counter-affidavits, in our opinion the motion should be granted. Rule 56(e) Fed.R.Civ.P. The affidavits establish that the photograph was taken about 1:00 o'clock P.M. November 25, 1973, while Neff was present on a dugout with a group of fans prior to a professional football game at Cleveland between the Cleveland Browns and the Pittsburgh Steelers. The photographer was on the field intending to take pictures of the Steeler players as they entered the field from the dugout. Neff and others were jumping up and down in full view of the fans in the stadium; they were waving Steeler banners and drinking beer; they all seemed to be slightly inebriated. One of the group asked the photographer for whom he was working and was told Sports Illustrated, whereupon the group began to act as if a television camera had been put on them; as the pictures were taken they began to react even more, screaming and howling and imploring the photographer to take more pictures. The more pictures taken of the group,

the more they hammed it up. All were aware that the photographer was covering the game for Sports Illustrated. There were no objections; they wanted to be photographed. Thirty pictures were taken of the group on the dugout from different angles.

During the period from July through December, 1973, this photographer took 7,200 pictures pursuant to his assignment to cover the Steelers. As part of his duty he edited the pictures and submitted one hundred to the magazine for selection by a committee of five employees. After several screenings of the thirty pictures of the group on the dugout, the committee selected Neff's picture with his fly open. Although Neff's fly was not open to the point of being revealing, the selection was deliberate and surely in utmost bad taste; subjectively, as to Neff, the published picture could have been embarrassing, humiliating and offensive to his sensibilities. Without doubt the magazine deliberately exhibited Neff in an embarrassing manner.

It appears that the pictures were taken to illustrate a book being written by one Blount about the Steeler fans, and three excerpts from the book were published in the magazine. Only three pictures, including Neff's, accompanied the article of August 5, 1974. The title to this article 'A Strange Kind of Love' could convey to some readers a derogatory connotation. Neff is not mentioned by name in the article; the Steeler-Cleveland game of November, 1973, is not mentioned in the article; Neff's photograph was not selected on the basis of its relationship to that game. The caption appearing adjacent to the photograph reads: 'In the fading autumn Sundays at Three Rivers, the fans joined the players in mean pro dreams.'

Three Rivers is the name of the stadium in Pittsburgh. Neff's photograph was selected because 'it represented the typical Steeler fan: a rowdy, strong rooter, much behind his team, having a good time at the game,' and 'it fitted in perfectly with the text of the story.' (See affidavit of Richard M. Gangel, Art Director for Sports Illustrated). It seems to us that art directors and editors should hesitate to deliberately publish a picture which most likely would be offensive and cause embarrassment to the subject when many other pictures of the same variety are available. Notwithstanding, '(t)he courts are not concerned with establishing canons of good taste for the press or the public.' *Aquino v. Bulletin Company*, 154 A.2d 422, 425 (1959).

The right of privacy is firmly established in Pennsylvania despite the fact that its perimeter is not yet clearly defined and its contours remain amorphous. *Vogel v. W. T. Grant Company*, 458 Pa. 124, 327 A.2d 133 (1974). From *Vogel* it seems that Pennsylvania follows the rules promulgated by the Restatement (Second) of Torts Secs. 652 B through E (Tent. Draft No. 13, 1967); that invasion of privacy is actionable under any one of four distinct, but coordinate, torts. These are concisely paraphrased in *Goldman v. Time, Inc.*, 336 F.Supp. 133, 136 (N.D.Cal.1971) as follows:

1. Intrusion upon the plaintiff's seclusion or solitude, or into his private affairs.
2. Public disclosure of embarrassing private facts about the plaintiff.
3. Publicity which places the plaintiff in a false light in the public eye.
4. Appropriation, for the defendant's advantage, of the plaintiff's name or likeness. Plaintiff's claim is based on 'appropriation of name or likeness' and 'publicity given to private life,' i.e., 4 and 2, supra. Plaintiff's brief, page 5. As to 4, supra, Sec. 652 C of the Restatement (Second) of Torts (Tent. Draft No. 21, 1975) states: 'One who appropriates to his own use or benefit the name or likeness of another is subject to liability to the other for unreasonable invasion of his privacy.' It is settled that this section is not applicable when a person's picture is used in a non-commercial article dealing with an accident, or the picture of a bystander at a political convention, or parade, or generally in the reporting of news. We think actions of excited fans at a football game are news as is a story about the fans of a professional football team. As stated in *Gautier v. Pro-Football, Inc.* 278 App.Div. 431, 435, 106 N.Y.S.2d 553, 557 (1st Dept. 1951), aff'd 304 N.Y. 354, 107 N.E.2d 485 (1953): 'Once an item has achieved the status of newsworthiness, it retains that status even when no longer current.' The fact that *Sports Illustrated* is a magazine published for profit does not constitute a 'commercial appropriation of Neff's likeness.' The fact that Neff was photographed in a public place for a newsworthy article, entitles the defendant to the protection of the First Amendment. *Time, Inc. v. Hill*, 385 U.S. 374, 397, 87 S.Ct. 534, 17 L.Ed.2d 456 (1967); *New York Times Co. v. Sullivan*, 376 U.S. 254, 84 S.Ct. 710, 11 L.Ed.2d 686 (1964). The tort described in 4, supra, and Sec. 652 C Restatement (Second) of Torts is not applicable to the facts in this case. As to 2, supra,

Sec. 652 D of the Restatement (Second) of Torts (Tent. Draft No. 13, 1967) states: 'One who gives publicity to matters concerning the private life of another, of a kind highly offensive to a reasonable man, is subject to liability to the other for invasion of his privacy.'

In the 1975 draft of the Restatement (Second) of Torts Sec. 652 D states: 'One who gives publicity to a matter concerning the private life of another is subject to liability to the other for unreasonable invasion of his privacy, if the matter publicized is of a kind which:
(a) would be highly offensive to a reasonable person, and
(b) is not of legitimate concern to the public.'

The article about Pittsburgh Steeler fans was of legitimate public interest; the football game in Cleveland was of legitimate public interest; Neff's picture was taken in a public place with his knowledge and with his encouragement; he was catapulted into the news by his own actions; nothing was falsified; a photograph taken at a public event which everyone present could see, with the knowledge and implied consent of the subject, is not a matter concerning a private fact. A factually accurate public disclosure is not tortious when connected with a newsworthy event even though offensive to ordinary sensibilities. The constitutional privilege protects all truthful publications relevant to matters of public interest. *Jenkins v. Dell Publishing Co.*, supra, family of victim of a murder; *Samuel v. Curtis Pub. Co.*, 122 F.Supp. 327 (N.D.Cal.1954), plaintiff attempting to dissuade woman hanging on bridge from committing suicide; *Berg v. Minneapolis Star & Tribune Co.*, 79 F.Supp. 957 (Minn.1948), courtroom; *Gill v. Hearst Pub. Co.*, 40 Cal.2d 224, 253 P.2d 441 (1953), plaintiff embracing his wife in a market place; *Jacova v. Southern Radio & Television Co.*, 83 So.2d 34 (Fla.1955), cigar store raid; *Themo v. New England Newspaper Pub. Co.*, 306 Mass. 54, 27 N.E.2d 753 (1940), police station; *Murray v. N.Y. Magazine Co.*, supra, parade; *Humiston v. Universal Film Mfg. Co.*, 189 App.Div. 467, 178 N.Y.S. 752 (1919), street; *Meetze v. Associated Press*, 230 S.C. 330, 95 S.E.2d 606 (1956), article reporting birth to 12 year old child; See *The Law of Torts*, by W. L. Prosser, Fourth ed. 1971 at pp. 811, 817. Cf. *Virgil v. Time, Inc.*, 527 F.2d 1122 (9th Cir. 1975). The tort described in 2, supra, and Sec. 652 D of the Restatement (Second) of Torts, supra, is not applicable to the facts in this case.

Of course, we are concerned that Neff's picture was deliberately selected by an editorial committee from a number of similar pictures and segregated and published alone. If his picture had appeared as part of the general crowd scene of fans at a game, even though embarrassing, there would be no problem. Although we have some misgivings, it is our opinion that the publication of Neff's photograph taken with his active encouragement and participation, and with knowledge that the photographer was connected with a publication, even though taken without his express consent, is protected by the Constitution.

An appropriate order will be entered.

Privileged Communications: When can one spouse testify against another in a criminal case?

At Common Law there were two related rules pertaining to the testimony of married persons against one another. The Spousal Privilege allowed one spouse to prevent the other from testifying against him or her. Typically, this meant, for example, that the prosecution could not call the wife to the stand to testify against the husband in a criminal trial, even if she wanted to so testify. As long as they were married, the defendant could prevent his (or her) spouse from testifying. This prohibition applied to all testimony- not just statements made by the defendant to the spouse. This privilege only lasted as long as the parties were married and was based on the public policy that a marriage would be destroyed were one spouse to testify against the other. Naturally there was an exception when one spouse was being tried for a crime alleged to have been committed against the other (assault, attempted murder, etc.). Many early commentators noted that the "privilege" was held by the wrong person - the defendant. They argued that it made more sense to give the privilege to the witness spouse. After all, if he or she wanted to testify against the other spouse, the relationship was probably not too good anyway.

A related rule is the "Marital Confidential Communication Rule." This rule applies only to communications between spouses while they are married. At Common Law, this rule provided that all such communications were privileged whether or not the parties were still married at the time of the trial. The public policy here was more concerned with the desire that spouses be able to communicate freely with one another. Thus, a wife could not testify about what was told in confidence to her by her husband, unless he agreed to her so testifying.

42 Pa.C.S. § 5913

§ 5913. Spouses as witnesses against each other

Except as otherwise provided in this subchapter, in a criminal proceeding a person shall have the privilege, which he or she may waive, not to testify against his or her then lawful spouse except that there shall be no such privilege:

(1) in proceedings for desertion and maintenance;

(2) in any criminal proceeding against either for bodily injury or violence attempted, done or threatened upon the other, or upon the minor children of said husband and wife, or the minor children of either of them, or any minor child in their care or custody, or in the care or custody of either of them;

(3) applicable to proof of the fact of marriage, in support of a criminal charge of bigamy alleged to have been committed by or with the other; or

(4) in any criminal proceeding in which one of the charges pending against the defendant includes murder, involuntary deviate sexual intercourse or rape.

§ 5914. Confidential communications between spouses

Except as otherwise provided in this subchapter, in a criminal proceeding neither husband nor wife shall be competent or permitted to testify to confidential communications made by one to the other, unless this privilege is waived upon the trial.

Statute of Limitations: How long do you have to file suit for each type of legal action?

Civil statutes of limitations are legislative enactments which state how much time an alleged injured party has to bring an action in law against the alleged wrongdoer. Most crimes (except the most serious) are also subject to statutes of limitations.

Equity actions are not subject to statutes of limitation, but rather to the equitable defense of laches. Unlike statutes of limitations that set specific, relatively inflexible time periods, laches is determined by looking at a variety of factors to determine whether it is fair to permit a party to bring suit after a certain amount of time has passed.

There are numerous public policy reasons for the limitation of such actions. It would be unfair for a plaintiff to be able to marshall and preserve all of the evidence he needs, then to wait for the passage of time to erase other evidence favorable to the defendant, and then to spring an action against an unsuspecting defendant who may, by then, have lost the opportunity to adequately defend himself.

In addition, society benefits from knowing that some behaviors and events, because of the passage of time, are settled and cannot be reopened. This balancing act between giving the plaintiff enough time to bring an action, and the public policies favoring quick resolutions, results in great variety among the states in the setting of statutes of limitations.

42 Pa.C.S. 5523

§ 5523. One year limitation

The following actions and proceedings must be commenced within one year:

(1) An action for libel, slander or invasion of privacy.

(2) An action upon a bond given as security by a party in any matter, except a bond given by a condemnor in an eminent domain proceeding.

(3) An action upon any payment or performance bond.

§ 5524. Two year limitation

The following actions and proceedings must be commenced within two years:

(1) An action for assault, battery, false imprisonment, false arrest, malicious prosecution or malicious abuse of process.

(2) An action to recover damages for injuries to the person or for the death of an individual caused by the wrongful act or neglect or unlawful violence or negligence of another.

(3) An action for taking, detaining or injuring personal property, including actions for specific recovery thereof.

(4) An action for waste or trespass of real property.

(5) An action upon a statute for a civil penalty or forfeiture.

(6) An action against any officer of any government unit for the nonpayment of money or the nondelivery of property collected upon on execution or otherwise in his possession.

(7) Any other action or proceeding to recover damages for injury to person or property which is founded on negligent, intentional, or otherwise tortious conduct or any other action or proceeding sounding in trespass, including deceit or fraud, except an action or proceeding subject to another limitation specified in this subchapter.

§ 5525. Four year limitation

The following actions and proceedings must be commenced within four years:

(1) An action upon a contract, under seal or otherwise, for the sale, construction or furnishing of tangible personal property or fixtures.

(2) Any action subject to 13 Pa.C.S. § 2725 (relating to statute of limitations in contracts for sale).

(3) An action upon an express contract not founded upon an instrument in writing.

(4) An action upon a contract implied in law, except an action subject to another limitation specified in this subchapter.

(5) An action upon a judgment or decree of any court of the United States or of any state.

(6) An action upon any official bond of a public official, officer or employee.

(7) An action upon a negotiable or nonnegotiable bond, note or other similar instrument in writing. Where such an instrument is payable upon demand, the time within which an action on it must be commenced shall be computed from the later of either demand or any payment of principal of or interest on the instrument.

(8)   An action upon a contract, obligation or liability founded upon a writing not specified in paragraph (7), under seal or otherwise, except an action subject to another limitation specified in this subchapter.

§ 5526. Five year limitation

The following actions and proceedings must be commenced within five years:

(1)   An action for revival of a judgment lien on real property.

(2)   An action for specific performance of a contract for sale of real property or for damages for noncompliance therewith.

(3)   An action to enforce any equity of redemption or any implied or resulting trust as to real property.

(4)   A proceeding in inverse condemnation, if property has been injured but no part thereof has been taken, or if the condemnor has made payment in accordance with section 407(a) or (b) (relating to possession and payment of compensation) of the Act of June 22, 1964 (Sp.Sess., P.L. 84, No. 6), known as the "Eminent Domain Code."

§ 5527. Six year limitation

Any civil action or proceeding which is neither subject to another limitation specified in this subchapter nor excluded from the application of a period of limitation by section 5531 (relating to no limitation) must be commenced within six years.

§ 5528. Fifteen year limitation

Except as otherwise provided by section 17 (relating to periods of limitation) of the act of August 9, 1971 (P.L. 286, No. 74), known as the "Disposition of Abandoned and Unclaimed Property Act," an action for escheat, or for payment into the State Treasury without escheat, must be commenced within 15 years after the property sought in such action shall have first escheated or become escheatable or payable into the State Treasury under any statute.

§ 5529. Twenty year limitation

(A)   EXECUTION AGAINST PERSONAL PROPERTY. An execution against personal property must be issued within 20 years after the entry of the judgment upon which the execution is to be issued.

(B)   INSTRUMENTS UNDER SEAL.

(1) Notwithstanding section 5525(7) (relating to four year limitation), an action upon an instrument in writing under seal must be commenced within 20 years.

(2) This subsection shall expire June 27, 1998.

§ 5530. Twenty-one year limitation

(A) GENERAL RULE. The following actions and proceedings must be commenced within 21 years:

(1) An action for the possession of real property.

(2) An action for the payment of any ground rent, annuity or other charge upon real property, or any part or portion thereof. If this paragraph shall operate to bar any payment of such a rent, annuity or charge, the rent, annuity or charge to which the payment relates shall be extinguished and no further action may be commenced with respect to subsequent payments.

(3) A proceeding in inverse condemnation, if property has been taken and the condemnor has not made payment in accordance with section 407(a) or (b) (relating to possession and payment of compensation) of the act of June 22, 1964 (Sp.Sess., P.L. 84, No. 6), known as the "Eminent Domain Code."

(B) ENTRY UPON LAND. No entry upon real property shall toll the running of the period of limitation specified in subsection (a)(1), unless a possessory action shall be commenced therefor within one year after entry. Such an entry and commencement of a possessory action, without recovery therein, shall not toll the running of such period of limitation in respect of another possessory action, unless such other possessory action is commenced within one year after the termination of the first.

§ 5531. No limitation

The following actions and proceedings may be commenced at any time notwithstanding any other provision of this subchapter except section 5521 (relating to limitations on foreign claims):

(1) An action against an attorney at law by or on behalf of a client to enforce any implied or resulting trust as to real property.

(2) An action by the Commonwealth, a county or an institution district against the real or personal property of persons who were public charges, including mental patients, to recover the cost of their maintenance and support.

(3) An action by the Commonwealth, a county or an institution district against the real or personal property of persons who were legally liable to pay for the maintenance and support of persons who were public charges, including mental patients, to recover the cost of their maintenance and support.

Sovereign Immunity: When Is The Government Immune?

That "the king can do no wrong," was the Common Law equivalent of "you can't sue City Hall." Although at one time, Pennsylvania enjoyed absolute sovereign immunity, the Pennsylvania Supreme Court abolished the doctrine in a 1978 decision (*Mayle v. Commonwealth*). The state legislature responded quickly by passing two acts: The Political Subdivision Tort Claims Act, 42 Pa. C.S. § 8541, et. seq. (pertaining to local governments and municipalities), and the Tort Claims Sovereign Immunities Act, 42 Pa. C.S. § 8521, et. seq. (pertaining to the Commonwealth of Pennsylvania). Both acts limit liability to specific types of cases, and limit the amount of damages available even in those cases for which there can be liability. In the following case, the Pennsylvania Supreme Court interpreted one section of the Political Subdivision Tort Claims Act in order to decide whether or not the plaintiff was entitled to sue Philadelphia for injuries she sustained while getting out of a city owned vehicle.

Political Subdivision Tort Claims Act
42 Pa.C.S. § 8541 - 8542

§ 8541. Governmental immunity generally

Except as otherwise provided in this subchapter, no local agency shall be liable for any damages on account of any injury to a person or property caused by any act of the local agency or an employee thereof or any other person.

§ 8542. Exceptions to governmental immunity

(A)   LIABILITY IMPOSED. A local agency shall be liable for damages on account of an injury to a person or property within the limits set forth in this subchapter if both of the following conditions are satisfied and the injury occurs as a result of one of the acts set forth in subsection (b):

   (1)   The damages would be recoverable under common law or a statute creating a cause of action if the injury were caused by a person not having available a defense under section 8541 (relating to governmental immunity generally) or section 8546 (relating to defense of official immunity); and

   (2)   The injury was caused by the negligent acts of the local agency or an employee thereof acting within the scope of his office or duties with respect to one of the categories listed in subsection (b). As used in this paragraph, "negligent acts" shall not include acts or conduct which constitutes a crime, actual fraud, actual malice or willful misconduct.

(B)   ACTS WHICH MAY IMPOSE LIABILITY. The following acts by a local agency or any of its employees may result in the imposition of liability on a local agency:

(1) Vehicle liability. . . .

(2) Care, custody or control of personal property. . . .

(3) Real property. . . .

(4) Trees, traffic controls and street lighting. . . .

(5) Utility service facilities. . . .

(6) Streets. . . .

(7) Sidewalks. . . .

(8) Care, custody or control of animals. . . .

Love v. City of Philadelphia
518 Pa. 370 (1988)

Justice McDermott delivered the opinion of the court.

Catherine Love appeals from an order of the Commonwealth Court reversing an order of the Philadelphia Court of Common Pleas which entered judgment for appellant against the City of Philadelphia.

The facts as found by the trial court are as follows. In approximately August of 1979, Catherine Love, then age 73, began attending the Mann Adult Center which was administered by the City of Philadelphia, Department of Public Health. Mrs. Love was transported to and from the Mann Center in a city owned van driven by Mr. Robert Kitchen. Mrs. Love was blind in one eye and had impaired vision in the other, and therefore required assistance boarding and alighting from the van. Mr. Kitchen usually parked the van at the curb in front of Mrs. Love's home. He would place a portable step at the doors to the van and would assist Mrs. Love in and out of the van.

On the afternoon of February 15, 1980, Mr. Kitchen transported Mrs. Love, the last occupant of the van that day, from the Mann Center to her home. Mrs. Love fell while alighting from the van, landing in the street with her feet approximately three feet from the curb line and her back approximately two feet from the portable step which had been placed next to the van.

Mr. Kitchen became aware that Mrs. Love had fallen and summoned the help of Mrs. Love's daughter-in-law and granddaughter. The Philadelphia Police were called and Mrs. Love was transported to Episcopal Hospital for treatment of her injuries. Mrs. Love suffered multiple injuries and was subsequently placed in a nursing home.

Catherine Love filed an action against the City of Philadelphia alleging that the city's negligence caused her injuries. The case was heard non-jury. At the conclusion of the trial the judge entered a verdict for Catherine Love against the city in the amount of $ 375,000.00. The court held that Mrs. Love's injuries were caused by the negligence of an employee of the City of Philadelphia who was acting within the scope of his employment, and that Mrs. Love's cause of action came within the "motor vehicle" exception to the Political Subdivision Tort Claims Act.

The city appealed to the Commonwealth Court which reversed the trial court's verdict, holding that the facts of this case did not fall under the "motor vehicle" exception. Hence, the city was held to be immune from suit.

Catherine Love petitioned this court for allowance of appeal, and we granted allocatur. Her appeal presents one issue: whether the act of entering into or alighting from a motor vehicle constitutes operation of that vehicle under 42 Pa.C.S. § 8542(b)(1). Local agencies are immune from tort liability except for certain specific exceptions enumerated in the Political Subdivision Tort Claims Act. One of those exceptions applies to vehicle liability, and it provides in relevant part that liability may result from "[t]he operation of any motor vehicle in the possession or control of the local agency . . ."

The statute does not define the word "operation", nor is it defined in the general definition section of the consolidated statutes. It is therefore our responsibility to derive the intent of the General Assembly in using the word.

In the recent case of *Mascaro v. Youth Study Center*, 514 Pa. 351, 523 A.2d 1118 (1987), this Court held that exceptions to governmental immunity were to be "narrowly interpreted . . . given the expressed legislative intent to insulate political subdivisions from tort liability." Therefore, we are constrained to strictly construe the crucial term, i.e. "operation".

Where terms are not otherwise defined "words and phrases shall be construed according to rules of grammar and according to their common and approved usage." We have generally used dictionaries as source material for determining the common and approved usage of a term....

Black's Law Dictionary defines the word "operate" as follows: This word, when used with relation to automobiles, signifies a personal act in working the mechanism of the automobile . . . Black's further defines "operation" as: the process of operating or mode of action." Black's

Law Dictionary, p. 984 (rev. 5th ed. 1979).

Similar definitions are found in the Oxford Dictionary. The American Heritage Dictionary defines "operation" as "[t]o run or control the functioning of: operate a machine"; and defines "operation" as "[t]he state of being operative or functioning in operation."

The trial court eschewed these dictionary definitions, choosing instead to look to the Pennsylvania No-Fault Act. By this analytical method the court found that "operation" included entering into or alighting from the vehicle. However, the definition relied upon by the trial court, found at 40 P.S. § 1009.103 referred to the "maintenance and use of a motor vehicle." It did not define "operation" of a vehicle and thus was inapplicable to this case. Furthermore, as the Commonwealth Court noted, the No-Fault Act was intended to be broadly construed to provide coverage wherever possible. As we have noted, that was not the legislative intention behind the motor vehicle exception to governmental immunity.

Reference to the No-Fault Act is instructive, however, on one point, in that it demonstrates that the General Assembly recognized a distinction between the term "operation" and the phrase "maintenance and use," since it carefully chose to use one term in one context but not in the other. The General Assembly does not lightly choose its words, and the choice of distinct descriptions cannot be ignored.

Thus the term "operates" must have been intended to mean something other than "maintenance and use." As we have illustrated, to operate something means to actually put it in motion. Merely preparing to operate a vehicle, or acts taken at the cessation of operating a vehicle are not the same as actually operating that vehicle. Thus, according to the common and approved usage of the word "operation", the van was not in operation at the time of Mrs. Love's accident. Getting into or alighting from a vehicle are merely acts ancillary to the actual operation of that vehicle.

In summary, we wish to emphasize that the issue here is not whether one may be tortiously injured entering or alighting from a stopped vehicle. Rather, the issue is the confining question of whether a political subdivision is immunized from suit when one is so injured, notwithstanding what may be the actual tort of their employees. The legislature, for reasons of policy, reasons we are not entitled to dilute for sympathy or even outrage at specific instances of blatant tort, has decided that such an immunity does exist, and we must abide, sometimes leaving dreadful injuries, negligently inflicted, uncompensated. The juridical concept that where there is a wrong there must be a right often depends on the wisdom and large responsibility of the legislature. What rights for what wrongs are generally their prerogative and apportioned in the exercise of their many responsibilities and competing needs. Their task, like ours, is never easy. However, it is our duty to respect and enforce their judgment, even with heavy hearts in particular instances.

Therefore, we affirm the order of the Commonwealth Court.

Papadakos, Justice, dissenting.

I respectfully dissent from the majority's construction of the term "operation" as contained in the motor vehicle exception to immunity from tort liability of the Political Subdivision Tort Claims Act. I agree that exceptions to governmental immunity under the Act are to be "narrowly interpreted." However, I do not believe that the legislature intended so narrow a construction as to permit avoidance of responsibility for the negligent conduct of the operator of a City vehicle where the conduct was within the course and scope of the operator's employment and, in my view, constituted operation of the vehicle. The majority, in the name of strict construction, has arrived at a result which is contrary to law, logic and fundamental justice.

Under the majority's interpretation, one can only be operating a vehicle if he actually puts it in motion or drives it. If the legislature so intended, I am sure it is capable of making such a distinction by using the appropriate language. The legislature used the term operation of a vehicle and this includes conduct which is generally within the intended use of the vehicle and entails the use of the vehicle's appurtenant parts. In construing the term operation for purposes of the drunk driving statute, it has been held that: "[a]driver may be in 'actual physical control' of his car and therefore 'operating' it while it is parked or merely standing still 'so long as [the driver is] keeping the car in restraint or is in a position to regulate its movements.'" Moreover, the term operation cannot be construed without regard to the facts of this case and the duties of the operator with respect to the vehicle and the Appellant. The operator was responsible not only for the transportation of Catherine Love to and from the Mann Adult Center, but also to help her in getting in and out of the van with the assistance of a stool that was to be used at all times. The operator also testified that it was his duty to deliver her safely on to the walk. In light of the fact that Mrs. Love was found in the street approximately three feet from the curb line with her back approximately two feet from the stool, it becomes clear that the operator did not get her safely to the sidewalk. The trial court found that Mrs. Love's injuries were incurred while alighting from the vehicle, that alighting from the vehicle is an adjunct of the operation of the vehicle since a stool was used to assist with the ingress and egress of the passenger. The court also found that the stool was an appendage of the vehicle and a necessary and indispensable component of the operation of the vehicle as it related to the transportation of Mrs. Love, and that alighting from the van by the use of the stool is an indivisible aspect of the operation of the vehicle. I agree with the trial court conclusion and would, for the reasons stated, reverse the decision of the Commonwealth Court and reinstate the judgment of the trial court.

Spousal Immunity: Can married persons sue one another?

The doctrine of spousal immunity grew out of the idea that a woman's identity legally merged into that of her husband when they married and they became a single legal entity. Strange as that sounds today, the idea meant that spouses, with some exceptions, could not sue one another because it is impossible to sue yourself! While Pennsylvania courts as recently as 1973 had upheld the doctrine of spousal immunity from tort liability, the Pennsylvania Supreme Court took advantage of a peculiar factual situation in 1981 to eliminate the doctrine.

After rejecting the argument that the doctrine was supported by sections of the *Married Persons Property Act*, the court then analyzed and rejected the policy grounds on which the doctrine had been based and concluded that [the] "marital relationship alone may not deny a party redress for injury" and abolished "the defense of interspousal immunity as a bar to suits in the courts of this Commonwealth."

In reaching a conclusion regarding spousal immunity, the Pennsylvania Supreme Court quotes from its own earlier opinion abolishing parental immunity (*Falco v. Pados*): "In the last analysis it is much to be preferred that we depend upon the efficacy of the judicial process to ferret out the meritorious from the fraudulent rather than using a broad broom to sweep away a class of claims, a number of which are admittedly meritorious."

Hack v. Hack
495 Pa. 300 (1981)

Justice Roberts delivered the opinion of the court.

Appellant, Judith Mazzochetti Hack, filed an action in trespass for damages incurred as a result of personal injuries sustained in an automobile accident on May 27, 1971, when she was a passenger in a car driven by appellee Joseph Steven Hack, owned by Joseph Steven Hack, Sr., and insured by Government Employees Insurance Company. Appellant averred in her complaint that the injuries she sustained were solely the result of the negligence of appellee. The Court of Common Pleas of Montgomery County granted appellee's motion for summary judgment on the ground that the action was barred by this Court's decision in *DiGirolamo v. Apanavage*, 454 Pa. 557, 312 A.2d 382 (1973) which affirmed the vitality of interspousal immunity. The Superior Court affirmed without opinion. This Court granted allowance of appeal.

Appellant and appellee Hack were unmarried at the time of appellee's alleged negligence. They married each other almost a year later on May 18, 1972. Approximately one year after their marriage, on April 26, 1973, appellant commenced this action. On September 9, 1974, appellant and appellee Hack were divorced. However, four months later, on January 16, 1975, they remarried. The record indicates that they continue to be married to each other at the present time.

On appeal, appellant argues that the interspousal immunity doctrine does not apply because of the peculiar factual and procedural posture of this case. First, she contends that appellee has waived the defense of interspousal immunity because the answer to the complaint, filed after the divorce and remarriage of appellant and appellee, pleads only the first marriage (now dissolved but in existence at the time the action was commenced) and not the second marriage (the only marriage in existence at the time the answer was filed). Appellant's second argument is that, even if the pleadings were proper, the defense of interspousal immunity should not apply where, as here, the marriage in effect at the time suit is instituted does not continue in effect throughout the litigation.

Adoption of either theory advanced by appellant would deny application of interspousal immunity as a defense in this action, but would leave unanswered the real question presented: whether interspousal immunity for personal injuries inflicted prior to or during marriage should continue as part of the common law of this Commonwealth. We reject the opportunity present on these facts to engraft exceptions onto an outmoded and unwarranted doctrine which denies a litigant, because of marital status and relationship, the opportunity to prove his or her claim in court. Instead, we conclude that a tortfeasor's immunity from liability because of his marital relationship with the injured party cannot be sustained on the basis of law, logic or public policy. Hence we abrogate the judicially-created doctrine of interspousal immunity.

I   This Court's most recent decision upholding the doctrine of interspousal immunity was rendered in *DiGirolamo v. Apanavage*, 454 Pa. 557, 312 A.2d 382 (1973). The majority of the Court specifically refused "to re-examine the reasoning underlying the rule, as well as the public policy considerations" stating that "the instant decision is controlled by a specific state statute." On an earlier occasion, however, this Court referred to the rule of interspousal immunity as *"both statutory and decisional,"* and as "now based upon social reasons and public policy." *Meisel v. Little*, 407 Pa. 546, 548, 180 A.2d 772, 773 (1962) (emphasis in original). A reading of these cases makes clear that interspousal immunity has survived as a doctrine in this Commonwealth only because this Court has erroneously interpreted the statutes relating to married women, 48 P.S. § 1-1 et seq. (1965), and adhered to outmoded common law concepts.

A.   In *DiGirolamo v. Apanavage*, supra, and *Meisel v. Little*, supra, the Court focused on whether the provision of the Married Persons Property Act which permits one spouse to sue the other "to protect and recover her [or his] separate property," 48 P.S. § 111 (1965), includes an action in tort for unliquidated damages. In answering this question in the negative, the majority overlooked relevant provisions and history of the statutes relating to married women.

The Married Persons Property Act, like similar statutes enacted in every state, was designed to abolish the common law "unity" of husband and wife, and thereby to secure to a married woman a separate legal identity from her husband with corresponding substantive and procedural rights.

At common law, the wife's identity merged upon marriage with that of her husband. Husband and wife were legally presumed to be one. That "one" was the husband, the wife having no independent rights. A married woman had no capacity to contract, to convey property, or to sue and be sued in her own name. In the words of one commentator, "[a] combination of all these incidents made it impossible at common law for one spouse ever to be civilly liable to the other for an act which would be a tort if the relation did not exist. Where the act occurred before marriage, a cause of action arose. If the man was the tortfeasor, the woman's right would be a chose in action, which upon marriage the man would have the right to reduce to possession. This union in one person of the right-duty relation discharges the duty as a matter of substance, and there is besides the procedural difficulty that the husband would be both plaintiff and defendant. If the woman was the tortfeasor, the man's right would be a chose in action against the woman, whose duty upon marriage would devolve upon the husband as a derivative duty, which would be discharged by union of the right and duty in the same person; and there is the same procedural difficulty. Where the act occurs during coverture, the matter is complicated by other factors . . . . the right and the duty to make compensation, if any can be said to exist, would be united eo instante in the same person, and no cause of action could arise; and even if it could be said to arise, there would be the procedural difficulty of the husband's being both plaintiff and defendant. The same reasoning would apply to acts which injure the person, whether done by husband to wife or by wife to husband . . . ." McCurdy, *Torts Between Persons in Domestic Relation*, 43 Harv.L.Rev. 1030, 1033-34 (1930).

The first Married Persons Property Act in this Commonwealth, enacted in 1848, guaranteed as a substantive right that "every species and description of property, whether consisting of real, personal or mixed, which may be owned by or belong to any single woman, shall continue to be the property of such woman, as fully after her marriage as before; and all such property of whatever name or kind, which shall accrue to any married woman during coverture by will, descent, deed of conveyance or otherwise, shall be owned, used and enjoyed by such married woman as her own separate property . . . ." Act of April 11, 1848, P.L. 536, § 6, 48 P.S. § 64 (1965). This language, which continues in force today as section 64 of Title 48, is supplemented by section 32.1 of that same title: "Hereafter, a married woman shall have the same right and power as a married man to acquire, own, possess, control, use, convey, lease or mortgage any property of any kind, real, personal, or mixed, either in possession or in expectancy, or to make any contract in writing or otherwise, and may exercise the said right and power in the same manner and to the same extent as a married man." Act of July 15, 1957, P.L. 969, § 1, 48 P.S. § 32.1 (1965). Both of these provisions granting to married women substantive property and contract rights are contained in Chapter 2, "Substantive Rights of Married Women," of Title 48.

In Chapter 3, "Remedies and Liabilities of Married Women," section 111 provides: "Hereafter a married woman may sue and be sued civilly, in all respects, and in any form of action, and with the same effect and results and consequences, as an unmarried person; but she may not sue her husband, except in a proceeding for divorce, or in a proceeding to protect and recover her separate property; nor may he sue her, except in a proceeding for divorce, or in a proceeding to protect or recover his separate property; nor may she be arrested or imprisoned for her torts." Act of June 8, 1893, P.L. 344, § 3, as amended, Act of March 27, 1913, P.L. 14, § 1, 48 P.S. § 111 (1965). Section 111, read in light of the substantive rights provided in Chapter 2 which it is intended to effectuate, compels the conclusion that "a proceeding to recover her [or his] separate property" includes the right to bring an action in tort. Clearly a claim for unliquidated tort damages falls within the language, "property of any kind, real, personal, or mixed, either in possession or in expectancy," 48 P.S. § 32.1 (1965), and "[e]very species and description of property, whether consisting of real, personal or mixed . . . and all such property of whatever name or kind, which shall accrue . . . by will, descent, deed of conveyance or otherwise, shall be . . . separate property," 48 P.S. § 64 (1965). The history of section 111 also compels

this result. Prior to the original enactment of section 111 in 1893, the statute governing the capacity of a married woman to sue and be sued provided: "A married woman shall be capable of entering into and rendering herself liable upon any contract relating to any trade or business in which she may engage, or for necessaries, and for the use, enjoyment and improvement of her separate estate, and for suing and being sued, either upon such contracts or for torts done to or committed by her, in all respects as if she were a feme sole, and her husband need not be joined with her as plaintiff, or defendant, or be made a party to any action, suit or legal proceeding of any kind brought by or against her in her individual right; and any debt, damages or costs recovered by her in any such action, suit or proceeding shall be her separate property, and any debt, damages or costs recovered against her in any such action, suit or other proceeding shall be payable out of her separate property and not otherwise . . . ." Act of June 3, 1887, P.L. 332, § 2. This language was interpreted as conclusively establishing that a married woman's right to recover for a tort is her separate property.

The acts of 1893 and 1913 subsequently abbreviated this language to its present form to provide that a married woman may bring an action "to protect or recover her separate property." 48 P.S. § 111 (1965). These acts did not repeat the explicit provisions of the act of 1887 that a wife's husband "need not be joined with her as plaintiff, or defendant, or be made a party . . ." and that "any debt, damages or costs recovered by her in any such action, suit or proceeding shall be her separate property . . . ." Nevertheless, since the act of 1887, it has never been questioned that a wife may sue in her own name without joining her husband as a party. Similarly, there is no legitimate statutory basis upon which to doubt that the definition of "separate property" provided in the act of 1887 was intended to apply equally to the acts of 1893 and 1913. Certainly neither act states otherwise.

The remedial purpose of the Married Persons Property Act, to enlarge a married woman's capacity to acquire and dispose of property and to sue and be sued, requires that any ambiguity in the statute's language must be read to expand, not restrict, the rights of married women. This Court has so demonstrated by consistently holding that a married woman may maintain an action in equity to protect and gain possession of her separate property, even during the period when that right was statutorily abridged at law.

These holdings were premised on the theory that the Married Persons Property Act, "an enabling and remedial statute," Heckman v. Heckman, 215 Pa. at 208, 64 A. at 426, was intended to enlarge the capacity of a married woman to sue and be sued by providing a cause of action at law, and not to restrict her capacity by eliminating equity as an alternative remedy. . . .

Thus, in light of the statute's language, history and purpose, it is reasonable to conclude that the acts of 1893 and 1913, like the act of 1887, intended that "separate property" include a claim for unliquidated tort damages.

Neither appellant nor appellee attempts to justify retention of the common law doctrine of interspousal immunity. Nevertheless, we address the social policy reasons which have traditionally been set forth as justifications for immunizing a tortfeasor-spouse from liability for his wrongs: "unity" of husband and wife; family harmony; prevention of collusion; and avoidance of trivial claims.

The first of these reasons, "unity" of husband and wife, clearly cannot be a legitimate basis for retaining interspousal immunity. As previously stated, the very purpose of the Married Persons Property Act was to abolish the validity of this concept at law and to establish a wife's separate legal identity and capacity. Despite the failure of prior decisions to abrogate interspousal immunity, these decisions have candidly recognized that interspousal immunity cannot be justified on the "unity" theory. Moreover, this Court has recently made clear that "[m]odern conditions demand that courts no longer engage in the automatic and unsupported assumption that one's pecuniary or proprietary interest is identical to that of one's spouse."

Although some decisions have purported to rely upon family harmony as a social policy supporting interspousal immunity, the family harmony theory, like the "unity" theory, is irreconcilable with this Court's decisions. The interspousal immunity doctrine as applied in this Commonwealth has barred an injured party from maintaining a direct tort suit against his or her spouse but has not barred an action against a third party, who may then bring in the negligent spouse as an additional defendant. Thus, although a direct suit against a spouse is not permitted, the object of such a suit --

recovery of damages from the spouse -- may nonetheless be achieved through indirect means.

If appellant had been injured in a two car collision and had filed a tort action against the driver of the second car, who then brought in appellee as a third-party defendant, appellant would have been permitted to proceed to trial. If both the original defendant and appellee had then been found liable as joint tortfeasors, appellant would have been able to recover her full judgment from the original defendant, and the original defendant would then have been able to enforce a right of contribution from appellee. If only appellee had been found liable, appellant would have been able to recover her full judgment directly from appellee.

Similarly, if appellant had been injured by the negligence of appellee while appellee was acting in the scope of his employment, and appellant had filed a tort action against appellee's employer who then brought in appellee as a third-party defendant, again unlike here, appellant would have been permitted to proceed to trial. Upon a finding of liability, the employer, responsible only on the theory of respondeat superior, would have been able to recover fully from appellee.

The only significant factor which presently operates to bar one spouse's suit against the other is the absence of the fortuitous circumstance of possible third-party liability. Clearly the presence or absence of a third party should not determine the rights and remedies of spouses inter se. Indeed, if the theory of family harmony were a valid justification for interspousal immunity, there could be no basis to allow recovery in any case.

In fact, where the tort is a negligent one, a lawsuit is less likely to impair family harmony than where the action is for breach of contract or conversion of property. These latter actions, unlike a claim of negligence, typically involve allegations of intentional wrongdoing and are not covered by insurance. Hence they are more likely to be disruptive of the marital relationship. Yet there is no question that such actions have been permitted at law since enactment of the Married Persons Property Act of 1856 and in equity even before then.

The facts of this case themselves belie any theory that interspousal tort litigation is inherently conducive to family disharmony. Although appellant and her husband were divorced approximately one year and four months after commencement of this action, the record does not indicate that the divorce was in any respect caused by marital discord resulting from the litigation. In fact, the parties' remarriage during the pendency of this litigation only four months after their divorce and their continued marriage to each other would indicate that the present action has not affected their marital felicity.

Especially, where as here the defendant-spouse is indemnified by insurance, there is no legitimate basis to believe that an action will adversely affect family harmony. If anything, the converse may be true. Denial of the action may itself promote marital discord by causing the husband and wife to rely on their own funds to pay expenses that otherwise would be paid for by insurance. Since the very purpose of liability insurance is compensation, its presence argues in favor of permitting an injured individual to establish the liability of his or her tortfeasor-spouse. Certainly it is "illogical to allow a wife to sue her husband's employer for injuries for which he is vicariously responsible, and to deny her a right to sue her husband for injuries sustained in an automobile accident in order to collect from his insurer on a contractual responsibility."

The third rationale advanced in support of interspousal tort immunity is that husband and wife may act collusively to recover unjustifiably from an insurance carrier. This rationale, however, is analytically inconsistent with the previous argument that tort litigation will disrupt family harmony. Moreover, it is wholly speculative.

Just as this Court rejected the possibility of collusion as justification for continuation of parental immunity, *Falco v. Pados*, so we reject it as justification for perpetuating interspousal immunity. The laws of contract and evidence are ample protection against any danger of fraud or collusion.

This Court's admonition in abolishing parental immunity applies equally here: "'In a day when automobile accidents are unfortunately becoming so frequent and the injuries suffered by the passengers are often so severe, it seems unjust to deny the claims of the many because of the potentiality for fraud by the few. Moreover, there is something wanting in a system of justice which permits strangers, friends, relatives and emancipated children to recover for injuries suffered as a result of their driver's negligence but denies this right to the driver's spouse and minor children who are also passengers in the same

vehicle.' . . . In the last analysis it is much to be preferred that we depend upon the efficacy of the judicial process to ferret out the meritorious from the fraudulent rather than using a broad broom to sweep away a class of claims, a number of which are admittedly meritorious."

The final justification for interspousal immunity, avoidance of trivial claims, is subject to the same analytical weakness as the argument regarding possible collusion and deserves the same response. The solution to fraudulent or trivial claims is not to prohibit all claims including the meritorious, but rather to rely on the judicial process to deny both the fraudulent and the frivolous. The adjudicatory process, which resolves causes on a case-by-case basis by applying legal principles to concrete factual situations, is well equipped to consider customs of human conduct.

As has been demonstrated, none of the justifications advanced in support of retention of interspousal immunity is persuasive. Thus we adopt here, as we have elsewhere, "the prevailing philosophy that liability follows tortious conduct."

II. This Court has full authority, and the corresponding duty, to examine its precedents to assure that a rule previously developed is not perpetuated when the reason for the rule no longer exists and when application of the rule would cause injustice. On previous occasions this Court has not hesitated to reconsider precedent in light of current social conditions and public policy.

The common law, which this Court is charged with the obligation to develop, is a constant "quest for reconciling authority with reason." This Court stated in *Estate of*

Grossman, supra: "It is the essence of common law courts today as in earlier times to view the body of the law as a living and developing legal system designed to serve societal needs in elevating the life and utility of the law rather than as a static set of rules. . . . 'Precedent speaks for the past; policy for the present and the future. The goal which we seek is a blend which takes into account in due proportion the wisdom of the past and the needs of the present.'

In accordance with these principles, we conclude that interspousal tort immunity is premised upon outmoded theories unsupported by today's social conditions and public policy and hence has no justification in contemporary society. Our conclusion is consistent with our duty to implement justice: "One of the great virtues of the common law is its dynamic nature that makes it adaptable to the requirements of society at the time of its application in court. There is not a rule of the common law in force today that has not evolved from some earlier rule of common law, gradually in some instances, more suddenly in others, leaving the common law of today when compared with the common law of centuries ago as different as day is from night. The nature of the common law requires that each time a rule of law is applied it be carefully scrutinized to make sure that the conditions and needs of the times have not so changed as to make further application of it the instrument of injustice. Dean Pound posed the problem admirably in his Interpretations of Legal History (1922) when he stated, 'Law must be stable, and yet it cannot stand still.'"

Having concluded that marital relationship alone may not deny a party redress for injury, we abolish the defense of interspousal immunity as a bar to suits in the courts of this Commonwealth.

Order of the Superior Court reversed, order of the trial court granting summary judgment vacated, and record remanded for proceedings consistent with this opinion.

Wrongful Life/Wrongful Birth: Are there any limits on medical malpractice liability?

In 1979, well before the legislature enacted the Actions for Wrongful Birth and Wrongful Life statute (42 Pa.C.S. 8305), the Pennsylvania courts were confronted for the very first time with the issue of "wrongful life." In the following incredible case, a man sought to become sterile to avoid passing on a crippling inherited disease to any more children (he already had two children who suffered from the disease, neurofibromatosis.) After one doctor allegedly assured him that his vasectomy was successful his wife became pregnant. A second doctor performed an abortion which he allegedly assured her was successful. Nonetheless, she gave premature birth to a child who suffered from the disease. Both doctors were sued. While liability is assumed, the measurement of damages in such a case poses considerable problems. Should the court award pain and suffering for the birth, plus the costs of birth? This is often dubbed a "wrongful birth" recovery. Alternatively, should the negligent physicians be responsible for the costs of raising the child? This is usually referred to as a "wrongful life" recovery. Should the wrongful life recovery be available only when the child is born unhealthy?

In the *Speck* case, the court addresses these issues. This case also asks, "who may be the plaintiffs?" Here, the creative lawyer includes as plaintiffs the parents (for their pain, suffering, expenses and anticipated costs of raising the child); the child herself (arguing that it would be better off for her to have not been born than be born with such a handicap); and even the siblings (arguing that their parents time and money will now have to be divided into three parts instead of two!). After an extended discussion, the court refused to allow recovery either for the costs of raising and caring for the child or for the emotional suffering of either the parents or the child. In effect, the court refused to recognize any cause of action for a "wrongful life" in Pennsylvania.

Speck v. Finegold
268 Pa. Super. 342 (1979)

Judge Cercone wrote the opinion for the court.

This case comes before us on plaintiffs' appeal from the lower court's order sustaining defendant-physicians' preliminary objections to certain allegations contained in plaintiffs' complaint. The intended effect of the preliminary objections is to terminate plaintiffs' lawsuit on grounds that plaintiffs' action is contrary to law and public policy. The matter before us, of first impression in the appellate courts of Pennsylvania, presents for judicial inquiry and decision the cognizability of an action in law brought by plaintiffs to recover damages against defendant- physicians whose alleged acts of negligence resulted in the birth of a child they feared would be born with mental and physical abnormalities. We affirm the order of the lower court in part and reverse and remand in part.

The difficulties presented in this case are aptly described in the words of Mr. Justice Blackmun in *Roe v. Wade*, (1973), a case overturning a Texas statute on constitutional grounds, concerning a woman's right to abortion: "We forthwith acknowledge our awareness of the sensitive and emotional nature of the abortion controversy, of the vigorous opposing views, even among physicians, and the deep and seemingly absolute convictions that the subject inspires. One's philosophy, one's experiences, one's exposure to the raw edges of human existence, one's religious training, one's attitudes toward life and family and their values, and the moral standards one establishes and seeks to observe, are all likely to influence and to color one's thinking and conclusions about abortion. . . .

"Our task, of course, is to resolve the issue by [resort to legal principles] free of emotion and predilection." From its earliest days, the common law held to the principle that "in civil court the death of a human being could not be complained of as an injury." *Baker v. Bolton* (1808). The reluctance of the judiciary to risk going beyond a principle that a tort died with its victim, became the impetus to legislative recognition of the cause of action since known as a "wrongful death" action, now an everyday source of litigation in the courts.

The courts today are now drawn into a new era of legal theory, one testing the validity of a cause of action generally termed "wrongful life." As stated by the New York Court of Appeals, "[e]ven as a pure question of law, unencumbered by unresolved issues of fact, the weighing of the validity of a cause of action seeking compensation for a wrongful causation of life itself casts an almost Orwellian shadow, premised as it is upon concepts of genetic predictability once foreign to the evolutionary process. It borders on the absurdly obvious to observe that resolution of this question transcends the mechanical application of legal principles." *Becker v. Schwartz* (1978).

However, this decision of the New York Court of Appeals, after raising the specter of improbabilities approaching the supernatural, comes to grips with reality and succumbs to the gravitational pull of human values when it finally concedes any such resolution, whatever it may be, must invariably be colored by notions of public policy, the validity of which remains, as always, a matter upon which reasonable persons may disagree.

Frank Speck, Jr. is a victim of the disease known as neurofibromatosis, a crippling disease of the fibrous structures of the nerves. In fact, his two children, Valerie and Lee Ann, are victims of this disease. In Lee Ann it is particularly crippling and disfiguring. Concerned with the possible recurrence of his affliction in a child conceived in the future, Frank and his wife, Dorothy, decided to limit the size of their family. Frank decided it would be best if he were made sterile in order to prevent such a consequence. For this reason he went to defendant-physician, Dr. Finegold, a licensed physician and surgeon in urology, for his advice and treatment with respect to a vasectomy procedure.

After examining Mr. Speck, Dr. Finegold represented to him that a vasectomy operation would sterilize him. Pursuant to an oral agreement to that effect reached between the parties on April 28, 1974, Dr. Finegold performed the vasectomy. Following the operation, Dr. Finegold assured Mr. Speck that he was made sterile and that he could engage in sexual relations with his wife without contraceptive devices. (The complaint does not state any specific time had passed before Dr. Finegold made his reassuring statement.) Mr. Speck followed this advice and Mrs. Speck became pregnant. Worried that Mrs. Speck's pregnancy might result in the dreaded consequences they wished to avoid, the Specks then sought advice and treatment by defendant-doctor, Dr. Schwartz, a physician and surgeon practicing in the field of obstetrics and gynecology. Pursuant to an oral agreement, the parents engaged Dr. Schwartz to perform an abortion on Mrs. Speck in order to terminate her pregnancy. On December 27, 1974, Dr. Schwartz performed the abortion procedure and subsequently represented to the Specks that the operation was a success and that Mrs. Speck's pregnancy had been terminated. However, sometime after the operation, Mrs. Speck informed Dr. Schwartz that she felt her pregnancy was continuing. The doctor "again and persistently" assured and represented to the Specks that Mrs. Speck's fetus had been aborted. However, on April 29, 1975, Mrs.

Speck gave birth to a premature child, Francine, afflicted with the crippling disease of neurofibromatosis. Throughout, the motivating purpose of the Specks' willingness to go through these procedures was to prevent the birth of another child who they feared might be born with mental and physical deficiencies.

Plaintiffs commenced this lawsuit based on a five-count complaint in trespass and assumpsit, seeking damages on behalf of the infant, Francine, for "wrongful life"; on behalf of their daughters, Valerie and Lee Ann, for economic hardship; and in their own right, for the pecuniary expenses they have borne and will in the future bear for the care and treatment of their child, Francine. Plaintiffs' complaint also seeks damages for emotional, mental and physical injuries and expenses suffered by plaintiff-parents as the result of the birth of Francine and damages suffered by Frank Speck, Jr. occasioned by the loss of his wife's services. Additionally, plaintiffs claim damages for their personal expenses, pain and suffering, and emotional distress incident to the alleged negligence in the vasectomy and abortion surgeries.

Plaintiffs allege, inter alia, that Francine's birth was the direct and proximate result of the physicians' acts of negligence, breach of contract and misrepresentation in their incorrect medical advice, in their negligent and unskillful diagnosis, care and treatment and for actions of negligence catalogued as: failure to properly perform the surgeries in the possession, employment and exercise of that degree and skill, learning and care required of them as physicians and specialists in their given fields of medicine; in failing to conduct tests to ascertain the success or failure of the vasectomy and abortion procedures; in failing to inform them of the risks involved; and in representing to the plaintiffs that the operations were successful and for the intended purposes, when, in fact, the doctors knew or should have known that they were not.

The lower court, on the basis of the defendant-doctors' demurrers, accepted the facts set forth in the complaint relating to the negligent acts alleged and found that plaintiffs had sustained and will sustain and suffer injuries and damages in the future, but held that no relief was cognizable in law which would permit plaintiffs to recover money damages arising out of or related to the life of Francine. The lower court allowed Mr. Speck's claim for damages incident to the vasectomy to stand for trial. It disallowed Mrs. Speck's claim for damages incident to the abortion procedure because she misjoined her counts in the complaint with those of her husband in violation of Pa.R.C.P. 1020(d)(1), 1020(b), 1028(a), 2228, 2229(a). The lower court, however, has allowed her to amend that part of the complaint and we agree.

In denying all claims of plaintiffs relating to the birth of Francine, the lower court based its decision on grounds that any allowance of damages for her birth is not recognized in law and is against public policy, and, in addition, that the damages are of such speculative nature as to be immeasurable. The basis of the lower court's view of public policy is that estimating the worth and sanctity of life as against non-life is a task that goes beyond the ken of human understanding or resolution. We hold that the lower court's denial of all damages arising out of the birth of Francine is untenable. According to the lower court, a cloak of inviolability protects doctors and others in the medical profession when their acts of negligence relate to "wrongful birth" cases despite established principles of law which do not protect these same persons in other categories of negligent care. Thus, we do not agree with the lower court in its blanket protection of a tort-feasor in these cases. To agree with the lower court in the instant case would be to allow an infringement of fundamental rights, which infringements are impermissible in other cases involving negligent conduct.

At the outset, the question presented for review is not to decide whether plaintiffs should ultimately prevail in this litigation, nor to decide what damages are recoverable if they do prevail, but rather to decide whether their complaint states a cognizable cause of action in law. Consequently, our problem, based on defendants' demurrers, is to decide whether plaintiffs have set forth a sufficiently cognizable lawsuit within the concept, purpose and function of the judicial process to have their claims considered by a court of law beyond and in addition to those allowed by the lower court. The merits of plaintiffs' claims, if cognizable at law, will be decided at trial where the doctors will also have the fullest opportunity to prove that they were not negligent nor responsible for plaintiffs' damages as alleged in plaintiffs' complaint. The question here, obstinate in its difficulty of solution, is whether and under what theory plaintiffs are entitled to recover.

The term "wrongful life" covers a multifaceted concept under which plaintiffs claim factually divergent wrongs in seeking judicial recognition and relief. In this context, the instant case may appropriately be considered to carry three labels: (a) "wrongful conception" wherein Mr. Speck underwent an unsuccessful vasectomy procedure and together with his wife seeks damages against Dr. Finegold for the "wrongful birth" of a child arising out of a negligent sterilization procedure. This kind of action, as we will see, meets with mixed reaction by the courts; (b) "wrongful birth" wherein Mr. and Mrs. Speck seek damages against Dr. Schwartz for the birth of a child attributed to a negligent abortion procedure, and a wrongful diagnosis of an existing pregnancy resulting in the deprivation of the mother's choice to terminate the pregnancy within the permissible time period; (c) a "wrongful life" action where an unplanned child seeks recovery for injuries suffered because of the negligent failure to prevent its birth. This kind of action has met with disapproval by the courts.

In reviewing the history of the cases on this subject, we find that the decisions which deny any recovery for "wrongful birth" do so, as did the lower court, primarily on the basis that the sanctity of life precludes a cognizable action in law and/or that it is impossible to measure damages between a child being born, defectively or not, and not being born at all. The courts which point to immeasurability as a reason for denying recovery for both parents and child hold that when a child or his parents claim it would be better if the child had not been born, they make it impossible for damages to be measured.

Although there is no appellate decision in our Commonwealth involving the question of whether parents and children can recover for damages arising out of a "wrongful birth", we do have in one of our lower courts in Pennsylvania an early case, *Shaheen v. Knight*, 6 Lyc.Rptr. 19, 11 Pa.D. & C.2d 41 (1957) (negligent sterilization), in which the court denied damages on grounds of public policy. The court's view was that although sterilization was not against public policy the recovery of damages for the birth of a normal child was foreign to the universal public sentiment of the people. The *Shaheen* court also enlarged on the public policy theme and said, "that it would be unjust for the physician to pay for the 'fun, joy and affection which plaintiff Shaheen will have in the rearing and education of this, defendant's [sic] fifth child'."

In the instant case, despite the added dimension of a mentally and physically deficient child, the lower court also held that the plaintiffs had set forth no cognizable cause of action in law for damages, because the purpose of life was procreation and the worth and sanctity of the child, regardless of the child's defects, was such that any recovery of money would be against public policy. But the lower court misses the point when it bases its opinion on this premise. The question is not the worth and sanctity of life, but whether the doctors were negligent in their surgical attempts at vasectomy and abortion.

Beside being against public policy, one of the arguments against recovery has been that abortion was against the law. *Stewart v. Long*

Island College Hospital (New York, 1972). In *Stewart* the verdict in favor of infant and parents was set aside on the ground that the action was not cognizable in law and further that it was impossible to measure damages in a "wrongful life" case. However, at this time abortion was illegal in New York. The last vestige of this public policy view was eliminated in two cases decided by the Supreme Court of the United States. In *Griswold v. Connecticut* the court held that a state statute proscribing the use of c o n t r a c e p t i v e s   w a s   a n unconstitutional intrusion upon the right of privacy and violated the Fourth and Fifth Amendments to the United States Constitution. In *Roe v. Wade*, the Supreme Court held that the constitutional right to privacy includes the woman's decision whether or not to terminate her pregnancy (absolute during first trimester, qualified during last two trimesters). The court in Roe said: ". . . Maternity, or additional offspring, may force upon the woman a distressful life and future. Psychological harm may be imminent. Mental and physical health may be taxed by child care. There is also the distress, for all concerned, associated with the unwanted child, and there is the problem of bringing a child into a family already unable, psychologically and otherwise, to care for it."

Since the *Griswold* and *Roe* cases, however, other public policy grounds are still made the basis for denial of recovery in "wrongful birth" cases. These include, inter alia: (1) the injury is too remote from the negligence; (2) the injury is too wholly out of proportion to the wrongdoer; (3) in retrospect it appears too highly extraordinary that the negligence should have brought about the harm; (4) allowance of recovery would be too unreasonable a burden on defendant; (5) allowance of recovery would open the way for fraudulent claims; (6) allowance for recovery would introduce a field of litigation that had no sensible or just stopping point. Usually one of these reasons sufficed to deny recovery in a "wrongful birth" case. It seems to us that these reasons ignore the judicial processes which daily meet other problems of equal difficulty and complexity with commendable results.

Prior to 1967, few courts had considered the question of whether the parents of an unplanned child could maintain an action against a physician for an improperly performed sterilization operation and, if so, the extent to which the compensatory damages were recoverable. The first of these cases was decided by the Minnesota courts in *Christensen v. Thornby*, 192 Minn. 123, 255 N.W. 620, 93 A.L.R. 570 (1934). In that case the plaintiff had undergone a vasectomy after his wife had experienced great difficulty in giving birth to her first child. When his wife subsequently became pregnant and delivered a healthy child, the plaintiff brought suit for his "anxiety and expenses" incident to the birth, claiming that the physician who had performed the vasectomy had deceived him into believing that the operation had been successful. The trial court sustained a demurrer to the complaint, and on appeal the trial court was upheld on the ground that the plaintiff had failed to allege that the false representation was made with fraudulent intent sufficient to support his allegation of deceit. Apart from the technical disposition made in this case, it was expressly held that sterilizations were not contrary to public policy and that an action, if properly pleaded, could be maintained against a physician for the improper performance of such an operation. Viewed in its correct posture, the *Christensen* case stands solely for the proposition that a cause of action exists for an improperly performed sterilization. The more troublesome question of damages, once liability on the part of a physician is established, was neither raised nor directly considered. Nevertheless, the following dicta from the *Christensen* opinion was later relied on by other courts to preclude parents from recovering damages for the economic costs of an unplanned child: ". . . [T]he plaintiff has been blessed with the fatherhood of another child. The expenses alleged are incident to the bearing of a child, and their avoidance is remote from the avowed purpose of the operation. As well might the plaintiff charge defendant with the cost of nurture and education of the child during its minority." What the court said in *Christensen*, supra, was that since the claim of damages was remote from the avowed purpose of protecting plaintiff's wife against the dangers of pregnancy, he had suffered no damages since his wife was not in any way injured and gave birth to a healthy child.

Christensen is not the same as the instant case. *Christensen* is not a case where the parents did not want a child, but one that the husband didn't want his wife's life endangered by childbirth. Since the wife suffered no harm, a wrongful life claim was remote from the purposes of the husband's sterilization. The facts in our instant case are certainly far

different from those in *Christensen*. Here plaintiff-parents did not want a child based on their deep-rooted and inextinguishable fear that such a child would be born with the dreaded disease affecting its nervous system.

In the years which followed the *Christensen* case, courts and commentators developed several theories to support the view that as a matter of public policy, parents should not be permitted to recover damages for the birth of either a defective or a healthy child, even though the infant may have been unplanned or unwanted at the time of conception. In *Gleitman v. Cosgrove*, supra, the New Jersey appellate court, in a tort claim arising out of the wrongful birth of a defective child, affirmed a judgment dismissing the complaint filed on behalf of an infant and its parents against a physician for his failure to inform the then two-month pregnant mother with German measles that her condition could possibly adversely affect the health of her child on grounds of the non-existence of cognizable damages. The court said it was impossible to measure in damages the difference between the infant's life with defects against the utter void of non-existence. By claiming he should not have been born at all, the court added, the infant made it impossible to measure the damages as required by compensatory remedies and thus not cognizable in law. The *Gleitman* court also held that to allow damages for the mother's emotional stress in raising a child or for the father's claim that it would be less expensive to have had an abortion performed on his wife than the expense of raising the child, made necessary the weighing of the intangible, unmeasurable and complex human benefits of motherhood and fatherhood against the alleged emotional and monetary injuries, which the court said was impossible to do.

Although not all of the early cases considering the issue expressed such a hostile view toward the parents' cause of action, the first major case holding that parents have a right to recover damages, including the cost of rearing an unplanned child born by reason of negligent sterilization procedures by defendant-physicians, was decided by the California Court of Appeals in the case of *Custodio v. Bauer*. The complaint was predicated on allegations of negligent performance of surgical procedures and medical advice and on breach of contract to successfully abort the plaintiff-wife. The trial court sustained the defendant's demurrer to the complaint and on plaintiffs' appeal the Court of Appeals reversed. The significance of the appellate decision, however, lies not in its holding that the plaintiffs' factual allegations were legally sufficient to state the several causes of action averred. The importance is in its decision on the extent of damages allowable, holding that the plaintiff-parents were entitled to not only costs arising out of the negligent medical procedures but to all costs which reasonably flowed from the negligence. The court in *Custodio* held that even if a woman survives the childbirth unharmed after a failed sterilization, there is still some loss which is compensable if the resultant additional child and change in family status can be measured economically. The court said that the birth of a child may be less than a blessing in

an economically deprived family, particularly if the sterilization had been intended to prevent the birth of a physically defective or mentally retarded infant and that childrearing costs are not remote from the avowed purpose of an operation undertaken for the purpose of avoiding child-bearing. See discussion of *Troppi v. Scarf*, 31 Mich.App. 240, 187 N.W.2d 511 (1971); 36 U. of Miami L.R. at page 1415, allowing a modified view relating to damages under Section 920, Restatement (Second) of Torts. In *Troppi*, supra, a pharmacist misfilled a prescription for an oral contraceptive; this mistake resulted in Mrs. Troppi's pregnancy and the birth of a healthy child. The court held that damages claimed by the parents were not unduly speculative, but within the scope of the generally applicable rule as to damages in tort actions, namely, that a tort-feasor is liable for all injuries resulting directly from his wrong acts, irrespective of whether they could have been foreseen by him, provided the damages are the legal and natural consequences of the wrong action imputed to the defendant. The *Troppi* court said that the difficulty in determining the amount to be deducted from gross damages under the benefit rule of § 920 would not justify "throwing up our hands and denying recovery altogether."

. . .

The most recent cases agree that the parents have a right in "wrongful birth" cases to claim and recover damages at trial for child-care costs arising out of the physicians' negligence. Forty-three years after the Minnesota case of *Christensen v. Thornby*, supra, was decided, the Minnesota Supreme

Court held in *Sherlock v. Stillwater Clinic* that parents had set forth a legally cognizable cause of action in a "wrongful life" case arising out of a negligent vasectomy. . . . [T]here is no paucity of cases as they apply to Dr. Finegold, the urologist, or to Dr. Schwartz, the obstetrician and gynecologist, which hold that a cognizable cause of action at law exists for recovery of damages on the part of the parents in "wrongful life" cases. It is not contended by plaintiffs that defendant-physicians' treatment of Mr. Speck in the sterilization procedure caused the abnormalities in their infant. But only that had plaintiffs been properly treated and cared for, their child would not have been conceived or born or if they had been sufficiently advised of the possibility of failed sterilization procedures they could have terminated the pregnancy within a prescribed time period by alternative methods of relief. This principle is included in plaintiff-parents' claim for breach of contract and misrepresentation. In the last analysis and evaluation, and irrespective of the category of claims made, we hold plaintiffs' complaint sounds essentially in negligence, tortious breach of contract, and/or medical malpractice. As in any cause of action based on these grounds, a successful plaintiff must demonstrate the existence of a duty, the breach of which may be considered the proximate cause of damages suffered by the injured parties. This case is predicated, primarily, on the doctors' assurances we accept as true based on defendant's demurrers.

Once the plaintiff has carried this burden, it is axiomatic that the tort-feasor is liable for all damages which ordinarily and in the natural course of things have resulted from the commission of the tort.

In the instant case, we deny Francine's claim to be made whole. When we examine Francine's claim, we find regardless of whether her claim is based on "wrongful life" or otherwise, there is a failure to state a legally cognizable cause of action even though, admittedly, the defendants' actions of negligence were the proximate cause of her defective birth. Her claims to be whole have two fatal weaknesses. First, there is no precedent in appellate judicial pronouncements that holds a child has a fundamental right to be born as a whole, functional human being. Whether it is better to have never been born at all rather than to have been born with serious mental defects is a mystery more properly left to the philosophers and theologians, a mystery which would lead us into the field of metaphysics, beyond the realm of our understanding or ability to solve. The law cannot assert a knowledge which can resolve this inscrutable and enigmatic issue. Second, it is not a matter of taking into consideration the various and convoluted degrees of the imperfection of life. It is rather the improbability of placing the child in a position she would have occupied if the defendants had not been negligent when to do so would make her nonexistent. The remedy afforded an injured party in negligence is intended to place the injured party in the position he would have occupied but for the negligence of the defendant. Thus, a cause of action brought on behalf of an infant seeking recovery for a "wrongful life" on grounds she should not have been born demands a calculation of damages dependent on a comparison between Hobson's choice of life in an impaired state and nonexistence. This the law is incapable of doing.

Finally, we hold that the impossibility of this suit as to Francine comes not so much from the difficulty in measuring the alleged damages as from the fact, unfortunately, that this is not an action cognizable in law. Thus, the recognized principle, not peculiar to traditional tort law alone, that it would be a denial of justice to deny all relief where a wrong is of such a nature as to preclude certain ascertained damages, is inapposite and inapplicable here. Accordingly, plaintiffs' complaint insofar as Francine's claim for damages for "wrongful life" is concerned, does not present a legally cognizable action at law.

Although we deny Francine's claim, we hold recovery is allowed in the parents' claim in this case. Here there is no dispute the pleadings allege the existence of a duty flowing from the defendant-physicians to themselves, the breach of which resulted in the birth of Francine. The alleged negligence and misrepresentations of both doctors and by the alleged breach of contract by Dr. Finegold has also been adequately pleaded. Unlike Francine's claim based on "wrongful life," plaintiff-parents' causes of action allege in traditional tort language that but for defendants' breach of duty to properly treat and advise plaintiff-parents they would not have been required to undergo the expenditures alleged. In these allegations plaintiff-parents set forth a duty owed to them by the doctors and breached by the doctors with

resulting injuries to the plaintiffs.

As to the emotional disturbance and mental stress claimed by plaintiff-parents due to the fact of Francine's birth, we hold these claims must be denied. In allowing recovery in favor of parents for pecuniary losses resulting from physicians' negligence in a "wrongful birth" case, the court in the case of *Park v. Chessin* and *Becker v. Schwartz* said: "Of course, this is not to say that plaintiffs may recover for psychic or emotional harm alleged to have occurred as a consequence of the birth of their infants in an impaired state. The recovery of damages for such injuries must of necessity be circumscribed." Unlike the measurability of pecuniary loss, to which plaintiff-parents are entitled, there is no legal realm of accountability to which they can look for claimed mental and emotional damages arising out of the birth of their child which could factually place them in a more favorable category than parents who generally, in the vicissitudes and vagaries of life, face the everyday potential of pain and suffering in the raising of their children. It is not possible to distinguish the mental and emotional travail which plaintiffs claim here from the pain and suffering of parents who raise a retarded child or whose infant is born blind or mongoloid or falls heir to one of the countless natural diseases or being healthy becomes permanently injured, disfigured or handicapped by reason of accident. The fact that plaintiffs did not want Francine does not alter the sameness in the quality and nature of pain and suffering experienced in the everyday work of parenthood.

In his Concurring and

Dissenting Opinion, Judge Spaeth states that, "[It]he majority says that many people have children who are unwanted for the same reasons, but with no negligence involved, and that their emotional and mental anguish is identical to that of the Specks." This is a misinterpretation of our position. Although the Specks feared the hereditary disease and economic hardships another child might bring, our denial of their recovery in no way means that all parents of "unwanted" children suffer the same stress. To the contrary, our position is that all parents suffer some degree of stress, especially if a child is born with a disabling condition. However, not all of these children are "unwanted" in any sense of that term, and the emotional anguish they suffer may be a normal, uncompensable price one pays for being a parent. Therefore, to allow plaintiffs' claim for mental and emotional stress would be to give them a societal advantage not conceivable in other cases of parenthood.

Order of the lower court affirmed in part, reversed in part and remanded for trial on the merits under the legal theories of tort and assumpsit as more specifically set forth in this opinion.

42 Pa.C.S. § 8305 (1990)

§ 8305. Actions for wrongful birth and wrongful life

(A) WRONGFUL BIRTH. There shall be no cause of action or award of damages on behalf of any person based on a claim that, but for an act or omission of the defendant, a person once conceived would not or should not have been born. Nothing contained in this subsection shall be construed to prohibit any cause of action or award of damages for the wrongful death of a woman, or on account of physical injury suffered by a woman or a child, as a result of an attempted abortion. Nothing contained in this subsection shall be construed to provide a defense against any proceeding charging a health care practitioner with intentional misrepresentation under the act of October 5, 1978 (P.L. 1109, No. 261), known as the Osteopathic Medical Practice Act, the act of December 20, 1985 (P.L. 457, No. 112), known as the Medical Practice Act of 1985, or any other act regulating the professional practices of health care practitioners.

(B) WRONGFUL LIFE. There shall be no cause of action on behalf of any person based on a claim of that person that, but for an act or omission of the defendant, the person would not have been conceived or, once conceived, would or should have been aborted.

(C) CONCEPTION. A person shall be deemed to be conceived at the moment of fertilization.

Punitive Damages: When may a court award punitive damages?

In general, punitive damages are available only where the defendant's tortious conduct has been found to be so outrageous as to be a shock to the community's conscience. In Arizona, for example, punitive damages may only be awarded where the "defendant's wrongful conduct was motivated by spite, malice, or intent to defraud" or where the defendant has demonstrated a "conscious and deliberate disregard or the interest and rights of others." *Volz v. Coleman Co.*, 748 P.2d 1191 (1987).

Clearly, one can imagine a driver of an automobile acting in such an outrageous fashion, and being held liable for punitive damages. But as the following case demonstrates, the law can be tricky.

Pennsylvania had passed a comprehensive No-Fault Motor Vehicle Insurance Act which dramatically changed the common law of torts as it applied to motor vehicle accidents. As such a revamping would necessarily entail the loss of certain rights by some, it was constitutionally required that there be some quid pro quo. Among other things, the No-Fault law provided that one would recover for medical expenses from one's own insurer regardless of fault. In exchange for the assurance of medical coverage regardless of fault, tort immunity was granted to the tortfeasor unless certain conditions were met (a certain threshold of injury), and recovery itself was basically limited, legislatively, to "general damages" (pain, suffering and the like).

Inasmuch as the statute did not explicitly preserve the common law recovery of punitive damages, the majority in the *Reimer* case felt it was no longer available in automobile accident cases. The majority opinion was "Per Curiam," meaning that no opinion was written by the majority. What follows is the dissent in which Justice Larsen argues that the statutory language regarding "nonreimbursable tort fine" should be interpreted as permitting punitive damages where the defendant has exhibited a "bad motive or reckless indifference to the rights of others."

Reimer v. Delisio
501 Pa. 662 (1983)

Per Curiam Opinion

Justice Larsen, concurring in part and dissenting in part.

I join the majority in affirming the order of the Superior Court at No. 16 M.D. Appeal Docket, 1982, granting a new trial due to the lower court's erroneous exclusions of medical testimony regarding the plaintiff's need for future surgery and of a motion picture depicting the plaintiff in physical therapy.

However, I dissent from the

majority's affirmance at No. 15 M.D. Appeal Docket, 1982, of the Superior Court's interpretation of the Pennsylvania No-Fault Act, 40 P.S. § 1009.101 et seq., as abolishing the right of a plaintiff to recover punitive damages in an action arising from a motor vehicle accident.

Initially, we are faced with the unfortunate consideration that, as with practically every case involving the interpretation of the No-Fault Act, the intention of its drafters is far from clear. Because of this pervasive ambiguity, and because, in my opinion, any enactment (or interpretation) which abolishes a common-law recognized remedy or cause of action without providing a substitute, statutory remedy or cause of action runs afoul of Article I, § 11 of our Constitution, see dissenting opinion of this author in *Carroll v. York*, 496 Pa. 363, 437 A.2d 394, 399 (1981) (joined by Flaherty and Kauffman, JJ.), I would hold that absent specific and explicit provisions to the contrary, any cause of action or remedy pre-dating the No-Fault Act, including punitive damages, remains in existence today. Thus, I would resolve all ambiguity in favor of no abolition and continued recognition of common-law remedies and causes of action.

I believe that such ambiguity exists regarding the effect of No-Fault upon recovery for punitive damages. Section 301(a) of the Act, 40 P.S. § 1009.301(a), provides in part:

Partial Abolition -- Tort Liability is abolished with respect to any injury that takes place in this State in accordance with the provisions of this Act if such injury arises out of the maintenance or use of a motor vehicle, except that: ...
(3) An individual remains liable for

intentionally injuring himself or another individual.

I would find punitive damages recoverable under § 301(a)(3). Punitive damages are appropriate to punish the actor for outrageous conduct, i.e. conduct exhibiting a bad motive or reckless indifference to the rights of others. *Chambers v. Montgomery*, 411 Pa. 339, 192 A.2d 355 (1963). For purposes of the No-Fault Act, I would hold that "intentional injury" includes the willful and reckless disregard for the safety, welfare and rights of others and would therefore hold the defendant's outrageous conduct in this case -- driving his car through a posted school zone which had caution lights flashing at a speed at least twice the speed limit of 25 m.p.h. -- renders him "liable for intentionally injuring . . . another individual" within the meaning of § 301(a)(3).

I would further hold that punitive damages are subsumed within the category of "nonreimbursable tort fine." Section 301(b) provides:

Nonreimbursable tort fine -- Nothing in this section shall be construed to immunize an individual from liability to pay a fine on the basis of fault in any proceeding based upon any act or omission arising out of the maintenance or use of a motor vehicle: Provided, That such fine may not be paid or reimbursed by an insurer or other restoration obligor. Both the trial court and the Superior Court recognized that, unless "nonreimbursable tort fine" is read to include punitive damages, the term, at present, would have no meaning in Pennsylvania. The Superior Court stated, 296 Pa.Super. 205, 442 A.2d 731: There is little doubt that, on its face, this provision admits of no ready interpretation, especially since the term "tort fine" appears to have been coined. In that regard, we empathize with the trial judge when he stated he did not know what a tort fine was. The Superior Court recognized that punitive damages are, in a manner of speaking, a penalty or fine imposed upon a person for engaging in particularly egregious conduct, payable to a victim as a kind of windfall, at least in the sense that the punitive damages are paid in addition to damages necessary to make the victim whole.

Yet, despite this recognition, the Superior Court chose to leave the term "nonreimbursable tort fine" essentially meaningless and unexplained. The basis of this interpretation, which is contrary to the canon of statutory construction presuming that the General Assembly desires the entire statute to be effective, Statutory Construction Act, 1 Pa.C.S.A. § 1921(a), is that the legislative history of proposed federal no-fault legislation indicated that punitive damages were not intended to be covered by the National No-Fault Motor Vehicle Act Senate Committee's definition of "tort fine."

The history of this proposed federal legislation offers dubious support for the Superior Court's interpretation. Even assuming, arguendo, however, that the lengthy passages quoted by the Superior Court were relevant to the interpretation of Pennsylvania's No-Fault Act, it seems to me they support a contrary conclusion. Those passages indicated the term "fine" does not mean solely a criminal penalty, but also includes "any charge, levy, assessment, order, condition or requirement that may be imposed 'in any proceeding.'" 296 Pa.Super. 205, 442 A.2d 731, quoting Report of the Senate Committee on Commerce, No. 93-382, Calendar No. 358 (August 15, 1973) at 73-74. The reason why punitive damages were not considered by that federal legislative panel on proposed federal legislation to be within the broad definition of "tort fine" was "in part because under some case law decisions awards for punitive damages may be paid by liability insurance, a practice which vitiates the purpose of a punitive damages judgment."

In Pennsylvania, however, it has been established that payment of punitive damages is not reimbursable by an insurance company as such reimbursement would be contrary to public policy. Accordingly, nonreimbursable punitive damages should be held to be within the meaning of § 301(b) "nonreimbursable tort fine." A contrary interpretation renders that section void of meaning.

For the foregoing reasons, I dissent and would reverse the order of the Superior Court at No. 15 M.D. Appeal Docket, 1982.

Statutory Vagueness: Does the activity of a massage parlor constitute prostitution?

The Fourteenth Amendment due process clause requires that all state criminal statutes be drafted so as to give "sufficient warning so that individuals may conform their conduct so as to avoid that which the law forbids." The following two cases involve claims of vagueness in the statute defining prostitution, the crime of engaging in sex as a business. The "business" part is not contested by either of the defendants; but each claims that they were not engaged in "sex". In *Robbins*, the co-owner of a Pennsylvania massage parlor complained to the Superior Court that her conviction for prostitution under §5902 of the Pennsylvania Crimes Code for engaging in "sexual activity as a business" should be reversed on the grounds that the law was too vague to give her sufficient warning that "allowing manual genital stimulation for the payment of money" was a forbidden behavior. In *Bleigh* the Superior Court addressed the issue of whether § 5902 could be constitutionally applied to punish a woman who engaged in self-masturbation for hire where there was no physical contact between the customer and the defendant.

Commonwealth of Pennsylvania v. Robbins
358 Pa. Super. 225 (1985)

Judge Tamilla delivered the opinion of the court.

This is an appeal from judgment of sentence entered after a jury convicted appellant of prostitution. A sentence of one year probation and a $ 750 fine was imposed. Appellant was charged under section (b) of Prostitution and related offenses, 18 Pa.C.S.A. § 5902, which states that it is an offense to "knowingly promote prostitution of another by owning, controlling, managing, supervising or otherwise keeping, alone or in association with another, a house of prostitution or a prostitution business . . . ." The jury found appellant in violation of this section for her co-owner status of the Body Clinic, an establishment where semi-nude female employees perform massages on nude male customers for a fee. The "massage" included masturbation of the genitalia. On appeal, appellant contends, inter alia, that section 5902 of the Pennsylvania Crimes Code, 18 Pa.C.S.A. § 5902, Prostitution and related offenses, is unconstitutionally vague and thus, void. Specifically, it is alleged that the term "sexual activity" is inadequately defined.

Section 5902 provides in pertinent part: (a) Prostitution. -- A person is guilty of prostitution; a misdemeanor of the third degree, if he or she: (1) is an inmate of a house of prostitution or otherwise engages in sexual activity as a business; . . . (Subsection (f) of section 5902 further defines sexual activity as "includ[ing] homosexual and other deviate sexual relations." In essence, appellant asserts she had no notice and fair warning as required by due process that she was violating the law by allowing manual genital stimulation for the payment of money. It is well settled that "[a] criminal statute must give reasonable notice of the conduct which it proscribes to a person charged with violating its interdiction. Statutes which are so vague that they fail to provide such notice violate the Due Process Clause of the Fourteenth Amendment to the United States Constitution." *Commonwealth v. Heinbaugh*, 467 Pa. 1, 5, 354 A.2d 244, 246 (1976). A statute will be deemed violative of due process if the terms of the statute ". . . are so vague that men of common intelligence must necessarily guess at its meaning and differ as to its application . . . ." *Connally v. General Construction Co.*, 269 U.S. 385, 391, 46 S.Ct. 126, 127, 70 L.Ed. 322, 328 (1926). However, the constitutional prohibition against vagueness does not invalidate every statute which could have been drafted with greater precision. Due process requires only that the law give sufficient warning so that individuals may conform their conduct so as to avoid that which the law forbids.

In addition to the aforementioned constitutional standards, this Court is mindful of the fact that ". . . a legislative enactment enjoys a presumption in favor of its constitutionality and will not be declared unconstitutional unless it clearly, palpably and plainly violates the constitution. All doubts are to be resolved in favor of constitutionality." *Parker v. Children's Hospital of Philadelphia*, 483 Pa. 106, 111, 394 A.2d 932, 937 (1978).

Our research has disclosed only two Pennsylvania cases which have examined the application of the prostitution statute to the activity of masturbation of a male by a nude or semi-nude female for hire. Both cases on point are decisions of the Pennsylvania Common Pleas Court. First, in *Commonwealth v. Dougan*, 5 D. & C.3d 406 (1978), the defendant, who had been charged with a violation of section 5902 for the masturbation of a male client for a fee at a "spa", motioned to quash the complaint. The court granted defendant's motion to quash on the basis that prostitution, as defined in section 5902(a), requires sexual activity involving at least some penetration. After reviewing the history of section 5902, the court opined that: The sexual activity contemplated by prior legislation and the cases interpreting that legislation were confined to sexual intercourse. In the present act, the legislature clarified the prior law to include "homosexual and other deviate sexual relations." In all of these activities there must be penetration however slight, before the act is committed. . . . It is important to note, however, that the court in *Dougan* did not undertake a detailed constitutional analysis of the prostitution statute to determine whether the term "sexual activity" was unconstitutionally vague. Conversely, Judge Wieand (now of this Court), while a Common Pleas Judge, in *Commonwealth v. Israeloff*,

8 D. & C.3d 5 (1978), concluded that the prostitution statute as applied to a genital massage for money is not unconstitutionally vague. Upon examination of the prostitution statute, in light of the aforementioned constitutional standards, the court concluded the statute does not fail for vagueness because: In the mind of a man of "common intelligence" the term sexual activity clearly encompasses masturbation as a business. Indeed, as we have already observed, it is difficult to believe that any man of common intelligence would consider the massaging of the genitals of an unclothed man by a nude or partially nude female to be anything other than sexual activity. Although we are not bound by either of these decisions, we find the analysis in Israeloff to be a more accurate application of the constitutional standards concerning vagueness. While the court in *Dougan* traced the history of the term "prostitution" from its common law origin, the court in *Israeloff* examined the term "sexual activity" in light of a constitutional void-for-vagueness challenge. We believe there is no question that appellant had notice and fair warning, as required by due process, that she was violating the

law by allowing manual sexual stimulation for the payment of money. This is clearly not a situation where the conduct prohibited is so intangible or vague as to require men of common intelligence to guess at its meaning and differ as to its application. The statute in question was enacted to provide an ascertainable standard of conduct directed at a defined evil; such evil being the commercial exploitation of sexual gratification. Furthermore, since the term "sexual activity" is undefined by the statute, we are obliged to construe that term according to its common and approved usage. When the term "sexual activity" is examined in light of the statute's underlying purpose of prohibiting commercial exploitation of sexual gratification and also in light of its common and approved usage, there is no doubt that masturbation for hire falls within the statute's proscription. Therefore, we find section 5902(a) is not unconstitutionally vague so as to cause appellant to seriously believe that she was not providing some form of sexual gratification for the payment of money. . . .

Accordingly, judgment of sentence is affirmed. . . .

Commonwealth of Pennsylvania v. Bleigh
586 A.2d 450 (1991) Pa. Super.

Judge Cirillo wrote the opinion for the court.

Ricki Lynne Bleigh, Virginia Lee Shipe, and John Andrews Thompson appeal from judgments of sentence entered on January 11, 1990 in the Cumberland County Court of Common Pleas. We affirm in part and vacate in part.

On October 13, 1988, Detective Michael Strine entered an adult bookstore. Upon entry, Detective Strine observed an array of sexually oriented materials including magazines, movies, and various devices. Additionally, the bookstore had booths available where patrons could view sexually explicit movies or, if they desired, a live female dancer. The booths contained a telephone, a waste can, and a roll of toilet paper. The patrons and the dancers were separated by a pane of glass. As such, they communicated by phone. Detective Strine entered a booth and placed money into a machine which opened a curtain and exposed Shipe draped in lingerie. Shipe informed Detective Strine that the curtain would remain open for five minutes and that if he placed five dollars through a slot in the wall marked "tips," she would take off her top, for ten dollars she would remove all her clothing and for twenty dollars she would put on a "show." Detective Strine placed twenty dollars through the slot and Shipe removed all of her clothing and masturbated. Later that same evening, Chief Barry Sherman of the Middlesex Township Police went to the same establishment, entered a private booth, placed twenty dollars through the slot and viewed Bleigh masturbate in the nude. Based upon this information, the police obtained a search warrant authorizing the seizure of "any and all sexually oriented materials, including magazines, movies, sexual devices, records of ownership/ occupancy/employment, any cash monies or proceeds derived from the sale of said material, and/or sexual activity." On October 14, 1988, the police executed the search warrant. Upon entering the building, which was open to the public at the time, they immediately arrested Thompson, who was working at the front counter. The police also arrested Shipe who was found in one of the booths, and Bleigh who was in the basement with her husband. A search of Shipe's pocketbook revealed the marked twenty dollar bill paid to her by one of the officers, a quantity of cocaine and drug paraphernalia. Additionally, a search of Bleigh's pocketbook following her arrest revealed the marked twenty dollar bill which had been paid to her by Chief Sherman the previous day. The police also observed Thompson's briefcase, and after searching it, discovered, among other things, a quantity of cocaine. After a jury trial Bleigh was convicted of prostitution.

Shipe was convicted of prostitution, unlawful possession of a controlled substance, and unlawful possession of drug paraphernalia. Thompson was convicted of promoting prostitution, unlawful possession of a controlled substance, and unlawful possession of drug paraphernalia. The defendants' post-verdict motions were denied, sentence was imposed and this timely appeal followed. The appellants' advance the following issues for our review:

I. (a) Does self-masturbation or simulated self-masturbation for hire constitute "prostitution" pursuant to 18 Pa.C.S. Section 5902(a); and if so, is Section 5902 constitutionally valid as applied in this case? (b) Was the evidence sufficient to sustain the Trial Court's failure to quash and/or dismiss the charge of promoting prostitution . . . against Mr. Thompson?

. . .

We are called upon once again to clarify what actions constitute the crime of prostitution in this Commonwealth. Specifically, we must determine if self-masturbation for hire with no physical contact between patron and performer constitutes prostitution. The legislature has provided: (a) Prostitution -- a person is guilty of prostitution; a misdemeanor of the third degree, if he or she: (1) is an inmate of a house of prostitution or otherwise engages in sexual activity as a business; . . . 18 Pa.C.S. § 5902(a) (emphasis added). Section 5902(f) states that sexual activity includes homosexual and other deviate sexual relations. 18 Pa.C.S. § 5902(f). Clearly, however, the conduct described in section 5902(f) is not the only activity that constitutes prostitution. Since the term "sexual activity" is neither specifically nor exhaustively defined in the prostitution statute, we must construe the term according to its common and approved usage. Consequently, it is necessary to trace the history and development of the prostitution statute. In *Commonwealth v. Lavery*, 247 Pa. 139, 142, 93 A. 276, [277-78] (1915), our Supreme Court said that prostitution was "not mere fornication or adultery confined to one man, but indiscriminate illicit intercourse for hire with any man seeking it," but in *Commonwealth v. Stingel*, 156 Pa.Super. 359, 361, 40 A.2d 140, 141 (1944), this Court held that "indiscriminate cohabitation" was no longer necessary, since "the Legislature ha[d] broadened the compass of the term" by the Act of June 24, 1939, P.L. 872, § 103; 18 Pa.C.S. § 4103. "Prostitution" was there defined as "offering or using of the body for sexual intercourse for hire.". . . In the present Act [18 Pa.C.S. § 5902], the Legislature did not eradicate the commonly understood definition of prostitution but merely clarified it to include "homosexual and other deviate sexual relations." It cannot be gainsaid that "prostitution" has persisted since Biblical times, and, as such, has acquired a traditional meaning, i.e. "indiscriminate illicit intercourse for hire." . . . In *Potts*, this court concluded that section 5902 was not unconstitutionally vague; rather, the court found it provided an ascertainable standard of conduct directed at a defined evil -- the commercial exploitation of sexual gratification. Other evils designed to be eradicated by the criminalization of prostitution are the spread of venereal disease; the corruption of law enforcement agencies; the incentive to coerce and exploit women; and criminal organizations living on the proceeds of prostitution. As the court in *Potts* stated, prostitution or sexual activity as a business, "has traditionally meant sexual intercourse for hire." Sexual intercourse, however, is not the only sexual activity proscribed by section 5902.

In *Cohen* and *Robbins*, this court held, after examining the statute's purpose, that the masturbation of a male by a female for money was sexual activity as a business and therefore prostitution. In both cases, as in *Potts*, the court also found that section 5902 was not unconstitutionally vague. Here, the Commonwealth argues that because Shipe and Bleigh engaged in self-masturbation for the sexual gratification of their customers, it was sexual activity as a business and therefore prostitution. We disagree. Having examined the evolution of the term prostitution, and the cases interpreting it, we conclude that self-masturbation for hire without any physical contact between performer and viewer is not the type of conduct intended to come within the purview of section 5902. Further, the definition of sexual activity in section 5902(f) states that it "includes homosexual and other deviate sexual relations." This clarification, while not controlling, indicates that sexual activity requires the physical interaction of two or more people.

Here, there was no physical interaction between the dancers and the patrons. As such, this conduct is more akin to commercial voyeurism; it is not, however, prostitution. Consequently, Bleigh's and Shipe's judgments of sentence for prostitution must be reversed. Likewise, since Thompson's conviction for promoting prostitution was based upon the actions of Bleigh and Shipe, his judgment of sentence is also reversed. See 18 Pa.C.S. § 5902(b). Clearly, if the activities promoted do not amount to prostitution, Thompson cannot be guilty of promoting prostitution. . . .

Since Shipe was sentenced to concurrent terms for prostitution, unlawful possession of a controlled substance, and unlawful possession of drug paraphernalia, we vacate the judgment of sentence for prostitution and affirm the judgments of sentence for possession of a controlled substance and for possession of drug paraphernalia. Likewise, since Thompson was sentenced to concurrent terms of imprisonment for promoting prostitution, possession of a controlled substance, and unlawful possession of drug paraphernalia, we vacate the judgment of sentence for promoting prostitution and affirm the judgments of sentence for unlawful possession of a controlled substance and unlawful possession of drug paraphernalia.

Affirmed in part; vacated in part.

Felony Murder: Can a felon who did not personally commit a homicide be convicted of murder?

The felony-murder rule has confounded jurist and student alike. At common law the issue was simple: one whose conduct brought about an unintended death in the commission of a felony was guilty of murder. The rationale of the rule was to act as a powerful deterrent to felons, a warning that even if an unintended death should occur during the commission of a felony, a murder conviction would be warranted against the felon.

Many jurisdictions, including Pennsylvania, have sought to moderate the harshness of the rule by limiting its scope. For example, the legislature has limited the phrase "perpetuation of a felony" to include only certain serious felonies. Additional limitation on the scope of the rule has been judicially created by focusing on the issue of causation. Fundamentally, the issue breaks down to "when it is fair to make the defendant murderously liable for the unintended death?"

In deciding that issue, should it matter "who pulled the trigger?" Or, "who died?" The common law felony-murder rule which permits a conviction for murder when a death results in the course of the commission of a felony produced has been modified and/or rejected in many states. In the following decision the Pennsylvania Supreme Court was faced with the issue of whether the felony-murder rule could be applied in a situation in which the shot which killed the victim was fired by a policeman responding to the crime rather than by one of the felons!

Commonwealth ex rel. James Smith v. Myers
438 PA 218 (1970)

Justice O'Brien wrote the opinion for the court.

This is an appeal from the order of the Court of Common Pleas of Philadelphia County, denying James Smith's petition for a writ of habeas corpus. The facts upon which the convictions of appellant and his cofelons, Almeida and Hough, rest are well known to this Court and to the federal courts. In addition to vexing the courts, these cases have perplexed a generation of law students, both within and without the Commonwealth, and along with their progeny, have spawned reams of critical commentary.

Briefly, the facts of the crime are these. On January 30, 1947, Smith, along with Edward Hough and David Almeida, engaged in an armed robbery of a supermarket in the City of Philadelphia. An off-duty policeman, who happened to be in the area, was shot and killed while attempting to thwart the escape of the felons. Although the evidence as to who fired the fatal shot was conflicting in appellant's 1948 trial, the court charged the jury that it was irrelevant who fired the fatal bullet:

"Even if you should find from the evidence that Ingling was killed by a bullet from the gun of one of the policemen, that policeman having shot at the felons in an attempt to prevent the robbery or the escape of the robbers, or to protect Ingling, the felons would be guilty of murder, or if they did that in returning the fire of the felons that was directed toward them." To this part of the charge appellant took a specific exception.

The jury convicted Smith of first degree murder, with punishment fixed at life imprisonment. He filed no post-trial motions, and took no appeal. Nor did Smith initiate any post-conviction proceedings until the instant case, despite the litigious propensities of his cofelons.

On February 4, 1966, appellant filed the present petition for a writ of habeas corpus. In his petition appellant raised the following contentions: first, that he had been denied his right to appeal and his right to the assistance of counsel on appeal from his conviction; second, that he was denied his constitutional right to a fair trial by reason of the knowing use of false testimony by the prosecution; and third, that he was denied his constitutional right to a fair trial by reason of the trial judge's charge to the jury, quoted above, which was allegedly inconsistent with the rule later announced by this Court in *Commonwealth v. Redline*, 391 Pa. 486, 137 A. 2d 472 (1958).

The court below held two hearings which were confined to the presentation of evidence in support of appellant's contention that he was denied his right to appeal. The other contentions raised by the appellant were briefed and argued to the court below, but not passed on below. The court below held that appellant had knowingly waived his right to appeal, and although the opinion does not discuss the question, the denial of relief necessarily manifested a belief by the court below that appellant was aware of his right to counsel on appeal. The other issues raised by appellant were not mentioned by the court, apparently of the view that they were cognizable only if it appeared that appellant had been denied his right to appeal, and was entitled to an appeal nunc pro tunc. We reverse, grant the writ, allow an appeal nunc pro tunc, and grant a new trial. . .

Appellant urges that he was denied due process by virtue of the trial court's charge that it was irrelevant who fired the fatal bullet. Such a charge was consistent with the dictum of this Court in *Commonwealth v. Moyer and Byron*, 357 Pa. 181, 53 A. 2d 736 (1947), and with the holding shortly thereafter in the appeal of appellant's cofelon, David Almeida, in *Commonwealth v. Almeida*, 362 Pa. 596, 68 A. 2d 595 (1949). In the latter case, by a stretch of the felony-murder rule, we held that Almeida could indeed be found guilty of murder even though the fatal bullet was fired by another officer acting in opposition to the felony. We adopted a proximate cause theory of murder: "[H]e whose felonious act is the proximate cause of another's death is criminally responsible for that death and must answer to society for it exactly as he who is negligently the proximate cause of another's death is civilly responsible for that death and must answer in damages for it." We thus affirmed Almeida's conviction, stating at page 607: "The felonious acts of the robbers in firing shots at the policemen, well knowing that their fire would be returned, as it should have been, was [sic] the proximate cause of Officer Ingling's death."

The proximate cause theory was taken a millimeter further by this Court in *Commonwealth v. Thomas*, 382 Pa. 639, 117 A. 2d 204 (1955). In that case the victim of an armed robbery shot and killed one of the felons, Jackson; the other felon, Thomas, was convicted of the murder.

Thomas was repudiated by this Court in *Commonwealth v. Redline*, 391 Pa. 486, 137 A. 2d 472 (1958). The facts there were virtually identical to those of *Thomas*; a policeman shot one fleeing felon and the other was convicted of murder. In an opinion by the late Chief Justice Charles Alvin Jones, this Court interred *Thomas* and dealt a fatal blow to *Almeida*. At the outset of this Court's opinion in *Redline*, we stated: "The decision in the *Almeida* case was a radical departure from common law criminal jurisprudence." The thorough documentation which followed in this lengthy opinion proved beyond a shadow of a doubt that Almeida and Thomas constituted aberrations in the annals of Anglo-American adjudicature.

Redline began with a rather general review of the entire felony-murder theory. If we may presume to elaborate a bit on that review, we should point out that the felony-murder rule really has two separate branches in Pennsylvania. The first, and the easier concept, is statutory. The Act of June 24, 1939, P. L. 872, § 701, 18 P.S. § 4701, provides, inter alia: "All murder which shall . . . be committed in the perpetration of, or attempting to perpetrate any arson, rape, robbery, burglary, or kidnapping, shall be murder in the first degree. All other kinds of murder shall be murder in the second degree." Clearly this statutory felony-murder rule merely serves to raise the degree of certain murders to first degree; it gives no aid to the determination of what constitutes murder in the first place. *Redline*, pointing out that except for one isolated situation there is no statutory crime of murder, directed us to the common law for a determination of what constitutes murder. It is here that the other branch of the felony-murder rule, the common law branch, comes into play. Citing *Commonwealth v. Drum*, 58 Pa. 9 (1868), the early leading case on murder in the Commonwealth, and IV Blackstone, Commentaries, *Redline* reaffirmed that the distinguishing criterion of murder is malice. The common law felony-murder rule is a means of imputing malice where it may not exist expressly. Under this rule, the malice necessary to make a killing, even an accidental one, murder, is constructively inferred from the malice incident to the perpetration of the initial felony.

The common law felony-murder rule as thus explicated has been subjected to some harsh criticism, most of it thoroughly warranted. It has been said to be "highly punitive and objectionable as imposing the consequences of murder upon a death wholly unintended." "An effect wholly unexpected and unconnected with the intention and act of the party, except by accident .

. . [is] made the foundation of criminal responsibility." *Redline* at page 494 related that "a widely accepted and quite plausible explanation of the origin of the doctrine is that at early common law many crimes, including practically all, if not all, felonies were punishable by death so that it was of no particular moment whether the condemned was hanged for the initial felony or for the death accidentally resulting from the felony." With a history like that it is hardly surprising that the rule has evoked bitter comment referring to it as "a holdover from the days of our barbarian Anglo-Saxon ancestors of pre-Norman days, [having] very little right to existence in modern society."

A more temperate commentator suggests that the rule should be modified, so that a killing committed during the perpetration of a felony would create merely a rebuttable presumption of intention, rather than the conclusive presumption now created. Other opponents of the felony-murder rule point out that it is hardly an essential weapon in the Commonwealth's arsenal. Our neighboring state of Ohio has managed quite well without a felony-murder rule since abolishing it over a century ago.

In fact, not only is the felony-murder rule nonessential, but it is very doubtful that it has the deterrent effect its proponents assert. On the contrary, it appears that juries rebel against convictions, adopting a homemade rule against fortuities, where a conviction must result in life imprisonment. If added deterrence is desired, the felony-murder rule is not the right approach. The situation was well-analyzed many years ago: "To punish as a murderer, every man who, while committing a heinous offence, causes death by pure misadventure, is a course which evidently adds nothing to the security of human life. . . . The only good effect which such punishment can produce will be to deter people from committing any of these offenses which turn into murders what are in themselves mere accidents. It is in fact an addition made in the very worst way . . . . If the punishment for stealing from the person be too light, let it be increased, and let the increase fall alike on all the offenders! Surely the worst mode of increasing the punishment of an offence is to provide that, besides the ordinary punishment, every offender shall run any exceedingly small risk of being hanged." To similar effect, Justice Oliver Wendell Holmes, in *The Common Law*, argued that the wise policy is not to punish the fortuity, but rather to impose severe penalties on those types of criminal activity which experience has demonstrated carry a high degree of risk to human life. In this respect, we note the recent amendment to The Penal Code, providing for increased penalties when certain crimes are committed with firearms.

We have gone into this lengthy discussion of the felony-murder rule not for the purpose of hereby abolishing it. That is hardly necessary in the instant case. But we do want to make clear how shaky are the basic premises on which it rests. With so weak a foundation, it behooves us not to extend it further and indeed, to restrain it within the bounds it has always known. As stated above, *Redline*, at page 495 et seq., demolished the extension to the felony-murder rule made in *Almeida*: "In adjudging a felony-murder, it is to be remembered at all times that the thing which is imputed to a felon for a killing incidental to his felony is malice and not the act of killing . . . .'

The malice of the initial offense attaches to whatever else the criminal may do in connection therewith.' . . . And so, until the decision of this court in *Commonwealth v. Almeida*, supra, in 1949, the rule which was uniformly followed, whether by express statement or by implication, was that in order to convict for felony-murder, the killing must have been done by the defendant or by an accomplice or confederate or by one acting in furtherance of the felonious undertaking.

"Until the *Almeida* case there was no reported instance in this State of a jury ever having been instructed on the trial of an indictment for murder for a killing occurring contemporaneously with the perpetration of a felony that the defendant was guilty of murder regardless of the fact that the fatal shot was fired by a third person acting in hostility and resistance to the felon and in deliberate opposition to the success of the felon's criminal undertaking."

Redline proceeded to discuss the cases, both within and without Pennsylvania, which establish the rule that murder is not present where the fatal shot is fired by a third person acting in opposition to the felon. We see no reason to repeat that discussion, and simply refer the reader to Redline, 497 to 503. The Court then summarized the rule by quoting, at pages 503-04, from 13 Ruling Case Law at pp. 753-754:

'"Thus, where persons conspire together to commit robbery, and while carrying out such conspiracy their victim, in self-defense, discharges a fire arm at his assailants, and accidentally kills a bystander, the conspirators are not guilty of the homicide.'. . ."

After this review of *Redline*, the uninitiated might be surprised to learn that *Redline* did not specifically overrule *Almeida*. This Court did overrule *Thomas*, holding that no conviction was possible for a justifiable homicide, where a policeman shot a felon, but "distinguished" *Almeida* on the ground that the homicide there, where an innocent third party was killed by a policeman, was only excusable. This distinction was rather remarkable in view of the cases relied upon by the Court -- almost all cases in which the victim was an innocent third party rather than a felon. . . .

In fact, even the majority in *Redline* seemed to realize that they were seizing upon a will-of-the-wisp in attempting to refrain from then overruling *Almeida*: "It is, of course, true that the distinction thus drawn between *Almeida* and the instant case on the basis of the difference in the character of the victims of the homicide is more incidental than legally significant so far as relevancy to the felony-murder rule is concerned: . . . In other words, if a felon can be held for murder for a killing occurring during the course of a felony, even though the death was not inflicted by one of the felons but by someone acting in hostility to them, it should make no difference to the crime of murder who the victim of the homicide happened to be."

The "distinction" *Redline*

half-heartedly tries to draw has not escaped criticism from the commentators. While the result reached in *Redline* and most of its reasoning have met with almost unanimous approval, the deus ex machina ending has been condemned. One learned journal has commented: "It seems, however, that *Almeida* cannot validly be distinguished from [*Redline*]. The probability that a felon will be killed seems at least as great as the probability that the victim will be an innocent bystander. Any distinction based on the fact that the killing of a felon by a policeman is sanctioned by the law and therefore justifiable, while the killing of an innocent bystander is merely excusable, seems unwarranted. No criminal sanctions now attach to either in other areas of criminal law, and any distinction here would seem anomalous. Indeed, to make the result hinge on the character of the victim is, in many instances, to make it hinge on the marksmanship of resisters. Any attempt to distinguish between the cases on the theory that the cofelon assumes the risk of being killed would also be improper since this tort doctrine has no place in the criminal law in which the wrong to be redressed is a public one -- a killing with the victim's consent is nevertheless murder. It is very doubtful that public desire for vengeance should alone justify a conviction of felony murder for the death of an innocent bystander when no criminal responsibility will attach for the death of a cofelon."

Redline concluded, at page 510, in this manner: "The limitation which we thus place on the decision in the *Almeida* case renders unnecessary any present reconsideration of the extended holding in that case. It will be time enough for action in such regard if and when a conviction for murder based on facts similar to those presented by the *Almeida* case (both as to the performer of the lethal act and the status of its victim) should again come before this court." The time is now. The facts are not merely similar to those of *Almeida*; they are identical, Smith and Almeida being cofelons. The case law of centuries and the force of reason, both dealt with in great detail in *Redline* and above, require us to overrule Almeida. . . .

Appellant is therefore in no way precluded from asserting his claim that Almeida should be overruled. We thus give Almeida burial, taking it out of its limbo, and plunging it downward into the bowels of the earth.

The order of the court below is reversed, an appeal is allowed nunc pro tunc, and a new trial is granted.

High Speed Police Pursuits: Is a police officer conducting a high speed chase liable when the fleeing suspect injures a third party?

High speed chases by police pose particularly difficult issues in both criminal and civil law contexts. In *Commonwealth v. Berggren*, 496 N.E. 2d 660 (1986), the Supreme Court of Massachusetts upheld the conviction of a fleeing felon for vehicular homicide where a police officer died while engaged in pursuit at a high rate of speed. More common, however, are cases in which innocent bystanders or the fleeing suspects or passengers riding with them are injured or killed during high speed chases and they seek to recover damages from either the police officer or the municipality which employs him.

In the following recent case the Pennsylvania Supreme Court addressed the issue of whether a police officer pursuing a fleeing vehicle at high speed can be held liable to an innocent party injured in a collision with the fleeing suspect. Justice Papadakos cites 42 Pa. C.S. 8542 and several earlier cases in concluding that the negligence of the fleeing suspect supersedes the police officer's decision to pursue and absolves him of any liability. As Justice Cappy points out, however, the majority opinion does "not eliminate liability claims against a municipality or its agents" where the police vehicle itself collides with the plaintiff's vehicle.

Dickens v. Horner et. al.
611 A.2d 693 (Superior Court, 1992)

Justice Papadakos delivered the opinion of the court:

This is the appeal of Upper Chichester Township and Officer Thomas Bush (Appellants) from the Opinion and Order of the Commonwealth Court affirming the order of the Court of Common Pleas of Delaware County which denied the Preliminary Objections of Appellants to a complaint brought against them by Denise Marie Dickens (Appellee).

The complaint alleges that Appellee was seriously injured on April 9, 1986, at 1:24 a.m., when an automobile driven by John Scott Horner (Horner) struck her. Horner was, at the time, fleeing at a high rate of speed from Officer Bush who had initiated a chase to stop Horner who was believed to be driving without a valid driver's license and under the influence of drugs.

There is no dispute that once Officer Bush identified Horner and decided to stop him, Horner sped away from the officer at a high rate of speed, ran a clearly marked stop sign, and collided with Appellee. Appellee brought this action against Horner and Officer Bush and the Township and alleges that while Horner was directly responsible for the accident, nevertheless, the decision of the officer to pursue Horner was a proximate cause of the accident.

Officer Bush and the Township filed preliminary objections to the complaint asserting immunity from suit under the provisions of the

Political Subdivision Tort Claims Act, 42 Pa.C.S. § 8541 et seq. (Tort Claims Act). The preliminary objections were denied by the Honorable Anthony R. Semararo of the Court of Common Pleas of Delaware County who then certified this interlocutory order for appeal, under our rules of Appellate Procedure Rules 1311 and 1312, as one involving a controlling question of law as to which there is a substantial ground for difference of opinion and that an immediate appeal would materially advance the termination of the matter. The Commonwealth Court granted the appeal and the proceedings in the Delaware County Court of Common Pleas were stayed pending the appeal. The Commonwealth Court, sitting en banc, affirmed the order of the trial court ruling that the allegations of a decision to initiate a pursuit and in failing to exercise due care in a chase could form the basis for a negligence action against a police officer and his employer Township, and that these acts do fall within the vehicle liability exception to governmental immunity at § 8542(b)(1) of the Tort Claims Act.

We granted Appellants' petition for allowance of appeal to review this conclusion in light of our case law concerning claims brought under the provisions of the Tort Claims Act.

That act provides that liability for negligent acts may be imposed if two conditions are satisfied, and if the injury occurs as a result of one of eight acts described at 42 Pa.C.S. § 8542(b). The two threshold conditions required are that: 1) damages would be recoverable under common law or a statute creating a cause of action against one not having an immunity defense, and 2) the injury must be caused by the negligent acts of the local agency or its employees acting within the scope of its office or duties, excepting therefrom acts of crime, fraud, malice or willful misconduct.

When considering whether an injury occurs as a result of one of the eight exceptions to the rule of absolute governmental immunity, we have indicated that all the exceptions must be narrowly interpreted given the expressed legislative intent to insulate political subdivisions from tort liability. *Walsh v. City of Philadelphia*, 526 Pa. 585 A.2d 445 (1991); *Love v. City of Philadelphia*, 518 Pa. 370, 543 A.2d 531 (1988); *Mascaro v. Youth Study Center*, 514 Pa. 351, 523 A.2d 1118 (1987). The acts of others are specifically excluded in the general immunity section and may not be imputed to the local agencies or its employees and, in *Mascaro*, we held that the Legislature has clearly precluded the imposition of liability on itself or its local agencies for acts of third parties and that it has not seen fit to waive immunity for these actors or their acts in any of the eight exceptions.

We viewed this conclusion as being consistent with the general rule that the criminal and negligent acts of third parties are superseding causes which absolve the original actor from liability for the harm caused by such third parties. This is also consistent with the Legislative determination that the criminal acts, actual fraud, actual malice or willful misconduct of its own agency or employees acting within the scope of their duties are not the subject of suit or liability and that it would be incongruous to interpret the Act in such a way that the municipality would be shielded from liability for the crimes of its agents and employees, yet responsible for the crimes of others.

These are the general principles of law which are applicable to this case, and which require us to reverse the opinion and order of the Commonwealth Court. In essence, Appellee seeks to impose liability on Officer Bush and the Township for an accident which was caused by the criminal acts of Horner.

It is alleged that Horner was driving without a valid license, under the influence of drugs, and that Horner created the chase by not stopping when he was being pursued by a police officer. Instead, Horner sped through residential streets in the early hours of the morning at 60 miles per hour, ignored a clearly marked stop sign, and rammed into Appellee. We cannot impose liability for the crimes of Horner on the Township or Officer Bush any more than we could the City or the Youth Study Center in *Mascaro* because the legislative scheme of immunity consistently excludes all criminal acts from liability, including the acts of one of such as Horner, who chooses to defy a lawful order to stop his car and commits a series of crimes which terminate in inflicting serious injuries to an innocent bystander like

Appellee. Nor should we overlook the fact that the control of preventing the accident was solely within the hands of Horner who only had to obey the law and stop when requested by the police.

Accordingly, the order of the Commonwealth Court is reversed, the Preliminary Objections of Appellants are granted, and the matter is remanded to the Court of Common Pleas of Delaware County so that Appellee may continue her case against Horner.

Mr. Justice Cappy wrote a concurring opinion.

I join in the opinion of the majority insofar as it establishes that a municipality and its agents cannot be held liable for the superseding criminal or negligent acts of a third party. I endorse the position that the decision of a police officer, acting within the scope of his duties, to initiate vehicular pursuit of a person suspected of committing a crime, cannot constitute negligence.

However, I write separately to emphasize that, in my view, the decision of the majority does not eliminate liability claims against a municipality or its agents in instances where its own actions, as opposed to those of a third party, are the proximate cause of the injury.

Insanity: What is the current test of insanity in Pennsylvania?

The finding that a criminal defendant is "not guilty by reason of insanity" has always been controversial since its first reported application in western jurisprudence - the *M'Naghten* case of 1843. The *M'Naghten* rule is a "cognitive" test: a person is not guilty by reason of insanity if (1) he suffers from a mental illness or disease that (2) causes a defect of reason, so (3) the defendant does not understand what it is he has done (or that what he did was wrong). Many commentators have argued that "humans are more than cognition." They suggest that there should be a second type of defense, a "volitional" test, based on a recognition of other factors of human psychology: a person should be found not guilty by reason of insanity, if he suffers from some mental illness such that he had an "irresistible impulse" to commit the criminal act.

In determining whether the defendant's impulse is truly "irresistible" (assuming that he knows exactly what it is he is doing), those jurisdictions that have the defense often rely on a colorfully titled "police officer at the elbow" test: would the defendant have committed the criminal act in the presence of the police, where his arrest would be inevitable and immediate.

Pennsylvania has never accepted a "volitional" test and continues to rely on the *M'Naghten* "cognitive" test when deciding on an insanity defense. The legislature has, however, provided an alternative to an insanity verdict, a finding that the defendant is "guilty, but mentally ill." The major difference is that with a finding of not guilty by reason of insanity, a defendant who subsequently becomes sane must be released. But while a defendant found guilty, but mentally ill will be sent to a mental hospital (just as one acquitted by reason of insanity), he will not be released if he regains his sanity before the expiration of what would have been his sentence. Instead, he will be sent to prison to serve out the remaining time.

Following the relevant statutory sections below is the *Heidnik* case in which the Court affirmed the defendant's conviction for gruesome murders despite his plea of insanity.

18 Pa.C.S. § 315

§ 315. Insanity

    (A) GENERAL RULE. The mental soundness of an actor engaged in conduct charged to constitute an offense shall only be a defense to the charged offense when the actor proves by a preponderance of evidence that the actor was legally insane at the time of the commission of the offense.

    (B) DEFINITION. For purposes of this section, the phrase "legally insane" means that, at the time of the commission of the offense, the actor was laboring under such a defect of reason, from disease of the mind, as not to know the nature and quality of the act he was doing or, if the actor did know the quality of the act, that he did not know that what he was doing was wrong.

18 Pa.C.S. § 314 (1991)

§ 314. Guilty but mentally ill

(A) GENERAL RULE. A person who timely offers a defense of insanity accordance with the Rules of Criminal Procedure may be found "guilty but mentally ill" at trial if the trier of facts finds, beyond a reasonable doubt, that the person is guilty of an offense, was mentally ill at the time of the commission of the offense and was not legally insane at the time of the commission of the offense.

(B) PLEA OF GUILTY BUT MENTALLY ILL. A person who waives his right to trial may plead guilty but mentally ill. No plea of guilty but mentally ill may be accepted by the trial judge until he has examined all reports prepared pursuant to the Rules of Criminal Procedure, has held a hearing on the sole issue of the defendant's mental illness at which either party may present evidence and is satisfied that the defendant was mentally ill at the time of the offense to which the plea is entered. If the trial judge refuses to accept a plea of guilty but mentally ill, the defendant shall be permitted to withdraw his plea. A defendant whose plea is not accepted by the court shall be entitled to a jury trial, except that if a defendant subsequently waives his right to a jury trial, the judge who presided at the hearing on mental illness shall not preside at the trial.

(C) DEFINITIONS. For the purposes of this section and 42 Pa.C.S. § 9727 (relating to disposition of persons found guilty but mentally ill):

> (1) "Mentally ill." One who as a result of mental disease or defect, lacks substantial capacity either to appreciate the wrongfulness of his conduct or to conform his conduct to the requirements of the law.

> (2) "Legal insanity." At the time of the commission of the act, the defendant was laboring under such a defect of reason, from disease of the mind, as not to know the nature and quality of the act he was doing or, if he did know it, that he did not know he was doing what was wrong.

(D) COMMON LAW M'NAGHTEN'S RULE PRESERVED. Nothing in this section shall be deemed to repeal or otherwise abrogate the common law defense of insanity (M'Naghten's Rule) in effect in this Commonwealth on the effective date of this section.

42 Pa.C.S. § 9727 (1991)

§ 9727. Disposition of persons found guilty but mentally ill

(A) IMPOSITION OF SENTENCE. A defendant found guilty but mentally ill or whose plea of guilty but mentally ill is accepted under the provisions of 18 Pa.C.S. § 314 (relating to guilty but mentally ill) may have any sentence imposed on him which may lawfully be imposed on any defendant convicted of the same offense. Before imposing sentence, the court shall hear testimony and make a finding on the issue of whether the defendant at the time of sentencing is severely mentally disabled and in need of treatment pursuant to the provisions of the act of July 9, 1976 (P.L. 817, No. 143), known as the "Mental Health Procedures Act."

(B) TREATMENT.

(1) An offender who is severely mentally disabled and in need of treatment at the time of sentencing shall, consistent with available resources, be provided such treatment as is psychiatrically or psychologically indicated for his mental illness. Treatment may be provided by the Bureau of Correction, by the county or by the Department of Public Welfare in accordance with the "Mental Health Procedures Act."

(2) The cost for treatment of offenders found guilty but mentally ill, committed to the custody of the Bureau of Correction and transferred to a mental health facility, shall be borne by the Commonwealth.

(C) DISCHARGE REPORT. When a treating facility designated by either the Bureau of Correction or the Department of Public Welfare discharges such a defendant from treatment prior to the expiration of his maximum sentence, that treating facility shall transmit to the Pennsylvania Board of Probation and Parole, the correctional facility or county jail to which the offender is being returned and the sentencing judge a report on the condition of the offender, together with the reasons for its judgments, which describes:

(1) The defendant's behavior.

(2) The course of treatment.

(3) The potential for recurrence of the behavior.

(4) The potential for danger to himself or the public.

(5) Recommendations for future treatment.

(D) PRERELEASE AND PAROLE CONDITIONS. An offender who is discharged from treatment may be placed on prerelease or parole status under the same terms and laws applicable to any other offender. Psychological and psychiatric counseling and treatment may be required as a condition of such status. Failure to continue treatment, except by agreement of the supervising authority, shall be a basis for terminating prerelease status or instituting parole violation hearings.

(E) PAROLE PROCEDURE. The paroling authority may consider the offender for parole pursuant to other law or administrative rules. When the paroling authority considers the offender for parole, it shall consult with the treating facility at which the offender is being treated or from which he was discharged.

(F) PROBATION.

(1) If an offender who is found guilty but mentally ill is placed on probation, the court may, upon recommendation of the district attorney or upon its own initiative, make treatment a condition of probation.

(2) Reports as specified by the trial judge shall be filed with the probation officer and the sentencing court. Failure to continue treatment, including the refusal to sentencing court, shall be a basis for the institution of probation violation hearings. The period of probation shall be the maximum permitted by law and shall not be reduced without receipt and consideration by the court of a mental health status report like that required in subsection (c).

(3) Treatment shall be provided by an agency approved by the Department of Public Welfare or, with the approval of the sentencing court and at individual expense, by private agencies, private physicians or other mental health personnel. A mental health status report, containing the information set forth in subsection (c), shall be filed with the probation officer and the sentencing court every three months during the period of probation. If a motion on a petition to discontinue probation is made by the defendant, the probation officer shall request a report as specified from the treating facility.

Commonwealth of Pennsylvania v. Heidnik
526 Pa. 458 (1991)

Justice Larsen wrote the opinion for the court.

On July 1, 1988, a jury in the Court of Common Pleas of Philadelphia County convicted appellant, Gary M. Heidnik, of two counts of murder of the first degree, six counts of kidnapping, five counts of rape, four counts of aggravated assault and two counts of involuntary deviate sexual intercourse. Following the verdict of guilty of two counts of murder of the first degree, a separate sentencing hearing was held pursuant to 42 Pa.C.S.A. § 9711, and the same jury sentenced appellant to death for each of the convictions of murder of the first degree. Post verdict motions were argued and denied, and the trial court imposed the sentences of death on March 2, 1989.

Following the imposition of sentence, appellant filed a direct appeal in this Court. Appellant has since expressed his desire to have his execution carried out as expeditiously as possible and has, consequently, instructed counsel not to pursue the aforesaid appeal. The purpose of an automatic direct appeal to this Court of a sentence of death is to ensure that the sentence comports with the Commonwealth's death penalty statute. *Commonwealth v. Appel*, 517 Pa. 529, 539 A.2d 780 (1989). In addition to our statutory obligation, this Court is required to review the sufficiency of the evidence for all death penalty convictions. *Commonwealth v. Zettlemoyer*, 500 Pa. 16, 454 A.2d 937 (1982), cert denied 461 U.S. 970, 103 S.Ct. 2444, 77 L.Ed.2d 1327 (1983).

When testing the sufficiency of the evidence, the applicable standard of review is whether, viewing all the evidence in the light most favorable to the Commonwealth as verdict winner, a jury could find every element of the crime beyond a reasonable doubt. In accordance with this standard, we find the evidence, as now set forth, sufficient beyond a reasonable doubt to sustain the jury's verdicts of murder of the first degree.

On March 24, 1987, the Philadelphia Police Department received a telephone call from a woman who stated that she had been held captive for the last four months. When police officers arrived at the pay phone from which the call was made, they observed a woman who was "visibly shaken" and who repeatedly stated to the officers, "You have to help me." (N.T. 6/21/88 at 274). After the officers were able to calm the woman, Josephina Rivera, she told them that she had been held captive in a basement by a man named Gary Heidnik (appellant) for the last four months and that three other women were still being held in the basement. Ms. Rivera explained that appellant was parked nearby, waiting for her to return from what appellant believed was a visit to her family.

Ms. Rivera also told the officers that appellant had killed two of the women he had held captive and that she feared for the lives of the three women remaining in the basement. Ms. Rivera provided the officers with a description of appellant and told them where he was parked. When the officers apprehended appellant, he asked, "What's this all about, Officer? Didn't I pay my child support?"

Proceeding upon the information Ms. Rivera had supplied, police officers entered appellant's home in North Philadelphia. In the basement of the home were two females lying on a mattress. The women were naked from the waist down, and their bodies were bruised. On the ankle of each woman was a heavy shackle with a long chain. In a corner of the basement the officers removed bags of dirt from a board covering a hole. In the hole lay a naked woman with her hands handcuffed behind her back and her ankle shackled. On returning to the first floor, the officers found in the kitchen six plastic bags containing human body parts.

Josephina Rivera and the women found by police in appellant's basement on March 24, 1987 had been brought there by appellant under similar circumstances over a period of four months. Each had agreed to accompany appellant to his home after being approached by him as he drove along the streets of North Philadelphia. Each had engaged in consensual sex with him before being choked until unconscious. While unconscious, each was carried to appellant's basement and chained to a sewer pipe. As many as three women at a time were confined in the hole appellant had dug in the basement floor. Each of the women was beaten by appellant, and with the exception of the last woman

taken captive, each was raped by appellant repeatedly. Although Josephina Rivera and the three women rescued on March 24, 1987 survived the brutalities inflicted on them by appellant, two other captives, Sandra Lindsay and Debra Dudley, did not.

In addition to beating and raping the captive women, appellant had devised a separate system of punishment for any of the women who screamed for help or attempted to escape. One method of punishment consisted of forcing the disobedient woman to stand suspended by her handcuffed wrist from a hook which appellant had installed in the basement rafters. Such punishment was administered to Sandra Lindsay for a period of three or four days in the first week of February, 1987. During that time, and for the preceding week, Ms. Lindsay was fed only bread and water. Also during that time, appellant forced one of the other captives to beat Ms. Lindsay because Ms. Lindsay was taking too long to eat the bread she was given. On the third or fourth day of her punishment, Ms. Lindsay collapsed after telling the other women that she felt sick. Appellant removed the handcuff from Ms. Lindsay's wrist and kicked her body into the hole in the basement floor. When appellant was unable to find Ms. Lindsay's pulse, he announced to the other women that Ms. Lindsay was dead and carried her body to the kitchen. He then decapitated and dismembered the body. Ms. Lindsay's head was placed in a large pot on the stove and boiled. Other of her body parts were shredded in a food processor and mixed with dog food, which appellant then fed to the other women. Still other parts of Ms. Lindsay's body were put into plastic bags and placed in his freezer.

In mid-March, appellant showed Ms. Lindsay's head, still in the pot on his stove, to another of the captives, Debra Johnson Dudley. Appellant told Ms. Dudley that unless she changed her attitude she would end up the same way Ms. Lindsay did. Appellant had previously stated to Ms. Rivera that he considered Ms. Dudley to be "a pain in the ass" and that he "wanted to get rid of her." On March 17, 1987, appellant administered an electrical shock to Ms. Dudley and two of the other captives as they lay trapped in the basement hole which appellant had filled with water. Appellant attached an electrical wire to Ms. Dudley's metal chain causing her to scream out in prolonged pain. When Ms. Dudley's screaming stopped abruptly, appellant lifted the board covering the hole and removed Ms. Dudley's body. Appellant then placed the body in a freezer in his basement; he later disposed of the body in a state forest in New Jersey. After Ms. Dudley's death, appellant ordered Josephina Rivera to write the following note: "Gary Heidnik and Josephina Rivera electrocuted Debra Dudley on March 17th in the basement of 3520 North Marshall Street by electrocution." Appellant then told Ms. Rivera that she would no longer need to be handcuffed because the incriminating note would prevent her from going to the police. Appellant also told Ms. Rivera that, even if he were arrested, he would simply go into court and "act crazy" by saluting the judge, among other things. Appellant explained to Ms. Rivera that somewhere in the law it states that if a person acts crazy for a certain amount of years, his case is eventually thrown out.

Appellant's mental condition at the time Sandra Lindsay and Debra Dudley died was an issue at trial. Appellant called three expert witnesses to establish that he was legally insane at the time of the deaths. The test for legal sanity and criminal responsibility in this Commonwealth is to be determined under the M'Naghten rule. *Commonwealth v. Banks*, 513 Pa. 318, 521 A.2d 1 (1987), cert. denied, 484 U.S. 873, 108 S.Ct. 211, 98 L.Ed.2d 162 (1987). Under M'Naghten, a defendant is legally insane and absolved of criminal responsibility if, at the time of committing the act, due to a defect of reason or disease of mind, the accused either did not know the nature and quality of the act or did not know that the act was wrong. *Commonwealth v. Tempest*, 496 Pa. 436, 437 A.2d 952 (1981). In order for insanity to constitute a defense, a defendant must prove insanity by a preponderance of the evidence. 18 Pa.C.S.A. § 315(a).

Dr. Clancy McKenzie, the first of two psychiatrists called by appellant, testified that appellant suffered from schizophrenia and that during the period in question appellant did not know right from wrong and was unable to understand the nature and quality of his acts. Dr. McKenzie stated that appellant's conduct during this time period was controlled by an "infant brain" with the chronological age of seventeen months. Dr. McKenzie reached this conclusion based on the fact that appellant's mother gave birth to another child when appellant was seventeen months old. When appellant's estranged wife notified appellant in October, 1986 that she had had a baby, Dr. McKenzie concluded that, "This took him back to the first time when the most important woman in the world to him, his mother, left him and had a baby. And at that point, the trauma in the present [being told that his estranged wife had borne a child] returned him to a trauma at age seventeen months, and he began to experience the world through the eyes of the seventeen month old. The reality is that mommy is never going to go away and leave me again."

Dr. Kenneth Kool, the second psychiatrist called by appellant, testified as to appellant's long-standing schizophrenic illness. Dr. Kool testified that appellant's schizophrenia affected him in such a manner that it prevented appellant from knowing the difference between right and wrong. It was Dr. Kool's opinion that appellant's acts were based on a "systematized delusion that God wanted him to produce a number of children, and this was essentially to him like a pact with God."

The third of appellant's expert witnesses was Jack A. Apsche, Ph.D., an expert in the field of counseling psychology. Dr. Apsche reviewed appellant's lengthy record of treatment for mental disorders dating back to 1962 and concluded that appellant did not know right from wrong and could not understand the nature and quality of his acts between November 26, 1986 and March 24, 1987, the period during which Ms. Lindsay and Ms. Dudley were murdered.

The Commonwealth presented several witnesses to rebut appellant's insanity defense. Dr. Robert Sadoff, a forensic psychiatrist, testified that

he had attempted to examine appellant but that appellant did not respond to any of the questions he was asked. Dr. Sadoff testified that appellant did, however, respond to his attorney's presence by saluting him. Dr. Sadoff thereafter reviewed appellant's extensive medical and psychiatric history, as well as information involving appellant's financial dealings, and his prior involvement with the criminal justice and family court systems. It was Dr. Sadoff's opinion that although appellant suffered from schizophrenia, his conduct between November 26, 1986 and March 24, 1987 indicates that his cognitive ability was intact and that he was able to understand the nature and quality of his acts at the time.

Doctor Sadoff testified that appellant's behavior during the relevant time (November 26, 1986 to March 24, 1987) showed that appellant knew what he was doing and knew that it was wrong. Other Commonwealth rebuttal witnesses included the following: 1) Ernestine Simpson, a social worker at a state hospital in New Jersey, testified that she interviewed appellant in the Fall of 1986 in order to determine whether appellant was sufficiently responsible to escort a patient, appellant's ex-wife, off hospital grounds. Ms. Simpson determined that appellant was sufficiently responsible and recalled that she viewed appellant as being neat, clean, courteous, calm, rational and intelligent. 2) Robert Kirkpatrick, appellant's stockbroker since 1974, testified that appellant was an astute investor who had raised his portfolio from $ 1,500 to $ 531,702 and that appellant had last placed an order for a purchase of stocks on November 17,

1986. 3) Shirley Carter, an acquaintance of appellant since 1978, testified that she had conversed with appellant in October and November of 1986. She testified that appellant's behavior appeared to be the same as it had been over the previous eight years. 4) Harold Wexler, a court reporter who had recorded proceedings involving appellant in family court in January of 1987, read the entire transcript of these family court proceedings to the within jury. The within trial court, in its Opinion in support of its Order denying appellant's post trial motions, characterized Appellant's behavior during the family court proceedings as cunning and deceptive in answering questions about his true worth and his obligation to support his wife and son, both of whom were on welfare. 5) David Pliner, a car salesman who recalled appellant coming to his showroom in November, 1986 to purchase a Cadillac, testified that appellant acted just like any other customer and that appellant had offered him advice on investing. 6) Richard W. Hole, M.D., a psychiatrist at the Veterans' Out-Patient Clinic in Philadelphia, testified that in December, 1986 appellant who had last been seen by Dr. Hole in February, 1986, asked to have his treatment reinstated. Appellant denied having any psychiatric symptoms, such as anxiety, hallucinations, depressions or delusions. Dr. Hole, nevertheless, prescribed thorazine, a tranquilizer widely used in managing schizophrenia, although he saw no ongoing problems at that time or when appellant returned in January and February of 1987. 7) Eva Wojciechowski, a court psychologist, testified that she had administered an intelligence test to appellant incidental to his attempt to gain partial custody of his son in March of 1987. Appellant's test showed that his I.Q. was 148. Ms. Wojciechowski testified that appellant's score placed him in the upper 1/2 of 1% of the total population.

The jury rejected appellant's insanity defense. Our review of the record establishes that the evidence is sufficient beyond a reasonable doubt to support the jury's conclusion that appellant was legally sane when he took the lives of Sandra Lindsay and Debra Dudley. And again, based upon the foregoing recitation of facts, we find the evidence to be sufficient beyond a reasonable doubt to sustain the jury's verdicts of murder of the first degree.

Our statutory obligation requires that we determine the following: 1) whether the sentences of death were the product of passion, prejudice or any other arbitrary factor; 2) whether the evidence fails to support the finding of at least one specified aggravating circumstance; or 3) whether the sentences are excessive or disproportionate to the penalty imposed in similar cases considering both the circumstances of the crime and the character and record of the defendant. 42 Pa.C.S.A. § 9711(h).

In the penalty phase of the proceedings, the jury found the existence of the following aggravating circumstances with regard to Ms. Lindsay's death: ". . . the defendant committed a killing while in the perpetration of a felony," 42 Pa.C.S.A. § 9711(d)(6); and "The offense was committed by means of torture," 42 Pa.C.S.A. § 9711(d)(8). For purposes of the sentencing statute, "torture" is understood as the infliction of a considerable amount of pain and suffering on a victim which is unnecessarily heinous, atrocious or cruel, manifesting exceptional depravity. *Commonwealth v. Pursell*, 508 Pa. 212, 495 A.2d 183 (1985). Sandra Lindsay's killing occurred during a kidnapping, supporting the finding that appellant committed a killing while in the perpetration of a felony. The evidence that Ms. Lindsay was hung by the wrist from a ceiling hook for three or four days, was fed only bread and water during that time, and was subjected to beatings as she hung from the hook is sufficient to support the finding of the sentencing jury that appellant killed Ms. Lindsay by means of torture.

With regard to Ms. Dudley's death, the jury found the existence of the same aggravating circumstances as were found in regard to Ms. Lindsay's death and found the following two additional aggravating circumstances: ". . . the defendant knowingly created a grave risk of death to another person in addition to the victim of the offense," 42 Pa.C.S.A. § 9711(d)(7); and "The defendant has been convicted of another murder, committed either before or at the same time of the offense at issue." 42 Pa.C.S.A. § 9711(d)(11). As with Ms. Lindsay, Ms. Dudley's death occurred during a kidnapping, supporting the jury's finding that appellant killed her during the perpetration of a felony. The evidence that Ms. Dudley's death occurred as the result of electrical charges being administered to her while she lay in a water-filled pit and screamed in agony, supports the jury's finding that Ms. Dudley also was killed by means of torture. The

fact that two other women in metal chains were in that water-filled pit with Ms. Dudley when appellant administered the electrical charge, supports the finding of a grave risk to others. The death of Ms. Lindsay, which occurred prior to Ms. Dudley's death, supports the finding of a murder committed before the offense at issue.

In addition to the foregoing aggravating circumstances, the sentencing jury found the existence of the following mitigating circumstance with regard to the murders of both Ms. Lindsay and Ms. Dudley: "The defendant has no significant history of prior criminal convictions." 42 Pa.C.S.A. § 9711(e)(1). The jury then unanimously found that this mitigating circumstance was outweighed by the aforementioned aggravating circumstances and, pursuant to 42 Pa.C.S.A. 9711(c)(1)(iv), fixed appellant's sentence at death for the murder of each woman.

Finally, we have examined the record and find that the sentence of death was a product of the evidence and not a product of "passion, prejudice or any other factor." 42 Pa.C.S.A. § 9711(h)(3). Based upon data supplied by the Administrative Office of Pennsylvania Courts we conclude that the sentences of death imposed upon appellant are neither excessive nor disproportionate to the penalty imposed in similar cases, considering the circumstances of the crime and the record of the accused.

For the foregoing reasons, we sustain the convictions of murder of the first degree and affirm the sentences of death.

Coercion/Duress Defense: Under what circumstances may a criminal defendant successfully raise the coercion defense?

Western jurisprudence has always recognized the defense of coercion or duress. The difficult question is where to draw the line on the continuum of duress -- from peer pressure at one extreme to a "gun to your head" at the other. Although § 309 of the Pennsylvania Crimes Code attempts to define the circumstances under which a criminal defendant is entitled to a defense of "duress", Pennsylvania courts continue to interpret how and when that defense may be raised. Must the defendant witness the violent acts of the person who has "coerced" him to commit a crime? Must the violent acts be close in time to the defendant's criminal act? In *Commonwealth of Pennsylvania v. Larry Russell* the Superior Court confronted the issue of whether a defendant seeking to show that he sold illegal drugs under duress is permitted to offer "evidence of violent acts, known to the defendant, committed by the alleged intimidating figure." The trial judge had found such evidence to be irrelevant, but the Superior Court ruled that prior assaults on those who refused to sell him drugs was relevant to a § 309 defense.

18 Pa.C.S. § 309

§ 309. Duress

(A) GENERAL RULE. It is a defense that the actor engaged in the conduct charged to constitute an offense because he was coerced to do so by the use of, or a threat to use, unlawful force against his person or the person of another, which a person of reasonable firmness in his situation would have been unable to resist.

(B) EXCEPTION. The defense provided by subsection (a) of this section is unavailable if the actor recklessly placed himself in a situation in which it was probable that he would be subjected to duress. The defense is also unavailable if he was negligent in placing himself in such a situation, whenever negligence suffices to establish culpability for the offense charged.

Commonwealth of Pennsylvania v. Russell
326 Pa. Super. 346 (1984)

Judge Cercone delivered the opinion of the court.

Appellant was arrested and charged with four counts each of delivery of a controlled substance and possession of a controlled substance with intent to deliver. He proceeded to trial before a jury. Appellant admitted selling the controlled substances, but claimed that, as a result of pressure applied by a Mr. Walburn, he had been coerced and entrapped to do so. He was convicted on all counts and sentenced to two (2) to four (4) years in prison on each count, to be served concurrently. He here appeals the judgment of sentence. On appeal appellant raises five (5) assignments of error all of which pertain to his entrapment defense. The first three claims address evidentiary ruling of the trial court. Finding merit to one of such claims, we are constrained to reverse and remand for a new trial. We choose to briefly address the other issues so to provide guidance to the trial court on remand.

Appellant contends that the trial court improperly restricted his cross- examination of an undercover investigator. He attempted to question the witness regarding the role of the Lewisburg Police Department in the investigation and the investigation's goal of apprehending appellant's supplier. The court found such inquiries irrelevant to the charges at hand and to the claim of entrapment. We

agree.

Evidence is relevant if it in some degree advances the inquiry, making the desired inference more probable than not. We find no error in excluding the above evidence for we fail to see how the proposed inquiry could further appellant's claim that he was entrapped or coerced by the conduct of an alleged agent of the Commonwealth. Next appellant argues that the court should have allowed him to introduce evidence as to the violent propensities of Walburn, who first brought appellant and the undercover agent together. He contended that it was out of fear of this person that he sold the illicit drugs. The trial court found the proffered evidence irrelevant. Appellant argues here, as he did in the court below, that such testimony was necessary to support his contention that he acted under duress, 18 Pa.C.S.A. § 309, and that he was entrapped due to his justifiable fear of Mr. Walburn. We agree.

In *Commonwealth v. Santiago*, 462 Pa. 216, 340 A.2d 440 (1975), the court was faced with a claim by the defendant that she had participated in the drug trade only because she had been coerced by her husband. The court held: If in fact a person is acting under duress or coercion, this provision, as under prior law, provides a defense. We can find no reason to employ a fiction which is without basis today. To do so would be to abort truth and to subvert the basic purposes of the adjudicative process. Thus, the issue for the trier of fact to resolve was whether [the defendant] was acting of her own volition or whether, in fact she was being coerced by her husband or any other person in her participation in this criminal activity.

Santiago in effect recognized the defense of duress in a prosecution for selling controlled substances, therefore, the issue becomes whether the proposed testimony should have been admitted for the purpose of showing duress. . . .

There is a lack of authority in the Commonwealth on the manner of establishing the defense of duress; however, the law on self-defense assists us in the disposition of this issue.

In *Commonwealth v. Amos*, 445 Pa. 297, 284 A.2d 748 (1971), we said testimony as to the victim's character is admissible for the following purposes: (1) to corroborate the defendant's alleged knowledge of the victim's violent character to corroborate the defendant's testimony that he had a reasonable belief his life was in danger and (2) to prove the allegedly violent propensities of the victim to show he was the aggressor. We further noted that, generally, character can be proved only by reputation evidence. In *Commonwealth v. Darby*, 473 Pa. 109, 373 A.2d 1073 (1977), we held that convictions and violent acts of a victim which did not result in

conviction, of which the defendant had knowledge, could be introduced for the first purpose mentioned in *Commonwealth v. Amos*.

Where self-defense is raised as a defense, the trial court should allow the defendant, who claims to have been aware of the victim's alleged violent propensities, to present evidence of specific acts of violence by the victim, of which the defendant was aware; the fact finder must then assess such evidence and determine if the defendant reasonably believed his health was in danger. Therefore, following the rationale of *Smith*, supra, when a defense of duress is proposed, the defendant should be permitted to present evidence of violent acts, known to the defendant, committed by the alleged intimidating figure.

In the current case appellant proposed to have a witness testify that the witness observed Walburn physically assault another, when that individual refused to sell Walburn drugs. Contrary to the court's ruling, such information was pertinent, under the holdings of the above case, as to whether appellant was coerced into participating in the drug transactions. This prior incident was sufficiently similar to the facts at hand that is should have been brought to the jury's attention. Therefore, as the jury should have been allowed to hear and weigh such a testimony a new trial is in order . . .

Judgment of sentence is reversed and the case is remanded for a new trial.

Rape: When Does "No" Not Mean "No"?

Under Section 3121 of the Pennsylvania Crimes Code, "A person commits a felony of the first degree when he engages in sexual intercourse with another person not his spouse: (1) by forcible compulsion; (2) by threat of forcible compulsion that would prevent resistance by a person of reasonable resolution. . ." While Pennsylvania law does not require the victim to physically resist the attacker, the law does permit the accused to introduce evidence the victim consented to have sex.

The use of force or threat of force, must be shown in order to prove the crime of rape. The crime is not simply defined in terms of non-consensual intercourse. But how much force is required to commit the crime of rape? How might the accused show that the victim consented? What must the victim do to demonstrate nonconsent? Does physical resistance by the victim demonstrate an absence of consent? The courts have not been consistent in answering these questions. In fact, the amount of resistance required to show nonconsent seems to depend on the relationship which the victim has with the accused. Though no resistance is legally required, defendants attempt to use the absence of resistance to show consent. Less resistance is required to show nonconsent in rapes by strangers than rapes by acquaintances.

From a purely legal perspective, the heart of the rape issue is whether it is to be viewed as a "general intent" or "specific intent" crime? If it is a general intent crime, it should be sufficient to show that the defendant intended the sexual intercourse and that the victim did not consent to the intercourse (focus on the victim's state of mind). If, however, rape is to be considered a "specific intent" crime (as in England), it must be found that the defendant intended to have sexual intercourse with the victim and that the defendant knew that the victim did not consent (focus on the defendant's state of mind).

In the recent case of *Commonwealth of Pennsylvania v. Robert A. Berkowitz* the Superior Court had to decide whether to permit a rape conviction where the victim had said "no," but offered no physical resistance, and the accused had used no force other than being "on top of the victim before and during intercourse..." These "facts show no more than what legal scholars refer to as 'reluctant submission.'" Despite the fact that the victim repeatedly said "no," the Superior Court reversed the conviction. At this writing, the case is on appeal.

Commonwealth of Pennsylvania v. Berkowitz
609 A.2d 1338 (Superior Court, 1992)

Per Curiam Opinion.

Appellant appeals from judgment of sentence imposed following convictions of rape and indecent assault. We are called upon to determine the degree of physical force necessary to complete the act of rape in Pennsylvania. We find that under the totality of the circumstances, evidence of sufficient force was not adduced herein. We are also asked to decide whether the trial court improperly excluded evidence of the victim's motive to fabricate the charge of indecent assault. We find that it did. Accordingly, we discharge appellant on the rape conviction and reverse and remand for a new trial on the indecent assault conviction.

I.   FACTS AND PROCEDURAL HISTORY

In the spring of 1988, appellant and the victim were both college sophomores at East Stroudsburg State University, ages twenty and nineteen years old, respectively. They had mutual friends and acquaintances. On April nineteenth of that year, the victim went to appellant's dormitory room. What transpired in that dorm room between appellant and the victim thereafter is the subject of the instant appeal. During a one day jury trial held on September 14, 1988, the victim gave the following account during direct examination by the Commonwealth. At roughly 2:00 on the afternoon of April 19, 1988, after attending two morning classes, the victim returned to her dormitory room. There, she drank a martini to "loosen up a little bit" before going to meet her boyfriend, with whom she had argued the night before. Roughly ten minutes later she walked to her boyfriend's dormitory lounge to meet him. He had not yet arrived.

Having nothing else to do while she waited for her boyfriend, the victim walked up to appellant's room to look for Earl Hassel, appellant's roommate. She knocked on the door several times but received no answer. She therefore wrote a note to Mr. Hassel, which read, "Hi Earl, I'm drunk. That's not why I came to see you. I haven't seen you in a while. I'll talk to you later, [victim's name]." She did so, although she had not felt any intoxicating effects from the martini, "for a laugh."

After the victim had knocked again, she tried the knob on the appellant's door. Finding it open, she walked in. She saw someone lying on the bed with a pillow over his head, whom she thought to be Earl Hassel. After lifting the pillow from his head, she realized it was appellant. She asked appellant which dresser was his roommate's. He told her, and the victim left the note.

Before the victim could leave appellant's room, however, appellant asked her to stay and "hang out for a while." She complied because she "had time to kill" and because she didn't really know appellant and wanted to give "a fair chance." Appellant asked her to give him a back rub but she declined, explaining that she did not "trust" him. Appellant then asked her to have a seat on his bed. Instead, she found a seat on the floor, and conversed for a while about a mutual friend. No physical contact between the two had, to this point, taken place.

Thereafter, however, appellant moved off the bed and down on the floor, and "kind of pushed [the victim] back with his body. It wasn't a shove, it was just kind of a leaning-type of thing." Next appellant "straddled" and started kissing the victim. The victim responded by saying, "Look, I gotta go. I'm going to meet [my boyfriend]." Then appellant lifted up her shirt and bra and began fondling her. The victim then said "no."

After roughly thirty seconds of kissing and fondling, appellant "undid his pants and he kind of moved his body up a little bit." The victim was still saying "no" but "really couldn't move because [appellant] was shifting at [her] body so he was over [her]." Id. Appellant then tried to put his penis in her mouth. The victim did not physically resist, but rather continued to verbally protest, saying "No, I gotta go, let me go," in a "scolding" manner.

Ten or fifteen more seconds passed before the two rose to their feet. Appellant disregarded the victim's continual complaints that she "had to go," and instead walked two feet away to the door and locked it so that no one from the outside could enter. Then, in the victim's words, "[appellant] put me down on the bed. It was kind of like -- he didn't throw me on the bed. It's hard to explain. It was kind of like a push but no. . . . . She did not bounce off the bed. "It wasn't slow like a romantic kind of thing, but it wasn't a fast shove either. It was kind of in the middle.

Once the victim was on the bed, appellant began "straddling" her again while he undid the knot in her sweatpants. He then removed her sweatpants and underwear from one of her legs. The victim did not physically resist in any way while on the bed because appellant was on top of her, and she "couldn't like go anywhere." She did not scream out at anytime because, "it was like a dream was happening or something."

Appellant then used one of his hands to "guide" his penis into her vagina. At that point, after appellant was inside her, the victim began saying "no, no to him softly in a moaning kind of way . . . because it was just so scary." After about thirty seconds, appellant pulled out his penis and ejaculated onto the victim's stomach. Immediately thereafter, appellant got off the victim and said, "Wow, I guess we just got carried away." To this the victim retorted, "No, we didn't get carried away, you got carried away." The victim then quickly dressed, grabbed her school books and raced downstairs to her boyfriend who was by then waiting for her in the lounge.

Once there, the victim began crying. Her boyfriend and she went up to his dorm room where, after watching the victim clean off appellant's semen from her stomach, he called the police.

Defense counsel's cross-examination elicited more details regarding the contact between appellant and the victim before the incident in question. The victim testified that roughly two weeks prior the incident, she had attended a school seminar entitled, "Does 'no' sometimes means 'yes'?" Among other things, the lecturer at this seminar had discussed the average length and circumference of human penises. After the seminar, the victim and several of her friends had discussed the subject matter of the seminar over a speaker-telephone with appellant and his roommate Earl Hassel. The victim testified that d u r i n g t h a t t e l e p h o n e conversation, she had asked appellant the size of his penis. According to the victim, appellant responded by suggesting that the victim "come over and find out." She declined. When questioned further regarding her communications with appellant prior to the April 19, 1988 incident, the victim testified that on two other occasions, she had stopped by appellant's room while intoxicated. During one of those times, she had laid down on his bed. When asked whether she had asked appellant again at that time what his penis size was, the victim testified that she did not remember.

Appellant took the stand in his own defense and offered an account of the incident and the events leading up to it which differed only as to the consent involved. According to appellant, the victim had begun communication with him after the school seminar by asking him of the size of his penis and of whether he would show it to her. Appellant had suspected that the victim wanted to pursue a sexual relationship with him because she had stopped by his room twice after the phone call while intoxicated, laying down on his bed with her legs spread and again asking to see his penis. He believed that his suspicions were confirmed when she initiated the April 19, 1988 encounter by stopping by his room (again after drinking), and waking him up.

Appellant testified that, on the day in question, he did initiate the first physical contact, but added that the victim warmly responded to his advances by passionately returning his kisses. He conceded that she was continually "whispering . . . no's," but claimed that she did so while "amorously . . . passionately" moaning. In effect, he took such protests to be thinly veiled acts of encouragement. When asked why he locked the door, he explained that "that's not something you want somebody to just walk in on you [doing.]"

According to appellant, the two then laid down on the bed, the victim helped him take her clothing off, and he entered her. He agreed that the victim continued to say "no" while on the bed, but carefully qualified his agreement, explaining that the statements were "moaned passionately." According to appellant, when he saw a "blank look on her face," he immediately withdrew and asked "is anything wrong, is something the matter, is anything wrong." He ejaculated on her stomach thereafter because he could no longer "control" himself. Appellant testified that after this, the victim "saw that it was over and then she made her move. She gets right off the bed . . . she just swings her legs over and then she puts her clothes back on." Then, in wholly corroborating an aspect of the victim's account, he testified that he remarked, "Well, I guess we got carried away," to which she rebuked, "No, we didn't get carried, you got carried away'"

After hearing both accounts, the jury convicted appellant of rape and indecent assault. Defense counsel filed post-verdict motions alleging numerous trial court errors. Before the trial court could rule on these motions, appellant retained new counsel who filed supplemental post-verdict motions. The trial court held a hearing on the motions and, finding no merit in them, denied appellant post-verdict relief. Appellant was then sentenced to serve a term of imprisonment of one to four years for rape and a concurrent term of six to twelve months for indecent assault. Post-trial bail was granted pending this timely appeal.

On appeal, counsel for appellant has presented this Court with the following issues.

1. Did the trial court err in failing to define "forcible compulsion" as requested by counsel, in accordance with *Commonwealth v. Rhodes*, 510 A.2d 1217 (1986)?

2. Did the trial court err in its denial of defendant's pre-trial motion to explore complaint's [sic] sexual infidelity to her boyfriend, which was the basis for continued arguments between them and provided a clear motive to fabricate a rape and thus was exculpatory to the defendant?

3. Is there sufficient evidence of "forcible compulsion" to support a rape conviction where the uncontroverted facts established "reluctant submission"?

4. Was trial counsel ineffective in his failure to explore the use of character witnesses to be called on behalf of the defendant to testify as to his reputation for honesty and peacefulness?

5. Did the prosecutor's comment during her closing that the jury should "rest assured that somebody in his (the defendant's) position in a case like this is not treated the same as a brutal stranger", relieve the jury of its sense of responsibility for its verdict and thus deprive defendant of a fair trial?

6. Did the trial court err in refusing defendant's motion for reconsideration requesting that defendant's sentence for indecent assault be vacated because of the doctrine of merger?

Since a finding of merit in the third issue would require the most encompassing relief for appellant, it is best addressed first.

II. SUFFICIENCY OF THE EVIDENCE

Appellant's argument in this regard was well summarized by appellant's counsel in his brief. The issues on appeal are real. At sentencing, they were recognized by the trial court as being on the cutting edge of the criminal jurisprudence of this Commonwealth:

The Court: Well, I'm comforted by the knowledge that whatever happens here today will certainly not end this case. This is going to go on and on for some time for just the very reason you suggested Mr. Mustokoff [present counsel for appellant], and that being that this case is on the cutting edge.

Mr. Berkowitz prays that this Court overturns his rape conviction. He asks that this Court define the parameters between what may have been unacceptable social conduct and the criminal conduct necessary to support the charge for forcible rape.

We contend that upon review, the facts show no more than what legal scholars refer to as "reluctant submission". The complainant herself admits that she was neither hurt nor threatened at any time during the encounter. She admits she never screamed or attempted to summon help. The incident occurred in a college dormitory in the middle of the afternoon.

There has never been an affirmed conviction for forcible rape under similar circumstances. Not one factor which this Court has considered significant in prior cases, exists here. The uncontroverted evidence fails to establish forcible compulsion.

The Commonwealth counters: Viewing the evidence and its inferences in the light most favorable to the Commonwealth, the jury's conclusion that the Defendant's forcible conduct overcame [the victim's] will is reasonable. The assault was rapid and the victim was physically overcome. Because she was acquainted with the Defendant, [the victim] had no reason to be fearful or suspicious of him and her resorting to verbal resistance only is understandable. More importantly, perhaps, it is only her lack of consent that is truly relevant. It is entirely reasonable to believe that the Defendant sat on her, pushed her on the bed and penetrated her before she had time to fully realize her plight and raise a hue and cry. If the law required active resistance, rather the simple absence of consent, speedy penetration would immunize the most violent attacks and the goal-oriented rapist would reap an absurd reward. Certainly a victim must communicate her objections. But, contrary to the Defendant's arguments, Pennsylvania law says she can "just say no." [The victim] said "no." She said it repeatedly, clearly and sternly. She

was rapidly, forcibly raped and deserves the protection of the law. With the Commonwealth's position, the trial court agreed. We cannot.

In viewing the evidence, we remain mindful that credibility determinations were a matter solely for the fact finder below. On appeal, we must examine the evidence in the light most favorable to the Commonwealth drawing all reasonable inferences therefrom. If a jury could have reasonably determined from the evidence adduced that all of the necessary elements of the crime were established, then the evidence will be deemed sufficient to support the verdict.

In Pennsylvania, the crime of rape is defined by statute as follows: A person commits a felony of the first degree when he engages in sexual intercourse with another person not his spouse: (1) by forcible compulsion; (2) by threat of forcible compulsion that would prevent resistance by a person of reasonable resolution; (3) who is unconscious; or (4) who is so mentally deranged or deficient that such person is incapable of consent. 18 Pa.C.S.A. § 3121.

A statutory caveat to this rule may be found in section 3107 of title 18. Resistance Not Required The alleged victim need not resist the actor in prosecution under this chapter: Provided, however, that nothing in this section shall be construed to prohibit a defendant from introducing evidence that the alleged victim consented to the conduct in question. The contours of Pennsylvania's rape statute, however, are not immediately apparent. As our Supreme Court explained in the landmark case, *Commonwealth v.*

Rhodes, 510 Pa. 537, 510 A.2d 1217 (1986): "Forcible compulsion" as used in section 3121(1) includes not only physical force or violence but also moral, psychological or intellectual force used to compel a person to engage in sexual intercourse against that person's will.

Closely related to section 3121(1) is section 3121(2) which applies to the situation where "forcible compulsion" is not actually used but is threatened. That section uses the phrase "by threat of forcible compulsion that would prevent resistance by a person of reasonable resolution." The Model Penal Code used the terminology "compels her to submit by any threat that would prevent resistance by a woman of ordinary resolution" and graded that offense as gross sexual imposition, a felony of the third degree. The Pennsylvania legislature rejected the concept that sexual intercourse compelled by "gross imposition" should be graded as a less serious offense and, therefore, enacted section 3121(2). By use of the phrase "person of reasonable resolution," the legislature introduced an objective standard regarding the use of threats of forcible compulsion to prevent resistance (as opposed to actual application of "forcible compulsion.")

The determination of whether there is sufficient evidence to demonstrate beyond a reasonable doubt that an accused engaged in sexual intercourse by forcible compulsion (which we have defined to include "not only physical force or violence, but also moral, psychological or intellectual force used to compel a person to engage in sexual intercourse against that person's will,"), or by the threat of such forcible compulsion that would

prevent resistance by a person of reasonable resolution is, of course, a determination that will be made in each case based upon the totality of the circumstances that have been presented to the fact finder. Significant factors to be weighed in that determination would include the respective ages of the victim and the accused, the respective mental and physical conditions of the victim and the accused, the atmosphere and physical setting in which the incident was alleged to have taken place, the extent to which the accused may have been in a position of authority, domination or custodial control over the victim, and whether the victim was under duress. This list of possible factors is by no means exclusive.

Before us is not a case of mental coercion. There existed no significant disparity between the ages of appellant and the victim. They were both college sophomores at the time of the incident. Appellant was age twenty; the victim was nineteen. The record is devoid of any evidence suggesting that the physical or mental condition of one party differed from the other in any material way. Moreover, the atmosphere and physical setting in which the incident took place was in no way coercive. The victim walked freely into appellant's dorm room in the middle of the afternoon on a school day and stayed to talk of her own volition. There was no evidence to suggest that appellant was in any position of authority, domination or custodial control over the victim. Finally, no record evidence indicates that the victim was under duress. Indeed, nothing in the record manifests any intent of appellant to impose "moral, psychological or intellectual" coercion upon the victim. See and compare *Commonwealth v. Rhodes*, supra (position of authority, isolated area of the incident and explicit commands sufficient to prove mental coercion); *Commonwealth v. Ables*, supra, 590 A.2d at 338 (position of trust and confidence coupled with emotional exploitation sufficient to establish moral coercion); *Commonwealth v. Ruppert*, Pa. Super., 579 A.2d 966 (1990) (father-daughter relationship coupled with showing of sexually explicit pictures sufficient to establish p s y c h o l o g i c a l c o e r c i o n); *Commonwealth v. Frank*, 395 Pa. Super. 412, 577 A.2d 609 (1990) (therapist-patient relationship coupled with threat sufficient for p s y c h o l o g i c a l c o e r c i o n); *Commonwealth v. Dorman*, supra (appellant's position of authority and trust and remote location of the incident sufficient to establish psychological coercion).

Nor is this a case of a threat of forcible compulsion. When asked by defense counsel at trial whether appellant had at any point threatened her in any manner, the victim responded, "No, he didn't." Moreover, careful review of the record fails to reveal any express or even implied threat that could be viewed as one which, by the objective standard applicable herein, would prevent resistance by a person of reasonable resolution." 18 Pa.C.S.A. § 3121(2). Compare *Commonwealth v. Poindexter*, 372 Pa.Super. 419, 547 A.2d 757 (1989) (father's reproaches and threats sufficient to establish coercion toward daughters); *Commonwealth v. Williams*, 294 Pa.Super. 93, 439 A.2d 765 (1982) (threat that victim would be killed if she resisted sufficient to establish forcible compulsion).

Rather, the Commonwealth contends that the instant rape conviction is supported by the evidence of actual physical force used to complete the act of intercourse. Essentially, the Commonwealth maintains that, viewed in the light most favorable to it, the record establishes that the victim did not consent to engage in the intercourse, and thus, any force used to complete the act of intercourse thereafter constituted "forcible compulsion."

In response, appellant urges that the victim's testimony itself precludes a finding of "forcible compulsion." Appellant essentially argues that the indisputable lack of physical injuries and physical resistance proves that the evidence was insufficient to establish rape. In beginning our review of these arguments, it is clear that any reliance on the victim's absence of physical injuries or physical resistance is misplaced. Although it is true that the instant victim testified that she was not physically hurt in any fashion," and that it was "possible that [she] took no physical action to discourage [appellant]," such facts are insignificant in a sufficiency determination. As our Supreme Court has made clear, "rape . . . is defined, not in terms of the physical injury to the victim, but in terms of the effect it has on the victim's volition."' Similarly, our legislature has expressly commanded that the "victim need not resist the actor in prosecutions under" Chapter 31. See 18 Pa.C.S.A. § 3107 (emphasis added). As the *Rhodes* Court observed, this legislative mandate was intended to make it clear that "lack of consent is not synonymous with lack of resistance."

Thus, while the presence of

actual injury or physical resistance might well indicate "forcible compulsion," we are compelled to conclude that the absence of either or both is not fatal to the Commonwealth's case.

What is comparatively uncertain, however, in the absence of either an injury or resistance requirement, is the precise degree of actual physical force necessary to prove "forcible compulsion." As the *Rhodes* Court has made clear, no precise definition of the term "forcible compulsion" may be found. The "force necessary to support convictions for rape and involuntary deviate sexual intercourse need only be such as to establish lack of consent and to induce the woman to submit without additional resistance . . . The degree of force required to constitute rape [or involuntary deviate sexual intercourse] is relative and depends upon the facts and particular circumstances of the case."

[The] *Rhodes* Court specifically refused to "delineate all of the possible circumstances that might tend to demonstrate that sexual intercourse was engaged in by forcible compulsion or by threat of forcible compulsion within the meaning of [title 18] section 3121 (1) and (2)." Rather, the Court left that delineation to evolve "in the best tradition of the common law -- by development of a body of case law. . . . Whether there is sufficient evidence to demonstrate . . . that an accused engaged in sexual intercourse by forcible compulsion . . . is, of course, a determination that will be made in each case based on the totality of the circumstances. . . ." Thus, the ultimate task for the fact finder remains the question of whether, under the totality of circumstances,

"the victim . . . was forced to . . . engage in sexual intercourse . . . against his or her will."

Here, the victim testified that the physical aspects of the encounter began when appellant "kind of pushed me back with his body. It wasn't a shove, it was just kind of a leaning-type thing." Compare *Commonwealth v. Rough*, supra (victim forced to floor and struck). She did not testify that appellant "pinned" her to the floor with his hands thereafter; she testified that he "started kissing me . . . [and] lift[ing] my shirt [and] bra . . . straddling me kind of . . . shifting at my body so that he was over me." Compare *Commonwealth v. Meadows*, 381 Pa. Super. 354, 553 A.2d 1006, 1008-09 (1989) (victim "pinned" to the ground despite physical resistance). When he attempted to have oral sex with her, appellant "knelt up straight . . . [and] tried to put his penis in my mouth . . . and after he obviously couldn't . . . he, we got up." Although appellant then locked the door, his act cannot be seen as an attempt to imprison the victim since she knew and testified that the type of lock on the door of appellant's dorm room simply prevented those on the outside from entering but could be opened from the inside without hindrance. *Compare Commonwealth v. Rhodes*, supra (victim imprisoned in car brought to isolated area). Appellant did not push, shove or throw the victim to his bed; he "put" her on the bed, not in a "romantic" way, but not with a "fast shove either." Once on the bed, appellant did not try to restrain the victim with his hands in any fashion. Compare *Commonwealth v. Irvin* (victim choked and her screams muffled by defendant's hands). Rather, while she was "just kind of laying there," he "straddled" her, "quickly undid" the knot in her sweatpants, "took off" her sweatpants and underwear, placed the "weight of his body" on top of her and "guided" his penis inside her vagina. Even in the light most favorable to the Commonwealth, the victim's testimony as to the physical aspects of the encounter cannot serve as a basis to prove "forcible compulsion." The cold record is utterly devoid of any evidence regarding the respective sizes of either appellant or the victim. As such, we are left only to speculate as to the coercive effect of such acts as "leaning" against the victim or placing the "weight of his body" on top of her. This we may not do. Moreover, even if the record indicated some disparity in the respective weights or strength of the parties, such acts are not themselves inconsistent with consensual relations. Except for the fact that appellant was on top of the victim before and during intercourse, there is no evidence that the victim, if she had wanted to do so, could not have removed herself from appellant's bed and walked out of the room without any risk of harm or danger to herself whatsoever. These circumstances simply cannot be bootstrapped into sexual intercourse by forcible compulsion.

Similarly inconclusive is the fact that the victim testified that the act occurred in a relatively brief period of time. The short time frame might, without more, indicate that the victim desired the sexual encounter as easily as it might that she didn't, given the fact that no threats or mental coercion were alleged. At most, therefore, the physical aspects of the encounter establishes that appellant's sexual advances may have been unusually rapid, persistent and virtually uninterrupted. However inappropriate, undesirable or unacceptable such conduct may be seen to be, it does not, standing alone, prove that the victim was "forced to engage in sexual intercourse against her will."

The only evidence which remains to be considered is the fact that both the victim and appellant testified that throughout the encounter, the victim repeatedly and continually said "no." Unfortunately for the Commonwealth, under the existing statutes, this evidence alone cannot suffice to support a finding of "forcible compulsion." Evidence of verbal resistance is unquestionably relevant in a determination of "forcible compulsion." At least twice previously this Court has given weight to the failure to heed the victim's oral admonitions. See *Commonwealth v. Meadows*, supra, 553 A.2d at 1009 (evidence sufficient to convict for rape where "appellant pinned [the victim] to the ground and knowingly disregarded her efforts to communicate the idea that she did not want to have intercourse."); see also *Commonwealth v. Dorman*, supra, 547 A.2d at 761 (finding evidence of rape sufficient where "despite the victim's protests, appellant . . . disrobed her, pushed her down on the seat of the car and had intercourse with her.") In each such case, however, evidence of verbal resistance was only found sufficient where coupled with a sufficient threat of forcible compulsion, mental coercion, or actual physical force of a type inherently inconsistent with consensual sexual intercourse. Thus, although evidence of verbal protestations may be relevant to prove that the intercourse was against the victim's will, it is not dispositive or sufficient evidence of "forcible compulsion."

If the legislature had intended to define rape, a felony of the first degree, as non-consensual intercourse, it could have done so. It did not do this. It defined rape as sexual intercourse by "forcible compulsion." Compare 18 Pa.C.S.A. § 3126 (defining indecent assault as "indecent contact with another not [the actor's] spouse . . . without the consent of the other person.") If the legislature means what it said, then where as here no evidence was adduced by the Commonwealth which established either that mental coercion, or a threat, or force inherently inconsistent with consensual intercourse was used to complete the act of intercourse, the evidence is insufficient to support a rape conviction. Accordingly, we hold that the trial court erred in determining that the evidence adduced by the Commonwealth was sufficient to convict appellant of rape. . . .

IV. CONCLUSION

For the foregoing reasons, we conclude that the evidence adduced by the Commonwealth was insufficient to convict appellant of rape, and that a new trial is warranted on the indecent assault charge. The remaining issues appellant raises need not be addressed in view of this disposition. Accordingly, we discharge appellant as to the rape conviction and reverse and remand for a new trial in accordance with this opinion.

Equal Protection: Does the state have the power to prohibit deviate sexual acts among unmarried persons?

In *Bowers v. Hardwick*, 106 S. Ct. 2841 (1986), the United States Supreme Court upheld a Georgia statute criminalizing oral and anal sex, even between consenting adults in the privacy of their homes. The statute did not differentiate between heterosexuals or homosexuals, nor between married and unmarried lovers, although the actual case involved homosexual sodomy. The opinion was quite controversial. Many states, including Pennsylvania, have statutes on the books, but rarely enforced, that prohibit certain sexual acts of consenting adults. Six years before *Bowers*, the constitutionality of Pennsylvania's statute regulating voluntary sexual conduct under the police power of the state was challenged in *Commonwealth of Pennsylvania v. Michael Bonadio*. It should be noted that there was one substantial difference between the Georgia statute and Pennsylvania's -- Pennsylvania's Crimes Code excluded married couples from prosecution by virtue of its definition of deviate sexual intercourse: "Sexual intercourse per os or per anus between human beings who are not husband and wife..."

The defendants in *Bonadio* were exotic dancers and other employees of an "adult" pornographic theater in Pittsburgh, and members of the audience with whom the dancers allegedly engaged in a variety of sexual acts. The defendants successfully argued that the statute prohibiting voluntary deviate sexual intercourse was both beyond the police power of the state and a violation of the Equal Protection clauses of both the Pennsylvania and United States Constitutions because it only prohibited such conduct among unmarried persons.

Commonwealth of Pennsylvania v. Bonadio
490 Pa. 91 (1980)

Justice Flaherty delivered the opinion of the court.

This is an appeal from an Order of the Court of Common Pleas of Allegheny County granting appellees' Motion to Quash an Information on the ground that the Voluntary Deviate Sexual Intercourse Statute is unconstitutional. Appellees were arrested at an "adult" pornographic theater on charges of voluntary deviate sexual intercourse and/or conspiracy to perform the same.

[The relevant portions of the statute are the following:

"A person who engages in deviate sexual intercourse under circumstances not covered by section 3123 of this title (related to involuntary deviate sexual intercourse) is guilty of a misdemeanor of the second degree." Act of December 6, 1972, P.L. 1482, No. 334 § 1, 18 Pa.C.S.A. § 3124 (1973).

"'Deviate sexual intercourse.' Sexual intercourse per os or per anus between human beings who are not husband and wife, and any form of sexual intercourse with an animal." Act of December 6, 1972, P.L. 1482, No. 334, § 1, 18 Pa.C.S.A. § 3101 (1973).]

The Commonwealth's position is that the statute in question is a valid exercise of the police power pursuant the authority of states to regulate public health, safety, welfare, and morals. Yet, the police power is not unlimited, as was stated by the United States Supreme Court in *Lawton v. Steele*, 152 U.S. 133, 137, 14 S.Ct. 499, 501, 38 L.Ed. 385 (1894).

"To justify the State in thus interposing its authority in behalf of the public, it must appear, first, that the interests of the public generally, as distinguished from those of a particular class, require such interference; and, second, that the means are reasonably necessary for the accomplishment of the purpose, and not unduly oppressive upon individuals."

The threshold question in determining whether the statute in question is a valid exercise of the police power is to decide whether it benefits the public generally. The state clearly has a proper role to perform in protecting the public from inadvertent offensive displays of sexual behavior, in preventing people from being forced against their will to submit to sexual contact, in protecting minors from being sexually

used by adults, and in eliminating cruelty to animals. To assure these protections, a broad range of criminal statutes constitute valid police power exercises, including proscriptions of indecent exposure, open lewdness, rape, involuntary deviate sexual intercourse, indecent assault, statutory rape, corruption of minors, and cruelty to animals. The statute in question serves none of the foregoing purposes and it is nugatory to suggest that it promotes a state interest in the institution of marriage. The Voluntary Deviate Sexual Intercourse Statute has only one possible purpose: to regulate the private conduct of consenting adults. Such a purpose, we believe, exceeds the valid bounds of the police power while infringing the right to equal protection of the laws guaranteed by the Constitution of the United States and of this Commonwealth.

With respect to regulation of morals, the police power should properly be exercised to protect each individual's right to be free from interference in defining and pursuing his own morality but not to enforce a majority morality on persons whose conduct does not harm others. "No harm to the secular interests of the community is involved in atypical sex practice in private between consenting adult partners." *Model Penal Code* § 207.5 -- Sodomy & Related Offenses. Comment (Tent. Draft No. 4, 1955). Many issues that are considered to be matters of morals are subject to debate, and no sufficient state interest justifies legislation of norms simply because a particular belief is followed by a number of people, or even a majority. Indeed, what is considered to be "moral" changes with the times and is dependent upon societal background. Spiritual leadership, not the government, has the responsibility for striving to improve the morality of individuals. Enactment of the Voluntary Deviate Sexual Intercourse Statute, despite the fact that it provides punishment for what many believe to be abhorrent crimes against nature and perceived sins against God, is not properly in the realm of the temporal police power.

The concepts underlying our view of the police power in the case before us were once summarized as follows by the great philosopher, John Stuart Mill, in his eminent and apposite work, *On Liberty* (1859): [T]he sole end for which mankind are warranted, individually or collectively, in interfering with the liberty of action of any of their number, is self-protection . . . [T]he only purpose for which power can be rightfully exercised over any member of a civilised community, against his will, is to prevent harm to others. His own good, either physical or moral is not a sufficient warrant. He cannot rightfully be compelled to do or forbear because it will be better for him to do so, because it will make him happier, because, in the opinions of others, to do so would be wise, or even right. These are good reasons for remonstrating with him, or reasoning with him, or persuading him, or entreating him, but not for compelling him, or visiting him with any evil in case he do otherwise. To justify that, the conduct from which it is desired to deter him must be calculated to produce evil to some one else. The only part of the conduct of any one, for which he is amenable to society, is that which concerns others. In the part which merely concerns himself, his independence is, of right, absolute. Over himself, over his own body and mind, the individual is sovereign.

It is, perhaps, hardly necessary to say that this doctrine is meant to apply to human beings in the maturity of their faculties . . .

But there is a sphere of action in which society as distinguished from the individual, has, if any, only an indirect interest; comprehending all that portion of a person's life and conduct which affects only himself, or if it also affects others, only with their free, voluntary, and undeceived consent and participation . . .

This, then, is the appropriate region of human liberty. It comprises, first, the inward domain of consciousness; demanding liberty of conscience, in the most comprehensive sense; liberty of thought and feeling; absolute freedom of opinion and sentiment on all subjects, practical or speculative, scientific, moral, or theological . . . Secondly, the principle requires liberty of tastes and pursuits; of framing the plan of our life to suit our own character; of doing as we like, subject to such consequences as may follow: without impediment from our fellow-creatures, so long as what we do does not harm them, even though they should think our conduct foolish, perverse, or wrong. Thirdly, from this liberty of each individual, follows the liberty, within the same limits of combination among individuals; freedom to unite, for any purpose not involving harm to others: the persons combining being supposed to be of full age, and not forced or deceived.

No society in which these liberties are not, on the whole, respected, is free, whatever may be its form of government; . . . The only freedom which deserves the name, is that of pursuing our own good in our own way, so long as we do not attempt to deprive others of theirs, or impede their efforts to obtain it. Each is the proper guardian of his own health, whether bodily, or mental or spiritual. Mankind are greater gainers by suffering each other to live as seems good to themselves, than by compelling each to live as seems good to the rest. This philosophy, as applied to the issue of regulation of sexual morality presently before the Court, or employed to delimit the police power generally, properly circumscribes state power over the individual.

Not only does the statute in question exceed the proper bounds of the police power, but, in addition, it offends the Constitution by creating a classification based on marital status (making deviate acts criminal only when performed between unmarried persons) where such differential treatment is not supported by a sufficient state interest and thereby denies equal protection of the laws. Assuming, without deciding, that no fundamental interest is at stake (i. e., the right of privacy), so that strict scrutiny of the classification is not required, the classification still denies equal protection under the following standard:

The Equal Protection Clause of [the state and federal] constitutions does not deny the State the power to treat different classes of persons in different ways, but does deny the right to legislate that different treatment be accorded to persons placed by a statute into different classes on the basis of criteria wholly unrelated to the objective of the particular statute. The classification must be reasonable,

not arbitrary, and must rest upon some ground of difference having a fair and substantial relation to the object of the legislation so that all persons similarly circumstanced shall be treated alike.

The Commonwealth submits that the classification is justified on the ground that the legislature intended to forbid, generally, voluntary "deviate" sexual intercourse, but created an exception for persons whose exclusion is claimed to further a state interest in promoting the privacy inherent in the marital relationship. We do not find such a justification for the classification to be reasonable or to have a fair and substantial relation to the object of the legislation. Viewing the statute as exceeding the proper bounds of the police power, however, since none of the previously discussed valid legislative interests in regulating sexual conduct are promoted by the statute, the classification itself could not bear a substantial relation to a valid legislative objective. Furthermore, even if the subject of the statute's regulation were properly within the police power, the marital status of voluntarily participating adults would bear no rational relationship to whether a sexual act should be legal or criminal. In *Eisenstadt v. Baird*, 405 U.S. 438, 453, 92 S.Ct. 1029, 1038, 31 L.Ed.2d 349 (1972) the Supreme Court of the United States stated: "[T]he State could not, consistently with the Equal Protection Clause, outlaw distribution [of contraceptives] to unmarried but not to married persons. In each case the evil, as perceived by the State, would be identical, and the underinclusion would be invidious." Similarly, to suggest that deviate acts are heinous if performed by unmarried persons but acceptable when done by married persons lacks even a rational basis, for requiring less moral behavior of married persons than is expected of unmarried persons is without basis in logic. If the statute regulated sexual acts so affecting others that proscription by law would be justified, then they should be proscribed for all people, not just the unmarried.

Order affirmed.

Justice Nix dissenting.

The majority tries to justify its novel and shocking ruling by suggesting that they are defending the individual from state intervention on questions of morality and personal conscience. Regrettably this theory ignores the facts of the case before the court. This is not a case of private, intimate conduct between consenting adults.

Appellees, Mildred Kannitz, known on the stage as "Dawn Delight" and Shanne Wimbel are "exotic" dancers. Appellees, Patrick Gagliano and Michael Bonadio are employees of the Penthouse Theater in downtown Pittsburgh, in which Ms. Delight and Ms. Wimbel perform. In March of last year, plainclothes police officers went to the Penthouse Theater, paid an admission fee, entered the theater, and viewed the performances of Ms. Delight and Ms. Wimbel. During the course of these performances Ms. Delight and Ms. Wimbel engaged in sexual acts with members of the audience. The police officers arrested the two performers, the patrons who participated in the sexual acts, as well as the theater's cashier, Bonadio, and the theater's manager, Gagliano. Ms. Delight and Ms. Wimbel were each charged by information with one count each of voluntary deviate sexual intercourse pursuant to 18 Pa.C.S.A. § 3124. Messrs. Bonadio and Gagliano were charged with one count each of criminal conspiracy.

The majority attempts to avoid the privacy issue by reasoning that there was not a valid exercise of the state's police power in the prohibition of this type of conduct. The absurdity of such a position does not require demonstration. Here we have a public display of the most depraved type of sexual behavior for pay. Any member of the public who pays the fee can witness and participate in this conduct. That the majority would suggest that this is beyond the state's power to regulate public health, safety, welfare, and morals is incredible. I assume that regulation of prostitution and hard core pornography are also now prohibited by todays ruling.

Finally, the majority's conclusion that the statute violates equal protection presents a "red herring." Concern over the marital exception contained within the voluntary deviate sexual intercourse statute, is misplaced, for the heart of this exception is the intimacy and warmth of a private marital sexual relationship. Here the sexual acts were performed in public and in return for monetary compensation. It is therefore clear that the marital status of the participants in this conduct would not have affected their culpability. To suggest that the marital exception was intended to insulate a marital couple who performed deviate sexual acts for public display for pay would distort the obvious legislative objective in providing for this exception. The marital exception was designed to protect the intimacy and privacy of the marital unit. It did not give married couples the license to publicly engage in lewd and lascivious public acts.

Contracting With Minors: When may a minor avoid a contract?

Western jurisprudence has consistently treated persons of "tender years" differently than adults. That a minor cannot be bound by contract (except for "necessaries") has been a generally accepted legal principle. For example, under the common law, a minor cannot contract for treatment by a physician without parental permission (except for emergencies where a parent's consent is inferred). There have been a few inroads in recent years where the legislature or judiciary has felt that parental permission should not always be required because of the nature of the care: abortion, contraception, mental illness, drug abuse.

In most situations, however, Pennsylvania follows the traditional common law policy of permitting minors to avoid liability for contract breaches by disaffirming the contracts into which they have entered. The minor may rescind the contract by simply returning the purchased item (or what is left of the product), and demand return of the purchase price. If the minor fails to make payments, the seller cannot recover for breach of contract, but can demand the return of the purchased item, but must return to the minor any payments already made. The Pennsylvania courts have further held that the minor cannot be held liable for tortious conduct if the real injury has arisen out of the minor's failure to perform his contractual obligation. In the following case a minor destroys an airplane which he has leased and escapes all liability for damage he has done to the plane. Note that the legislature has changed the age of majority to 18 years of age since this case was decided.

Central Bucks Aero, Inc. v. Smith
226 Pa. Super. 441 (1973)

Judge Spaeth wrote the opinion for the court.

This is an appeal from the granting of defendant-appellee's motion for summary judgment. The issue is whether we should overturn the longstanding common law doctrine that a minor by disaffirming a contract can avoid liability under the contract.

Appellee, when twenty years of age, leased an airplane from appellant. In the process of landing, appellee damaged the airplane beyond repair, and also damaged the landing field. After appellant filed suit in trespass, appellee disaffirmed the lease.

When a minor disaffirms a contract, unless the contract is for necessaries, the other party cannot recover the value of any item that the minor has obtained pursuant to the contract. The only remedy the other party has is an action in replevin to recover the item itself. If the minor no longer has the item, the other party is remediless. An action in trespass, which is the form of action selected by appellant, will not lie. As stated in *Penrose v. Curren*, 3 Rawle 351, 353 (1832): "The foundation of the action is contract, and disguise it as you may, it is an attempt to convert a suit, originally in contract, into a constructive tort so as to charge the infant." And see *Spangler Co. v. Haupt*, 53 Pa. Superior Ct. 545, 551 (1913): "In *Wilt v. Welsh*, 6 Watts, 9, Gibson, J., said: 'Indeed the privilege would be little worth if it might be eluded by fashioning the action into a particular shape.' The principle there maintained was, that whenever the substantive ground of an action against an infant is contract, as well where the contract is stated as incident to a supposed tort, as where it is not, the plaintiff cannot recover. In the course of his discussion of the cases in which infants may be sued in tort and those in which they cannot be, Judge Cooley says: 'The distinction is this: If the wrong grows out of contract relations, and the real injury consists in the nonperformance of a contract into which the party wronged has entered with an infant, the law will not permit the former to enforce the contract indirectly by counting on the infant's neglect to perform it, or omission of duty under it as a tort. The reason is obvious: To permit this to be done would deprive the infant of that shield of protection which, in matters of contract, the law has wisely placed before him:' 1 Cooley on Torts, 3d ed. 181." This principle is followed in most jurisdictions.

It may be granted that upon occasion the courts have decided to remove an immunity from legal responsibility by overruling the cases that created the immunity. *Ayala v. Philadelphia Board of Education*, 453 Pa. 584, 305 A. 2d 877 (1973); *Flagiello v. Penna. Hospital*, 417 Pa. 7486, 208 A. 2d 193 (1965). In the present case, however, such a decision would be inappropriate.

In cases such as *Ayala* and *Flagiello*, supra, the court was responding to an injustice; by removing the immunity in question the court extended protection to persons unable to protect themselves. No such situation is presented here. A businessman may protect himself from loss incident to a minor's disaffirmance of a contract by finding out whether the person with whom he is dealing is a minor. Ordinarily this will present no difficulty. If the person is a minor, or if it is not clear that he is an adult, the businessman may decline to deal with him, or may require that someone he knows is an adult join in the contract. Inasmuch as appellant neglected such precautions, it has only itself to blame for its inability to recover for the damage to its airplane and landing field.

Apart from these considerations, to overrule the cases that permit disaffirmance would involve the court in a legislative function. Some age must be established as the age below which disaffirmance will be permitted; perhaps a twenty year old person should not be protected, but surely an eight year old should be. If the age is to be changed, the legislature is better equipped than the court to decide whether the change should be to age 19, 18, 16, or some other age. (Indeed, the legislature has recently made this determination, selecting age 18. Act of June 16, 1972, P. L. 472, No. 151, § 1, 73 P.S. § 2021). In cases such as *Ayala* and *Flagiello* it was not necessary for the court to become involved in such legislative line drawing.

The order of the court below is affirmed.

23 Pa.C.S. § 5101

§ 5101. Attainment of full age

(A) AGE FOR ENTERING INTO CONTRACTS. Any individual 18 years of age and older shall have the right to enter into binding and legally enforceable contracts and the defense of minority shall not be available to such individuals.

(B) AGE FOR SUING AND BEING SUED. Except where otherwise provided or prescribed by law, an individual 18 years of age and older shall be deemed an adult and may sue and be sued as such.

Dividing Marital Property: Should the educational achievements of one spouse be treated as "marital property?"

Pennsylvania joined the 20th century of marital law in 1980 with the adoption of the Divorce Code, P.L. 63, April 2, 1980. Prior to this law, Pennsylvania was one of only a handful of states that (1) did not provide for a dissolution of a marriage except for fault, (2) did not provide for alimony, and (3) did not provide for equitable property distribution. Thus, upon a divorce in Pennsylvania prior to 1980, common law rules applied to the division of property. Property in the husband's name would belong to him. Property in the wife's name belonged to her. Property owned by the husband and wife together would belong to the both of them equally. The problem was that, stereotypically, there would be much more property in the man's name than in the woman's -- particularly where the man had a pension plan.

In determining whether a person should be awarded alimony (and under what terms), the Divorce Code now provides for certain factors to be considered (see § 3701.) These factors are similar, but not identical, to those factors to be considered in the division of property (§ 3502.) In the *Bold* case that follows, note that the issue is not one of alimony, but rather of property distribution.

Of particular difficulty has been the situation in which one partner has sacrificed and provided financial support for the other's education only to face divorce when the education has been completed. The supporting spouse in these cases often believes that he or she has enriched the earning capacity of the supported spouse and is entitled to recover the value of that support as part of a divorce settlement. As explained by Justice Flaherty, Pennsylvania recognizes the right of the supporting spouse to equitable reimbursement for the contribution made to the education of the other. Is this an appropriate way to handle the difficult but not unusual situation where one spouse has substantially assisted the other complete his (or her) education?

23 Pa.C.S. § 3701

(a)   Where a divorce decree has been entered, the court may allow alimony, as it deems reasonable, to either party, only if it finds that alimony is necessary.

(b)   In determining whether alimony is necessary, and in determining the nature, amount, duration, and manner of payment of alimony, the court shall consider all relevant factors including:

(1)   The relative earnings and earning capacities of the parties.

(2)   The ages, and the physical, mental and emotional conditions of the parties.

(3)   The sources of income of both parties including but not limited to medical, retirement, insurance or other benefits.

(4)   The expectancies and inheritances of the parties.

(5)   The duration of the marriage.

(6)   The contribution by one party to the education, training or increased earning power of the other party.

(7)   The extent to which the earning power, expenses or financial obligations of a party will be affected by reason of serving as the custodian of a minor child.

(8)   The standard of living of the parties established during the marriage.

(9)   The relative education of the parties and the time necessary to acquire sufficient education or training to enable the party seeking alimony to find appropriate employment.

(10)   The relative assets and liabilities of the parties.

(11)   The property brought to the marriage by either party.

(12)   The contribution of a spouse as homemaker.

(13)   The relative needs of the parties.

(14)   The marital misconduct of either of the parties during the marriage; however, the marital misconduct of either of the parties from the date of final separation shall not be considered by the court in its determinations relative to alimony.

(15)   The Federal, State and local tax ramifications of the alimony award.

(16)   Whether the party seeking alimony lacks sufficient property, including, but not limited to, property distributed under Chapter 4, to provide for the party's reasonable needs.

(17)   Whether the party seeking alimony is incapable of self-support through appropriate employment.

Bold v. Bold
524 Pa. 487 (1990)

Justice Flaherty wrote the opinion for the court.

The question in this case is whether a spouse who supports his or her marital partner during the time that person is in school is entitled to recoup the value of that support upon a divorce, and if so, under what circumstances.

The facts of this case are that the parties were married in 1974, and Mrs. Bold came to the marriage with a college degree; Mr. Bold had completed some college. From 1974 through 1979 the parties lived in California, where Mr. Bold pursued a course of college study culminating in his graduation from the Los Angeles College of Chiropractic in 1979. Mr. Bold received veteran's benefits in excess of $ 12,000 while he was in school; he took out a student loan in the amount of $1,187; and he earned approximately $ 19,000 working at odd jobs during this period. During the years Mr. Bold was in school, Mrs. Bold earned more than $ 97,000.
. . .

The couple moved to Pennsylvania, where Mrs. Bold accepted a job earning $ 17,000 and Mr. Bold accepted a job earning $ 200 per week. He earned $ 3470 for the year. In February of 1980 Mr. Bold opened his own chiropractic practice and Mrs. Bold remained at the same job. Mrs. Bold moved out of the marital home in October, 1981 at the request of Mr. Bold, and moved into a one bedroom apartment. . .

On May 12, 1981, Mrs. Bold filed a complaint seeking a divorce, equitable distribution, counsel fees, costs and expenses. A bifurcated divorce decree was entered by stipulation on April 26, 1984, and a master heard economic claims and filed a report and recommendation on January 24, 1986. . .

The trial court made the following distribution. . .

EQUITY AWARD

IT IS FURTHER ORDERED that defendant pay to plaintiff the sum of $ 33,000.00 in reimbursement equity in equal monthly installments of $ 550.00 without interest to commence upon entry of this decree and continue sixty (60) months; should any installment be more than five (5) days overdue, defendant shall pay interest at ten percent (10%) per annum on the over due amount. Both parties appealed this decree. Superior Court indicated that although it was aware of this Court's decision in *Hodge v. Hodge*, 513 Pa. 264 (1986) concerning whether alimony may be granted for reimbursement as well as for rehabilitation, the issue of reimbursement alimony was not preserved for appellate review. Superior Court, therefore, limited its review to the propriety of the award as an equitable reimbursement. . . The panel then held that equitable reimbursement is available "only when one party has been unjustly enriched by financial contributions rendered which exceed that imposed by law."

Because the evidence indicated that Mrs. Bold did not actually pay educational bills associated with Mr. Bold's academic degree, although she did work and support her husband while he attended school, her contributions did not exceed that required by law for the benefit of the family. The court determined, therefore, that Mr. Bold was not unjustly enriched and that the lower court's order directing Mr. Bold to pay $ 33,000 was in error. Superior Court also reviewed other matters not germane to this appeal, and on May 5, 1988 it reversed and vacated the decree of the trial court and remanded the case for proceedings consistent with its opinion. 374 Pa.Super. 317, 542 A.2d 1374. On July 18, 1988, Mrs. Bold filed a Petition for Allowance of Appeal, and this Court granted allocatur in order to address the question of when, if ever, equitable reimbursement is available to a spouse who has supported his or her marital partner while that person was in school.

As mentioned earlier, Section 501 of the Divorce Code, concerning alimony, is not asserted as a ground of recovery; instead, Mrs. Bold, the supporting spouse, relies upon Section 401(c), providing that Courts of Common Pleas shall have full equity power to protect the interests of the parties and effectuate the purposes of the act:

(c) In all matrimonial causes, the court shall have full equity power and jurisdiction and may issue injunctions or other orders which are necessary to protect the interests of the parties or to effectuate the purposes of this act, and may grant such other relief or remedy as equity and justice require against either party or against any third person over whom the court has jurisdiction and who is involved in or concerned with the disposition of the cause. 23 P.S. § 401(c).

It is axiomatic that an equity court is primarily interested in effecting fairness between the parties. It is equally plain that in order to do this, the court will consider, of necessity, all of the circumstances of the case, including, presumably, those circumstances mentioned in Section 501(b). Among the considerations listed in 501(b), is: "[t]he contribution by one party to the education, training or increased earning power of the other party." 23 P.S. § 501(b)(6). (Unchanged in the 1988 amendment). It follows, then, that Mrs. Bold's contribution to Mr. Bold's education is a factor to consider in determining whether she should be awarded any reimbursement under Section 401.

Superior Court apparently felt, however, that in order for Mrs. Bold's contribution to her husband's education to be considered, the contribution would have to exceed an amount she was legally required to contribute to her family. In other words, she would first have to show that she contributed more than was legally required, then Superior Court would consider her claim for equitable reimbursement. According to Superior Court, Mrs. Bold's contributions were merely legally mandated amounts, and Mr. Bold was not, therefore, unjustly enriched, but only the recipient of what was justly his.

Underlying Superior Court's decision is its concern that "[m]arriage is not a business enterprise which requires a strict economic accounting for all financial aid rendered during its course. Rather, each party owes the other a duty of support . . . . [E]quity will intervene only when one party has been unjustly enriched by financial contributions rendered which exceed that imposed by law." At 328, 542 A.2d at 1379.

A different view of the case is reflected in the rationale offered by the master, as described by the trial court: He [the master] took into consideration the fact that defendant spent the first five years of the marriage in school. As a result of his education, defendant now has a substantial increase in his earning capacity. Defendant contributed approximately $ 5,300 per year, while plaintiff annually contributed three times that amount. That is, from 1974 through 1979, plaintiff invested $ 34,000 more than the defendant did into the marriage. Second, the master considered that the parties separated when defendant's increased earning potential was only beginning to be realized. Thus, plaintiff was precluded from enjoying the benefits of her five year investment in defendant, that is, in his potential for increased earnings. During that time, she sacrificed her ability to accumulate and to save assets, and her lifestyle. Finally, the master considered the different lifestyles that the parties now enjoy. Defendant has the benefit of tax deduction [sic], savings accounts, retirement plans, and expensive automobiles, while plaintiff drives a 1974 Volkswagen and lives in an apartment without the luxury of a shower.

Because there was insufficient marital property to compensate Mrs. Bold for her financial contributions to the marriage in excess of those made by Mr. Bold, the master and the trial court awarded Mrs. Bold a cash amount which the master called "reimbursement alimony" and which the trial court called "equitable reimbursement."

While we agree with Superior Court that marriage is not a business enterprise in which strict accountings are to be had for moneys spent by one spouse for the benefit of the other, it appears to us that this case does not involve strict accountings, but gross accountings. Supporting spouses in these cases feel entitled to reimbursement, we believe, not because they have sacrificed to support the other spouse, but because they are, to use a strong word, "jettisoned" as soon as the need for their sacrifice, albeit in part a legal obligation, comes to an end. In retrospect, perhaps unintentionally, the supporting spouse in such a case can be said to have been "used." At least this is the perception of the supporting spouse, and we believe that this perception is not totally without foundation in all cases. On the other hand, we cannot completely disregard the legally imposed obligation of support. With a view to balancing the extremes, we hold, therefore, that separate and apart from the equitable distribution of marital property, consistent with fairness, the supporting spouse in a case such as this should be awarded equitable reimbursement to the extent that his or her contribution to the education, training or increased earning capacity of the other spouse exceeds the bare minimum legally obligated support as reflected in the guidelines promulgated by this Court.

Finally, Mr. Bold argues that even if equitable reimbursement should be awarded his wife, it should not be awarded in the form of cash payments when there is sufficient marital property available for distribution. We agree in principle with Mr. Bold's argument, but the property which the lower courts described as available for distribution does not equal the amount of Mrs. Bold's equitable distribution plus the amount of her equitable reimbursement, as determined by the trial court. Whether all of the existing property or some greater portion of the existing property should be distributed to the supporting spouse in an effort to decrease the amount of cash payments of "equitable reimbursement" is a matter for the sound discretion of the trial court, and we perceive no abuse of discretion in this case.

For the foregoing reasons, the judgment of Superior Court is vacated and the case is remanded to the Court of Common Pleas of Lehigh County for calculation of an amount of equitable reimbursement due Mrs. Bold consistent with this Opinion.

Zappala, Justice, dissenting.

Today, the majority has grafted a new provision onto the Divorce Code not heretofore provided for or intended by the Legislature. In addition to equitable distribution and alimony, we now have "equitable reimbursement". This judicial creation provides monthly payments which cannot be awarded as alimony because the spouse did not qualify, and is in lieu of equitable distribution in instances when no property exists for distribution. The rationale for creating this new provision is that the supporting spouse has been "used". That rationale defiles the fundamental concept of marriage by reducing it to a balance sheet retroactively weighing individual efforts made at a time when the individual labors on behalf of the family unit.

Even under the Uniform Partnership Act, 15 Pa.C.S.A. § 8301 et seq., when a partnership dissolves, partners are not required to retroactively account for all expenditures undertaken throughout the relationship. Now, before entering into the ultimate partnership, each partner will be required to create a legal partnership under the Uniform Partnership Act, to protect themselves from any unforeseen consequences should their marriage partnership dissolve. To me, such action appears absurd. Because I cannot agree with this rationale nor the legal gymnastics employed by the majority to reach its result, I must dissent. The Court's holding today will only further exasperate an at times already very volatile and emotional union with the requirement that prospective spouses not only keep a strict accounting of finances during the marriage, but view "marriage" as an investment that requires the investor to continually monitor his or her "investment portfolio"

Section 102 of the Divorce Code sets forth the intended purpose of the Code:
(1) Make the law for legal dissolution of marriage effective for dealing with the realities of matrimonial experience.

* * *

(3) Give primary consideration to the welfare of the family rather than the vindication of private rights or the punishment of matrimonial wrongs.

* * *

(6) Effectuate economic justice between parties who are divorced or separated and grant or withhold alimony according to the actual need and ability to pay of the [sic] parties and insure a fair and just determination and settlement of their property rights.

The Legislature has directed us to take these objectives into consideration when construing provisions of the Code. 23 P.S. § 102(b). In the 1980 version of § 501, alimony was arguably conditioned upon the inability to provide for oneself. This controversy was confronted and unresolved in Hodge v. Hodge, 513 Pa. 264, 520 A.2d 15 (1986). In that case, I adopted the view expressed by Judge Wieand in *Lehmicke v. Lehmicke*, 339 Pa.Super. 559, 573-574, 489 A.2d 782, 790 (1985) with regard to the realities of a marital relationship and its attending responsibilities:

The duty of support is imposed by rule of law on both spouses. Compliance with this legal duty does not result in unjust enrichment to the other. Marriage is for better or worse. It is not entered with a conscious intent that at some future time there will be an accounting of and reimbursement for moneys contributed to the support of the family. To inject such a concept would in my judgment, have far-reaching and unfortunate consequences. If I am correct in my view regarding the duty of spousal support, then it is difficult to perceive good reason for creating an exception which would reimburse a spouse for support contributed while the other is attending an institution of higher learning or otherwise obtaining advanced training.

Because § 501 clearly prohibits equitable alimony, the Appellant must rely upon § 401(c). But to support the application of § 401(c), the majority refers to the factors set forth in § 501(b). The majority accomplishes indirectly what it cannot accomplish directly.

This is not a situation in which one spouse is seeking reimbursement for expenditures that directly increase the other spouse's earning capacity. As the majority notes, Mrs. Bold did not actually pay educational expenses associated with her husband's academic degree. Rather, Appellant is seeking and the court is awarding a return of funds expended for the necessities of life. We now will require reimbursement of a spouse for a roof, food and clothing. This clearly was not intended by the Legislature.

Even under § 501, as amended, such a position is untenable. While I realize that the Legislature has removed the "inability to provide" prerequisite for alimony as alluded to in Hodge, alimony continues to be based on need and the Legislature has set forth the factors to be considered in evaluating that need. One such factor is the contribution made by one spouse to the education, training or increased earning power of the other party. 23 P.S. § 501(b)(6).

Thus, if a spouse is in need of assistance for a period of time to increase her/his earning capacity, alimony may be appropriate. Likewise, a spouse may receive a greater percentage, if not all, of the marital assets, if such an award is found to be appropriate after a review of all of the factors set forth in § 401. The legislature has provided a comprehensive scheme to resolve the economic issues in a failed marriage, keeping in mind the purposes set forth in § 102. This Court is now imposing new provisions that run contrary to those purposes. For the foregoing reasons I cannot agree with the majority and therefore dissent.

Parental Duties: What are the obligations of parents to pay for the college education of their children?

Until 1992, Pennsylvania law seemed settled that divorced parents were liable for their children's post-high school education (up to age 23). In every case since the Superior Court held in *Commonwealth v. Gilmore*, 97 Pa. Super 303 1929, that "parental duty involves, in addition to provision for mere physical needs, such instruction and education as may be necessary to fit the child reasonably to support itself. . ." Pennsylvania courts had interpreted this decision to mean that noncustodial parents had a duty to pay college tuition for their children. This rule has been relied upon by many college students over the years.

Then came the following case - literally "out of the blue" which changed the expectation of everyone. The Supreme Court ruled that the *Gilmore* case only required that parents support the high school education of their children, not college. After reading the case, one may ask why is it that only the children of separated parents can sue for educational support, while the children of intact families cannot. The rationale has always been that the court should not get involved in how an intact family spends its money. Thus, routinely, (and stereotypically) a wife's complaint that her husband did not give her enough money, would be dismissed if they were still living together (with the exception of the claim that "necessities" were not being met. The law's answer to the wife has consistently been -- if the conditions are unbearable, then separate from him and file for support.

Criticism of the Court's ruling prompted a quick response in the legislature where a bill is pending as this book goes to press which would reverse the Supreme Court's interpretation by enacting into law the understanding of the *Gilmore* case which had prevailed until the *Blue* decision.

Blue v. Blue
616 A.2d 628 (Pa. Supreme Court, 1992)

Justice Zappala wrote the opinion for the court.

In this appeal, we are asked to determine to what extent a parent must pay for a child's college education and whether that child must contribute to his or her own college education through the use of loans and grants. This scenario is but another fall-out from a failed marriage, and results in a son suing his father for assistance in paying for his college education.

Reginald V. Blue's father and mother separated in October of 1987, with the mother leaving the marital residence. At the time of the support hearing in this matter in January of 1989, a divorce action was pending. Prior to separation, Reginald had attended three semesters of college at Pennsylvania State University. However, the emotional trauma of his parents' separation caused him to take a leave of absence during his second year at Penn State.

The father is an assistant professor at Lehigh County Community College with an annual salary of approximately $43,000.00. Reginald's mother is also employed by the college, as a secretary, with an annual gross income of approximately $12,000.00. Prior to separation, while Reginald was attending Penn State, all college expenses were paid for by Reginald's parents from their joint incomes. Reginald's parents did not require him to seek any financial assistance for his college education. Although in his brief Reginald disputes any plan to fund his college education, if necessary, through lifetime investments made by his parents, his father presented uncontradicted testimony that he and Reginald's mother had saved funds through stock purchases and individual retirement accounts to pay for Reginald's college education as well as any post graduate education.

During the spring of 1988, with the encouragement of his father, Reginald attended Lehigh County Community College. Because Reginald's parents were employees of the college, no tuition had to be paid. It is also during this time that Reginald resided with his father in the marital residence. The monthly mortgage on the marital residence was $280.00. In addition, it appears that the father alone paid for all of Reginald's needs including $40.00 a week spending money, a car payment and automobile insurance.

During the summer and fall of 1988, Reginald worked as a ride operator at Dorney Park and as a temporary for Kelly services. Through both jobs, Reginald earned approximately $ 6,265.44. During the hearing, it was disputed as to how much remained of Reginald's earnings. His father seemed to argue that Reginald would have realized approximately $ 4,000.00 if he had not spent much of his money on his girlfriend, while Reginald testified that he only saved $ 2,200.00 after paying his car payment, automobile insurance and food expenses incurred while working 12-hour shifts at Dorney Park.

In August of 1988, Reginald's father decided that he needed to "get on with his life" and purchased a $114,000.00 five-bedroom home without any down payment being required. The monthly mortgage payment for this new home was $1,187.00 a month or a monthly mortgage payment increase of $900.00. The father then left his son and the marital residence and moved into his new home with his girlfriend and her two minor children where the father pays all the monthly living expenses except for the girlfriend's car payment and her medical expenses. Approximately 30 days after father left the marital residence, mother, her boyfriend and his emancipated son moved into the marital residence. During his semester breaks, Reginald now lives with his mother who provides free room and board.

Sometime during the summer of 1988, Reginald reapplied and was accepted to resume his college studies at Penn State commencing with the fall term of 1988. Because he did not have the funds to pay the required college expenses, Reginald postponed returning to Penn State until

January 1989. At that time, the cost of tuition, room and board was approximately $6,440.00 with an additional $400.00 needed for books and other expenses.

As of the January 1989 hearing, $2,000.00 had been paid towards Reginald's bill, $1,000.00 from his earnings/savings and $1,000.00 from a loan from his mother. Reginald did testify that he did apply for grants beginning with the January 1989 term. He had not applied sooner because he believed his application would be rejected because he lived with his father during 1988 and his father's income was too high.

After taking testimony and giving both parties the opportunity to offer legal authority in support of his position, the trial court entered an order requiring the father to pay $4,600.00 a year towards Reginald's college education. In addition, the trial court required Reginald to apply for and accept any educational loans or grants he received. The father would then be entitled to a reduction in support to the extent of any grants and/or loans received.

On appeal, the Superior Court affirmed the assessment of support in the amount of $4,600.00 a year, but reversed the trial court with regard to the requirement that Reginald Seek financial assistance and that the father's support obligation be reduced by the amount of any assistance received. In its memorandum opinion Superior Court reasoned that since parents bear the financial responsibility for college expenses, a child should not have to obtain loans and/or grants but should that child choose to do so, a parent's obligation to provide support should not be reduced.

We granted the father's Petition for Allowance of Appeal to address the issue of parental responsibility to provide college educational support and reverse the Superior Court's determination.

The scope of review in a typical support matter is whether the trial court has abused its discretion. *Costello v. LeNoir*, 462 Pa. 36, 337 A.2d 866 (1975). Even though this appeal does not present a typical support matter, we see no reason for adopting a different scope of review. In essence, we are reviewing an order requiring a parent to provide support, albeit not monthly support but rather educational support. Therefore, an abuse of discretion is the appropriate standard of review.

This Court has defined an abuse of discretion as follows: Not merely an error of judgment, but if in reaching a conclusion the law is overridden or misapplied or the judgment exercised is manifestly unreasonable, or the result of partiality, prejudice, bias, or ill-will, as shown by the evidence or the record, discretion is abused. *Kelly v. County of Allegheny*, 519 Pa. 213, 217, 546 A.2d 608, 610 (1988) citing *In Re: Woman's Homeopathic Hospital of Philadelphia*, 393 Pa. 313, 316, 142 A.2d 292, 294 (1958).

The trial court and the superior Court differed as to a parent's responsibility for college expenses. Relying upon *Leonard*, the Superior Court held that parents bear the primary financial responsibility for their child's reasonable college expenses. The Superior Court then determined that the trial court misapplied Leonard and shifted the primary obligation for college expenses to Reginald.

The trial court determined

that the father caused his own undue hardship as the result of his real estate purchase. Therefore, the trial court determined that the father had a duty to provide financial assistance to Reginald. However, the trial court also concluded that the father did not have limitless financial resources and therefore Reginald had the primary obligation for his own college education. This added requirement to the holdings of *Miller* and *Leonard* is what caused Superior Court to reverse the trial court.

Upon closer scrutiny, what has been accepted as fact is actually fiction. Neither statute nor specific case law had enunciated the legal axiom relied upon by the lower courts. To the contrary, all that had been articulated was that set forth in *Emerick v. Emerick*.

In *Emerick v. Emerick* the mother and father had entered into an agreement subsequently incorporated into the divorce decree which required the father to provide a four-year college education for each of his children commensurate with his financial ability. When the father refused to pay the educational expenses of two college age children, the mother sought enforcement of the agreement and decree. In reversing both the Superior Court and the trial court, which had dismissed the mother's claim for educational expenses, we were persuaded by the fact that the father had entered into an agreement to pay educational expenses. We did not unequivocally adopt a legal principle that a parent has a legal obligation to provide college expenses but rather permitted recovery of college expenses if a parent had the financial ability to do so, because the parties' agreement had required that result. Therefore,

our research having found no legal authority to require a parent to provide for college educational support, we must reverse the Superior Court and decline to adopt the reasoning of either lower courts.

Since *Emerick*, this court has not reviewed this particular issue although the Superior Court has been faced with this issue in varying forms. See *Leonard v. Leonard*, 353 Pa. Super. 604, 510 A.2d 827 (1986) (the proper determination in evaluating the parents' ability to pay college expenses is the parents' earning capacity rather than his actual income); *Miller v. Miller*, 353 Pa. Super. 194, 509 A.2d 402 (1986) (the independent resources of a college age child may be considered in determining the child's need for support); *Brake v. Brake*, 271 Pa. Super. 314, 413 A.2d 422 (1979) (a support order may be entered against a parent for a child's college education, even in the absence of an agreement to support the child past the age of 18, as long as this obligation would not result in undue hardship to the parent); *Lederer v. Lederer*, 291 Pa. Super. 22, 435 A.2d 199 (1981) (factors to be considered in awarding college education support is whether the child is able and willing to successfully pursue his course of studies, the adequacy of the income of the child, and whether the parent has sufficient estate, earning capacity or income to provide for the education without undue hardship); and *Ulmer v. Sommerville*, 200 Pa. Super. 640, 190 A.2d 182 (1963). In each instance, the Superior Court assumed that a legal obligation existed and molded a remedy in response to that obligation. The Superior Court's reasoning seems to have evolved from its opinion in *Commonwealth v.*

Gilmore, 97 Pa. Super. 303 (1929). In *Gilmore*, a father obligated to pay support for his minor son, attempted to terminate support upon his son reaching the age of 16. The father argued that state law only mandated attendance at school until age 16 and that sufficient employment opportunities existed within the community for his son to obtain a job to support himself. Therefore, since attendance at school was no longer required, the need to provide support for his minor son ceased. In response, the father's minor son testified as to his progress in school and his desire to continue with his education and complete high school.

In refusing to grant the father's petition to terminate support, the trial court (whose opinion was adopted by the superior Court) noted that case law tended to include some education within the purview of a parent's obligation to provide support and maintenance. "The law, apart from statute has come to recognize that parental duty involves, in addition to provision for mere physical needs, such instruction and education as may be necessary to fit the child reasonably to support itself and to be an element of strength rather than one of weakness in the social fabric of the state. 97 Pa. Super. at 308.

At that time, an education was deemed to be a necessity in the preparation of a child for the rigors of life and to assist that child in becoming useful in society. However, the term "education" in this context did not contemplate collegiate or professional education but rather was confined to elementary and vocational education. The reason for this distinction was that elementary education was considered a necessary element of support much like food, clothing and housing. The duty to provide educational support beyond the minimum state-required attendance, however, was tempered by the parent's ability to pay and the child's commitment to completing his high school studies.

In recent history, the Superior Court has adopted and applied the *Gilmore* analysis to college educational support of a child. In essence, the Superior Court has transferred this "principle of necessity" of a basic fundamental education to a requirement that each child be entitled to an "enhanced" education. We do not agree with this transformation.

Under the common law, a parent had a duty to support a minor child. In its wisdom, our General Assembly has bestowed adulthood on minor children at age 18. Consequently, the common law duty to support a minor child must by necessity cease at age 18. Although several states have imposed a statutory duty upon a parent to provide college educational support for a child no longer considered a minor, our General Assembly has not. Accordingly, since no legal duty has been imposed by our legislature, nor have we developed such a duty by our case law, we decline to do so. Since our legislature has taken an active role in domestic matters through amendments and reenactment of the Divorce Code and the Domestic Relations Act, we feel the more prudent course is to await guidance from that body rather than creating duties and obligations by judicial pronouncement.

A basic education as guaranteed by our Commonwealth constitution must be available to all

Commonwealth citizens. In many instances, high school students reach their 18th birthday prior to graduation from high school. It would make no sense to terminate a support order while a child is attending high school. The rigors of high school are difficult enough without worrying about how a child is going to support himself for the remaining days of his high school education. Therefore, notwithstanding a child reaching majority at age 18, a parental duty of support is owed until a child reaches 18 or graduates from high school, whichever event occurs later. This will ensure that children have a minimum education in order to prepare them for the challenges of life.

The judgment of the Superior Court is reversed and the complaint for support for aid to higher education is dismissed.

Mr. Justice Larsen Dissenting

I dissent. I do not see this case as involving an abuse of discretion would affirm the Superior Court's order as to the holding that parents have an obligation to provide college support for their children. I would reverse the Superior Court order as to the parents not getting a reduction or credit toward this obligation from the children's grants, scholarships, loans, financial worth, etc. No windfalls should occur here.

Proposed Amendment

(A)   When liability may be found.   Parents may be liable for an unemancipated child's reasonable and necessary post high school educational expenses. The responsibility to provide for post high school educational expenses is a shared responsibility between both parents. The duty of a parent to provide a post high school education for a child is not as exacting a requirement as the duty to provide food, clothing, and shelter for a child of tender years is unable to support himself. In determining whether a parent may be so liable, the court shall consider the following:

1.   Whether the child is able and willing to successfully pursue his course of studies in a reputable institution of higher education which is appropriate and commensurate with the ability and aptitude of the child.
2.   The adequacy of the income and separate estate of the child.
3.   The ability of the child to receive scholarships, grants, and loans.
4.   Whether the parent has sufficient estate, earning capacity or income to provide for the education.
5.   Any willful estrangement between parent and child caused by the child.
6.   Any other relevant factors.

(B)   When liability may not be found.   A court shall not order support for educational expenses if any of the following circumstances exist:

1.   Undue financial hardship would result to the parent.
2.   The educational support would be a contribution for postcollege graduate school expenses.
3.   The order would extend support for the child beyond the child's twenty-third birthday.

(C)   Exceptional circumstances.   If exceptional circumstances exist, the court may order educational support for the child beyond the child's twenty-third birthday.

Statute of Frauds: What contracts must be in writing to be enforceable?

Many have heard that "an oral contract isn't worth the paper it is not written on." In reality, however, the vast majority of contracts are not in writing. When you purchase something in a store, enter a bus, or place an order at a restaurant, you are making a contract either orally, or by your actions. There are certain types of contracts, however, that are only enforceable if they are in writing. The laws requiring that some contracts be in writing are known as Statutes of Frauds, named after the celebrated English statute of 1677. Among the types of contracts that require some writing evidencing the agreement are: sale of real estate, agreeing to pay the debt of another person, and leases of longer than one year.

33 P.S. § 1 (1990)

§ 1.   Parol leases, etc.; estates in lands not to be assigned, etc., except by writing

From and after April 10, 1772, all leases, estates, interests of freehold or term of years, or any uncertain interest of, in, or out of any messuages, manors, lands, tenements or hereditaments, made or created by livery and seisin only, or by parol, and not put in writing, and signed by the parties so making or creating the same, or their agents, thereunto lawfully authorized by writing, shall have the force and effect of leases or estates at will only, and shall not, either in law or equity, be deemed or taken to have any other or greater force or effect, any consideration for making any such parol leases or estates, or any former law or usage to the contrary notwithstanding; except, nevertheless, all leases not exceeding the term of three years from the making thereof; and moreover, that no leases, estates or interests, either of freehold or terms of years, or any uncertain interest, of, in, to or out of any messuages, manors, lands, tenements or hereditaments, shall, at any time after the said April 10, 1772, be assigned, granted or surrendered, unless it be by deed or note, in writing, signed by the party so assigning, granting or surrendering the same, or their agents, thereto lawfully authorized by writing, or by act and operation of law.

§ 2.   Declarations of trusts and grants thereof to be in writing

All declarations or creations of trusts or confidences of any lands, tenements or hereditaments, and all grants and assignments thereof, shall be manifested by writing, signed by the party holding the title thereof, or by his last will in writing, or else to be void: Provided, That where any conveyance shall be made of any lands or tenements by which a trust or confidence shall or may arise or result by implication or construction of law, or be transferred or extinguished by act or operation of law, then and in every such case such trust or confidence shall be of the like force and effect as if this act had not been passed.

§ 3.   Promise to answer for debt of another

No action shall be brought whereby to charge any executor or administrator, upon any promise to answer damages out of his own estate, or whereby to charge the defendant, upon any special promise, to answer for the debt or default of another, unless the agreement upon which such action shall be brought, or some memorandum or note thereof, shall be in writing, and signed by the party to be charged therewith, or some other person by him authorized.

§ 4.   Contracts for less than twenty dollars excepted

This act shall not go into effect until the first day of January next, or apply to or affect any contract made or responsibility incurred prior to that time, or for any contract the consideration of which shall be a less sum than twenty dollars.

§ 5.   Acceptances to be in writing

No person within this state shall be charged, as an acceptor on a bill of exchange, draft or order drawn for the payment of money, exceeding twenty dollars, unless his acceptance shall be in writing, signed by himself, or his lawful agent.

§ 6.   When written instruments without consideration valid

A written release or promise, hereafter made and signed by the person releasing or promising, shall not be invalid or unenforceable for lack of consideration, if the writing also contains an additional express statement, in any form of language, that the signer intends to be legally bound.

§ 7.   Uniformity of interpretation

This act shall be so interpreted and construed as to effectuate its general purpose to make uniform the law of those states which enact it.

§ 8.   Short title

This act may be cited as the Uniform Written Obligations Act.

Adverse Possession: When can property be obtained by "adverse possession?"

A common retort to the refrain that "the meek shall inherit the earth" is "yeah, but not the mineral rights." This retort encapsulates a recurrent theme in the law: meekness is often not a legal virtue. Indeed, it is often a liability (as where meekness is construed as a waiver). In fact, in the law of real property, there are times when assertiveness, even outright "aggression," is rewarded. A person who does not have legal title to property, for example, may acquire such an interest by treating another's property as his own for a long enough period of time. This is reflected in the doctrine of adverse possession.

This rule is often criticized as rewarding a "thief's mentality," for it requires that the party know that the property legally belongs to another, but nevertheless continues to treat the property as his own. If the use is *permitted* by the rightful owner, then no time is counted for purposes of establishing adverse possession. Pennsylvania, like most other states, has set the time for adverse possession at twenty one years. This means that a person, to be able to claim legal title to property not initially titled in his name, must take possession of the property "openly, actually, continuously, exclusively, visibly and notoriously, for at least 21 years." In the following case, the additional question asked is whether you can "tack on" the years that your predecessor so treated another's property to your use of the property to reach the 21 year requirement.

Glenn v. Shuey
407 Pa. Super 213 (1991)

Judge Cirillo delivered the opinion of the court.

Ronald and Holly Shuey ("the Shueys") appeal from the judgment entered in the Court of Common Pleas of Centre County following appellee H. Parker Glenn's action in ejectment. We affirm.

This appeal arises from a dispute concerning the boundary between two parcels of real estate situated in Howard Township, Centre County. Both parcels ("parcel A" and "parcel B") were at one time owned by Ronald Curtin. On January 18, 1833, Curtin conveyed what eventually became the Shueys' property, parcel B, to Michael Leyman by a deed recorded in Centre County deed book K, page 397. On March 25, 1842, Curtin conveyed parcel A to John Leathers by a deed recorded in Centre County deed book N, page 422.

The Shueys are owners of parcel B by virtue of a deed dated

July 12, 1967, and recorded July 13, 1967 in Centre County deed book 294, page 596. Glenn's sources of title in parcel A are two deeds, one recorded July 5, 1957 in deed book 238, page 389, by which he became the owner of one-half interest, and the other recorded in deed book 247, page 257 on June 18, 1959, which vested title to the remaining one-half interest.

During 1987, a survey of parcel B was performed by Fred Henry on behalf of the Shueys. Subsequent to Henry's survey, Glenn employed Kerry H. Uhler and Associates for the purpose of surveying parcel A. The Uhler survey located the boundary line between parcels A and B as passing within a few feet west of the Shueys' home. In contrast, the Henry survey located that line as passing 25 feet west of the line as determined by the Uhler survey.

Until the completion of the Henry Survey in May, 1987, the Shueys' use of the disputed tract was limited to a twelve-foot wide gravel driveway passing along the western edge of the Shueys' home and ending at the rear of the Shueys' porch. The driveway extends from the rear of the Shuey home to the township road. Subsequent to the Henry survey, the Shueys placed a rope barrier along the line which they claimed to be the proper boundary between their property and that of Glenn. The Shueys also placed a large propane tank in the disputed tract at the southern end of the driveway. Prior to the placement of the barrier, the entire disputed tract, with the exception of the gravel driveway, was used exclusively by Glenn. Glenn's use of the disputed area included, 1) mowing the grass strip between the gravel driveway and the property line as claimed by Glenn, 2) the maintenance of various shrubs, grapevines and berry bushes in the disputed tract south of the end of the driveway, and 3) mowing and/or cutting grass in the disputed tract including cutting hay for livestock.

Glenn commenced an action in ejectment in the Court of Common Pleas of Centre County, alleging that the Shueys' actions deprived him of a portion of property to which he possessed legal title by virtue of deeds dated October 30, 1956 and June 18, 1959. Glenn's complaint also averred that he and his predecessors in title were in open, visible and notorious possession of the disputed area since January 30, 1923, for a period of over 65 years.

In their answer and new matter, the Shueys disputed the accuracy of the Uhler survey and alleged that all of their activity, including the erection of the rope barrier, transpired upon their own property as depicted by the Henry survey. The Shueys claimed ownership of the disputed property by virtue of their deed. Alternatively, the Shueys averred that they and their predecessors in title had used and maintained the driveway running along the western edge of the Shuey home for a period in excess of 21 years. Similarly, the Shueys maintained that they and their predecessors were in open, visible and notorious possession of the driveway and the entire parcel as depicted by the Henry survey for a period in excess of 21 years. Consequently, the Shueys claimed legal title to the disputed area by virtue of adverse possession.

The case proceeded to a non-jury trial, the Honorable David

E. Grine presiding. In his first opinion and order, filed July 25, 1989, Judge Grine determined that the Uhler survey correctly determined the boundary between parcel A and parcel B. Consequently, the court held that the line between the properties passed within a few feet west of the Shueys' home and therefore Glenn possessed legal title to the majority of the gravel driveway. In addition to establishing title by survey to within a few feet of the Shueys' home, the court opined that Glenn established title to the western edge of the Shueys' driveway by adverse possession as he exercised exclusive, visible and notorious control over the tract for a period of 21 years.

The trial court further held that because the Shueys had occupied their own property for a period of 20 years and 11 months as of the time of Glenn's ejectment action, they failed to establish ownership rights in the disputed tract by adverse possession. The court rejected the Shueys' allegation that they established the requisite 21 year period for acquiring title by adverse possession by tacking on their predecessor's possession of the disputed tract.

The trial court reasoned that the Shueys could not satisfy the requirements of section 72 by tacking because: 1) no relationship existed between the Shueys and their predecessor; 2) the predecessor had not claimed title to the disputed property; and 3) the deed conveying title to the Shueys made no reference to the disputed tract.

The Shueys' motion for post-trial relief was denied, and the trial court entered an opinion and order on September 26, 1989. On September 28, 1989, counsel for the Shueys sent Judge Grine a letter requesting that the court reconsider its order denying post-trial relief. Subsequently, on October 10, 1989, the court filed an amended opinion and order denying the Shueys' motion for post-trial relief.

The Shueys present the following issues for our consideration:

1) Did appellants [the Shueys] establish ownership of a driveway adjacent to their home by adverse possession?

2) Can appellants [the Shueys] tack their period of adverse possession and use of the driveway onto periods of adverse possession and use of the same by their predecessors in title?

Since the Shueys' issues are intertwined, we combine them for purposes of discussion.

It is well settled that a party claiming title to real property by adverse possession must affirmatively prove that he or she had "actual, continuous, exclusive, visible, notorious, distinct, and hostile possession of the land for twenty-one years." . . .

Broadly speaking, "actual possession" of land is dominion over the land; it is not equivalent to occupancy. There is no fixed rule, however, by which the actual possession of real property by an adverse claimant may be determined in all cases. The determination of what constitutes actual possession of property for purposes of adverse possession depends on the facts of each case, and to a large extent on the character of the premises. Id.

The words "visible and notorious possession," as applied to the adverse holding of land by a party without color of title, mean that the claim of ownership must by evidenced by conduct sufficient to place a reasonable person on notice that his or her land is being held by the claimant as his own.

　　To constitute distinct and exclusive possession for purposes of establishing title to real property by adverse possession, the claimant's possession need not be absolutely exclusive. Rather, it need only be a type of possession which would characterize an owner's use. For example, in *Reed*, the appellees, Robert and Audrey Reed, asserted title by adverse possession to a lot adjacent to their residence. The Reeds had maintained the lot by cutting the lawn and by planting and maintaining thereon various shrubbery and flowering plants. In affirming the trial court's determination that the Reeds had established title to the lot by adverse possession, Judge Wieand, writing for a unanimous court, opined:

Thus, the exclusive character of appellees' [the Reeds] possession was not destroyed because other persons occasionally passed unobserved over the lot. It was enough that appellees' possession was to the general exclusion of others and that they remonstrated with persons who attempted, without permission, to use the land.

　　The word "hostile," as an element of adverse possession does not mean "ill will" or "hostility," but implies an assertion of ownership rights adverse to that of the true owner and all others. Simply stated, the possession must be "such as to import a denial of the owner's title." 3 Am.Jur.2d § 50, at 143-144. Furthermore, if all of the elements of adverse possession other than hostility are established, the element of hostility is implied.

　　Finally, in order for adverse possession to ripen into title, it is necessary to show that such possession has been continuous and uninterrupted for the full statutory period. In this Commonwealth, as in most jurisdictions, the statutory period is twenty-one years. See 42 Pa.C.S. § 5530(a)(1). The law does not require that the claimant remain continuously on the land and perform acts of ownership from day to day. A temporary break or interruption, not of unreasonable duration, does not destroy the continuity of the adverse claimant's possession.

　　Here, the trial court focused primarily on the Shueys' failure to show that they exercised dominion over the driveway for the statutory period of 21 years. In arguing that they acquired title to the driveway by adverse possession, the Shueys allege that the trial court erred in concluding that they could not tack the period of adverse possession of their predecessors onto their own possession. The Shueys do not dispute the trial court's factual determination that Glenn commenced his action in ejectment on June 25, 1988, twenty years and eleven months after the occupancy of parcel B by the Shueys. Since it appears that the Shueys must show that they were entitled to tack the adverse possession of the previous occupants to their own possession in order to establish title to the driveway, we turn our attention to prior cases in which tacking was at issue.

　　In *Wittig v. Carlacci*, 370 Pa.Super. 584, 537 A.2d 29 (1988), a panel of this court reviewed the principles of law applicable when a party attempts to tack the adverse possession of his or her predecessor onto his or her own time of possession: "The possession of successive occupants may be tacked, but only where there is privity between them . . . . For our purposes, "privity" refers to a succession of relationship to the same thing, whether created by deed or other acts or by operation of law . . . . But a deed does not itself create privity between the grantor and the grantee as to land not described in the deed but occupied by the grantor in connection therewith, although the grantee enters into possession of the land not described and uses it in connection with that conveyed * * * The deed, in itself, creates no privity as to land outside its calls. Nor is privity created by the bare taking of possession of land previously occupied by the grantor." The *Wittig* court noted: "Each predecessor must have claimed title to the property in dispute, and in transferring to his successors must have purported to include it." Thus, a grantee cannot tack his grantor's adverse possession of land when the grantor does not convey such land to him. . . .

Here, the trial court held that the failure of the Shueys to show that their immediate predecessor in title claimed the disputed tract was evidenced by the testimony of Ken Bitner. Bitner testified that he lived in his parents' home, now the Shueys' home, for approximately ten years beginning in 1954. When asked who lived in the Shuey house after he moved out but before the Shueys moved in, Bitner stated that Joseph Leathers lived there. The Shueys argue that their immediate predecessors in title are John A. and Tracie M. Barnhart who leased the premises to Leathers.

The record indicates that the Barnharts, rather than Ken Bitner, were the Shueys' immediate predecessors in title to parcel B. The Shueys acquired title to parcel B from the Barnharts by a deed recorded July 13, 1967 in Centre County deed book 294, page 596. Similarly, the deposition testimony of Joseph C. Leathers refutes the trial court's apparent conclusion that Bitner is the Shueys' immediate predecessor in title to parcel B. Leathers testified as follows:

Q: So you lived in that house through the 40s, 50s and so forth, or?

A: [Leathers] Yes. When I moved out of the house across the street, I moved in the house that Holly Shuey lives in now and I don't have my dates quite exact . . . . but I know I was in there before 1964 and I was in there after 1964. Now I was there for probably, in the neighborhood of 4 to 5 years.

Q: Did you rent that property?

A: Yeah, I rented that off of Barnhart.

* * *

Q: Do you remember when you moved out? Is that when Holly Shuey moved in?

A: Yeah. She moved . . . I . . . Correct me there. I moved out and she moved in shortly after, now I think the house sat empty a few months before she moved in. I would say I moved out probably right around in '66 [sic] if I remember correctly.

* * *

Leathers testified that he and his family parked cars in the driveway, and he noted that the driveway was the only means of access to the coal chute at the back corner of the house. Leathers further noted that Glenn never used the driveway because there was a garage situated directly on the driveway approximately 40 feet behind the Shueys' house.

In their appellate brief, the Shueys argue that Leathers' testimony clearly establishes that their predecessors in title claimed title to the driveway. While Leathers' testimony demonstrates continuous use of the driveway, it is unclear whether he occupied the Shuey home during June, 1967, the month preceding the Shueys' acquisition of parcel B. Leathers noted that he believed that the Shuey home may have been empty for a few months before Holly Shuey moved in and that he probably moved out sometime in 1966. Hence, our determination of whether there exists sufficient privity between the Shueys and their immediate predecessors is contingent upon whether John and Tracie Barnhart asserted ownership rights over the gravel driveway.

In *Plott*, there was no privity between Cole and his predecessors because none of Cole's predecessors asserted ownership to the disputed property nor did they express an intention to convey anything more than what was set forth in their respective deeds. Likewise, in the instant case, the Barnharts' deed makes no mention of the disputed tract, and the record offers no indication that they intended to convey the gravel driveway to the Shueys. The Shueys have not shown privity by the bare taking of the possession of the driveway which was previously occupied by Leathers until some undetermined date. (". . . nor is privity created by the bare taking of possession of land previously occupied by the grantor."). The Shueys note that by statute in this Commonwealth all appurtenances, unless specifically excepted in a deed,

are passed to the next owner. See 21 P.S. § 3. The Shueys rely upon a nineteenth century case, *Scheetz*, in support of their conclusion that the deed by which they acquired title to parcel B did not necessarily have to include a description of the driveway. In Scheetz our supreme court opined that a mill-pond held under a base fee, no longer used in conjunction with a mill and occupied adversely as arable land, passed under a conveyance of the mill with its appurtenances.

Here, the Shueys have made no showing that they possessed the driveway in a manner adverse to Glenn. Unlike the party claiming adverse possession of the filled in mill-pond in *Scheetz*, the Shueys have failed to demonstrate that the driveway was an appurtenance belonging to parcel B. To the contrary, a review of the record indicates that the Shueys and their predecessors may have used the gravel driveway with Glenn's permission. Compare *Stevenson v. Williams*, 188 Pa.Super. 49, 145 A.2d 734 (1958) (en banc) (evidence insufficient to establish prescriptive easement rights in appellees' use of driveway where their use of the driveway and their predecessors' use began and continued as a result of friendly and accommodating permission by appellants) with *Waltimyer v. Smith*, 383 Pa.Super. 291, 556 A.2d 912 (1989) (title owner of portion of driveway located on border of abutting property failed to demonstrate that abutting landowner's use of common driveway was permissive). For example, prior to the Shueys' separation, Glenn ordered the removal of an antenna which had been placed on the Glenn side of the driveway. Glenn indicated that Ron Shuey complied with his request. Glenn also noted that he directed a bulldozer operator to utilize the driveway in 1962 to gain access to the rear of his property for the purpose of digging out a cesspool. He also stated that he used the driveway at various times for heavy hauling. Hence, it does not appear that the Shueys or their predecessors in title kept their respective "flags flying" in an attempt to prevent Glenn from utilizing the gravel driveway. *Klos*, 355 Pa.Super. at 402, 513 A.2d at 492.

Although not expressly stated in his opinion of July 25, 1989, it appears that Judge Grine characterized the Shueys' use of the driveway as "permissive." Stevenson, supra. We agree with his determination that the testimony adduced during the trial not only supports Glenn's ejectment action but also defeats any claim by the Shueys against the entire disputed tract.

The Shueys also rely on *Hughs v. Pickering*, 14 Pa. 297 (1850), for the proposition that when a subsequent holder enters property with the permission of the previous holder, the former has the right to tack one possession to another. In Hughs, the plaintiff, John Pickering, brought an action in ejectment to recover possession of a tract of land which he owned but which was occupied by Hughs. Hughs had acquired the property from Mrs. Bartlett for the sum of approximately $ 5.00. Subsequently, Bartlett gave half of this sum to George Mason, her brother. At trial, Mason testified that he had chopped logs, saplings and brush on the disputed property in addition to erecting a ten by twelve foot shanty on the property. The issue in Hughs was whether Hughs had the right to tack Mason's possession of the tract to his own in order to satisfy the 21 year requirement for establishing title by adverse possession. Our supreme court held that Pickering was not entitled to oust Hughs from the portion of the tract which had been improved by Mason, as Hughs had established title to the property by adverse possession. Id. at 302. The court opined that it was not necessary that Mason actually possess the disputed tract at the time of the sale in order to preserve the continuity of possession between Hughs and Mason. Writing for the unanimous court, Justice Rogers observed: "Had Mason abandoned the property absolutely, or had Hughs taken possession without authority, these would present such a case of want of continuity as would be fatal to the defence [Hughs' defense]. That Hughs paid consideration for and took possession of the disputed tract pursuant to an agreement of sale were critical factors in the court's analysis.

Here, in contrast, it does not appear that the Shueys were authorized to use the driveway by anyone other than Glenn. Hence, Hughs does not support the Shueys' claim that they had established privity between themselves and their predecessors in title to parcel B. Consequently, the Shueys may not tack the adverse possession of their predecessors onto their use of the gravel driveway. The Shueys have therefore failed to show that they had "actual, continuous, exclusive, visible, notorious, distinct and hostile possession" of the gravel driveway for twenty-one years. We find no error of law or abuse of discretion.

Judgment affirmed.

Retail Theft: What powers do merchants have to prevent shoplifting?

Retail theft, commonly referred to as shoplifting, is extremely common. The prevalence of this crime adds significantly to the cost of many products because of the need to recoup losses, provide adequate security, and create otherwise "needless" packaging to discourage such theft. People often have a misconception about when a person may be legally stopped by a store employee who suspects him of shoplifting, and what type of investigation may be conducted. First, it is clear that security personnel need not wait until a suspect has left the store before stopping him. The law presumes an intent to steal by virtue of certain behavior. Second, it is clear that even one who is falsely accused of retail theft and involuntarily held and searched, does not automatically have a tort case against the store. The law clothes the store and its employees with immunity for such errors so long as if there was probable cause to detain and search.

18 Pa.C.S. § 3929

§ 3929. Retail theft

(A) OFFENSE DEFINED. A person is guilty of a retail theft if he:

(1) takes possession of, carries away, transfers or causes to be carried away or transferred, any merchandise displayed, held, stored or offered for sale by any store or other retail mercantile establishment with the intention of depriving the merchant of the possession, use or benefit of such merchandise without paying the full retail value thereof;

(2) alters, transfers or removes any label, price tag marking, indicia of value or any other markings which aid in determining value affixed to any merchandise displayed, held, stored or offered for sale in a store or other retail mercantile establishment and attempts to purchase such merchandise personally or in consort with another at less than the full retail value with the intention of depriving the merchant of the full retail value of such merchandise;

(3) transfers any merchandise displayed, held, stored or offered for sale by any store or other retail mercantile establishment from the container in or on which the same shall be displayed to any other container with intent to deprive the merchant of all or some part of the full retail value thereof; or

(4) under-rings with the intention of depriving the merchant of the full

retail value of the merchandise.

(B) GRADING.

(1) Retail theft constitutes a:

(i)   Summary offense when the offense is a first offense and the value of the merchandise is less than $150.

(ii)   Misdemeanor of the second degree when the offense is a second offense and the value of the merchandise is less than $ 150.

(iii)   Misdemeanor of the first degree when the offense is a first or second offense and the value of the merchandise is $ 150 or more.

(iv)   Felony of the third degree when the offense is a third or subsequent offense, regardless of the value of the merchandise.

(2) Amounts involved in retail thefts committed pursuant to one scheme or course of conduct, whether from the same store or retail mercantile establishment or several stores or retail mercantile establishments, may be aggregated in determining the grade of the offense.

(C) PRESUMPTIONS. Any person intentionally concealing unpurchased property of any store or other mercantile establishment, either on the premises or outside the premises of such store, shall be prima facie presumed to have so concealed such property with the intention of depriving the merchant of the possession, use or benefit of such merchandise without paying the full retail value thereof within the meaning of subsection (a), and the finding of such unpurchased property concealed, upon the person or among the belongings of such person, shall be prima facie evidence of intentional concealment, and, if such person conceals, or causes to be concealed, such unpurchased property, upon the person or among the belongings of another, such fact shall also be prima facie evidence of intentional concealment on the part of the person so concealing such property.

(C.1)   EVIDENCE. To the extent that there is other competent evidence to substantiate the offense, the conviction shall not be avoided because the prosecution cannot produce the stolen merchandise.

(D) DETENTION. A peace officer, merchant or merchant's employee or an agent under contract with a merchant, who has probable cause to believe that retail theft has occurred or is occurring on or about a store or other retail mercantile establishment and who has probable cause to believe that a specific person has committed or is committing the retail theft may detain the suspect in a reasonable manner for a reasonable time on or off the premises for all or any of the following purposes: to require the suspect to identify himself, to verify such identification, to determine whether such suspect has in his possession unpurchased merchandise taken from the mercantile establishment and, if so, to recover such merchandise, to inform a peace officer, or to institute criminal proceedings against the suspect. Such detention shall not impose civil or criminal liability upon the peace officer, merchant, employee, or agent so detaining.

(E) REDUCTION PROHIBITED. No justice of the peace or other magistrate shall have the power to reduce any other charge of theft to a charge of retail theft as defined in this section.

(F) DEFINITIONS.

"CONCEAL." To conceal merchandise so that, although there may be some notice of its presence, it is not visible through ordinary observation.

"FULL RETAIL VALUE." The merchant's stated or advertised price of the merchandise.

"MERCHANDISE." Any goods, chattels, foodstuffs or wares of any type and description, regardless of the value thereof.

"MERCHANT." An owner or operator of any retail mercantile establishment or any agent, employee, lessee, consignee, officer, director, franchisee or independent contractor of such owner or operator.

"PREMISES OF A RETAIL MERCANTILE ESTABLISHMENT." Includes but is not limited to, the retail mercantile establishment any common use areas in shopping centers and all parking areas set aside by a merchant or on behalf of a merchant for the parking of vehicles for the convenience of the patrons of such retail mercantile establishment.

"STORE OR OTHER RETAIL MERCANTILE ESTABLISHMENT." A place where merchandise is displayed, held, stored or sold or offered to the public for sale.

"UNDER-RING." To cause the cash register or other sales recording device to reflect less than the full retail value of the merchandise.

(G) FINGERPRINTING. Prior to the commencement of trial or entry of plea of a defendant 16 years of age or older accused of the summary offense of retail theft, the issuing authority shall order the defendant to submit within five days of such order for fingerprinting by the municipal police of the jurisdiction in which the offense allegedly was committed or the state police. Fingerprints so obtained shall be forwarded immediately to the Pennsylvania State Police for determination as to whether or not the defendant previously has been convicted of the offense of retail theft. The results of such determination shall be forwarded to the Police Department obtaining the fingerprints if such department is the prosecutor, or to the issuing authority if the prosecutor is other than a police officer. The issuing authority shall not proceed with the trial or plea in summary cases until in receipt of the determination made by the State Police. The district justice shall use the information obtained solely for the purpose of grading the offense pursuant to subsection (b).

Lie Detectors: May employers require employees or prospective employees to submit to polygraph testing?

Theft by employees poses yet another problem for retailers. Such criminal conduct ranges from taking home pens and paperclips, to the embezzlement of millions of dollars. It is often difficult to catch such acts of thievery because of the employees' access to business assets and the need of an employer to trust employees to some degree. Thus, employers find the "polygraph" or "lie detector" an attractive means of preventing and uncovering dishonest employees. The polygraph is simply a machine that registers a person's physiological responses -- perspiration, respiration, pulse -- to questions posed by the examiner. The theory is that certain physiological responses involuntarily accompany dishonest answers.

There has been considerable debate about the reliability of such devices as well as their potential for abuse. Opinions vary from F. Lee Bailey who routinely uses them and advocates their expanded role to the late Senator Sam Irvin of the U.S. Senate Judiciary Committee who investigated the matter and personally concluded that "it was 20th century witchcraft." Pennsylvania's public policy about the polygraph is expressed in the following statute. Note that in criminal cases, the law continues to take the position that the results of such tests are generally inadmissible at a trial.

18 Pa.C.S. § 7321

(A) OFFENSE DEFINED. A person is guilty of a misdemeanor of the second degree if he requires as a condition for employment or continuation of employment that an employe or other individual shall take a polygraph test or any form of a mechanical or electrical lie detector test.

(B) EXCEPTION. The provisions of subsection (a) of this section shall not apply to employees or other individuals in the field of public law enforcement or who dispense or have access to narcotics or dangerous drugs.

Medical Malpractice: Is a physician liable to a non-patient who is harmed by the physician's negligent care of a patient?

In general, one cannot be held liable to another, unless there is a duty owed to that person. Even if one might have acted in complete safety, one has neither committed a crime, nor exposed oneself to civil liability, if one chooses not to help another who is in danger. Thus, a physician may be liable for missing a melanoma (a type of deadly skin cancer) visible on a patient's body, but not liable for failing to tell a person he meets socially that such a melanoma is obvious.

In the following case we are faced with the issue of the physician's patient causing harm because she was not advised that she posed a risk of contagion to her husband. Her husband then became ill, and sued his wife's physician. It is extremely important to note that this case does not deal with the related issue (discussed later in this book) of whether a physician has a duty to warn the non-patient. Liability in the *DiMarco* case is based on the doctor's alleged failure to advise his own patient of the fact that she carried and could transmit hepatitis by engaging in sexual intercourse.

Joseph R. DiMarco v. Lynch Homes
525 Pa. 558 (1990)

Justice Larsen delivered the opinion of the court.

This appeal presents the issue of whether a physician owes a duty of care to a third party where the physician fails to properly advise a patient who has been exposed to a communicable disease, and the patient, relying upon the advice, spreads the disease to the third party.

On June 18, 1985, Janet Viscichini, a blood technician, went to the Lynch Home in Kimberton, Pennsylvania, to take a blood sample from one of the residents. During the procedure, the patient struck or kicked Ms. Viscichini, whose skin was accidentally punctured by the needle which she had used to take blood from the patient. When Ms. Viscichini learned that the patient was a carrier of hepatitis and other diseases, she immediately sought treatment from Doctors Giunta and Alwine, appellants herein. The appellants advised her that if she remained symptom free for six weeks, she would not have been infected by the hepatitis virus. Ms. Viscichini was not told to refrain from sexual relations for any period of time following her exposure to the disease, but she practiced sexual abstinence until eight weeks after the exposure. As she had remained symptom free during that time, she resumed sexual relations with appellee, Joseph DiMarco, to whom she was not married. In September of 1985, Ms. Viscichini was diagnosed as suffering from hepatitis B; in December of 1985, appellee was diagnosed as having the same disease.

Appellee brought an action in the Court of Common Pleas of Philadelphia County against appellants and the Lynch Home. Among appellee's claims is the assertion that it was negligent for the appellants not to have warned Ms. Viscichini that having sexual relations within six months of the exposure could cause her sexual partner to contract hepatitis. The trial court granted appellants' preliminary objections and dismissed appellee's complaint with prejudice on the ground that the appellants owed appellee no duty of care because there was no privity between appellee and the appellants. The trial court suggested, however, that a duty may be owed under these facts where the patient and the third party are married.

Appellee filed an appeal to Superior Court, which reversed, holding that the appellants "had a duty to act reasonably in advising [Viscichini] regarding her ability to transmit her communicable disease." To support its conclusion that appellants owed appellee a duty, Superior Court cites the Restatement (Second) of Torts, § 324A, which provides: One who undertakes, gratuitously or for consideration, to render services to another which he should recognize as necessary for the protection of a third person or his things, is subject to liability to the third person for the physical harm resulting from his failure to exercise

reasonable care to protect his undertaking, if (a) his failure to exercise reasonable care increases the risk of such harm, or (b) he has undertaken to perform a duty owed by the other to the third person, or (c) the harm is suffered because of reliance of the other or the third person upon the undertaking. Restatement (Second) of Torts § 324A. Specifically, Superior Court found that subsection (c) provided the basis for liability in this case. Accordingly, Superior Court found that appellee had pled a cause of action in negligence, and the case was remanded for trial. We granted the appellants' petition for allowance of appeal, and we now affirm the decision of the Superior Court.

On an appeal from the sustaining of preliminary objections in the nature of a demurrer, "we accept as true all well-pleaded material facts set forth in the complaint as well as all inferences reasonably deducible therefrom." In the instant case, appellee averred in his complaint that he contracted hepatitis after he had intimate relations with a woman who had been exposed to hepatitis eight weeks prior to the sexual relations; that this woman had been told by her doctors, appellants herein, that if she remained symptom free for six weeks, she would not have been infected by the hepatitis virus; that in reliance upon that advice, the woman abstained from sexual relations for eight weeks; and that the advice of the appellants was wrong in that the waiting period should have been twenty-six weeks.

In *Cantwell v. Allegheny County*, 506 Pa. 35, 41, 483 A.2d 1350, 1353-54 (1984), this Court stated:

In order to state a cause of action under § 324A, a complaint must contain factual allegations sufficient to establish the legal requirement that the defendant has undertaken "to render services to another which he should recognize as necessary for the protection of a third person" (in this case, the plaintiff, appellee). This is essentially a requirement of foreseeability.

When a physician treats a patient who has been exposed to or who has contracted a communicable and/or contagious disease, it is imperative that the physician give his or her patient the proper advice about preventing the spread of the disease. Communicable diseases are so named because they are readily spread from person to person. Physicians are the first line of defense against the spread of communicable diseases, because physicians know what measures must be taken to prevent the infection of others. The patient must be advised to take certain sanitary measures, or to remain quarantined for a period of time, or to practice sexual abstinence or what is commonly referred to as "safe sex."

Such precautions are taken not to protect the health of the patient, whose well-being has already been compromised, rather such precautions are taken to safeguard the health of others. Thus, the duty of a physician in such circumstances extends to those "within the foreseeable orbit of risk of harm." If a third person is in that class of persons whose health is likely to be threatened by the patient, and if erroneous advice is given to that patient to the ultimate detriment of the third person, the third person has a cause of action against the physician, because the physician should recognize that the services rendered to the patient are necessary for the protection of the third person.

As Superior Court Judge Frank J. Montemuro, Jr., writing for the majority, so cogently noted: [T]his case involves a communicable disease. It hardly needs to be said that the prevention and control of communicable diseases is a momentous task which is of the utmost importance to the health and welfare of our citizens. The Disease Prevention and Control Law of 1955 requires a physician who treats or examines a person suffering from or who is suspected of having a communicable disease to make a prompt report to the local board of health or, if necessary, to the State Health Center of the Department. See 35 P.S. § 521.3; 28 Pa.Code § 27.21(a) and (b). We note that 28 Pa.Code § 27.115 specifically requires physicians to report cases of Hepatitis B. Further, several provisions of the Pennsylvania Code set forth procedures to be followed to prevent the contamination of our blood banks with blood from donors who suffer from or may have been exposed to viral hepatitis. See 28 Pa.Code §§ 25.71 and 30.30(7)(i). 384 Pa.Super. 463, 470, 559 A.2d 530, 533 (1989). Clearly, such measures are mandated by law specifically to protect third persons who will come into contact with those who have been exposed to or who have contracted a communicable disease.

We find, therefore, on the basis of the averments set forth in appellee's complaint, that appellee has stated a cause of action against the appellants. We further hold that the class of persons whose health is likely to be threatened by the patient includes any one who is physically intimate with the patient. Those, like the trial court, who insist that we cannot predict, or foresee, that a patient will engage in sexual activity outside of the marital relationship and that thus, we need not protect those who engage in "casual" sex, are exalting an unheeded morality over reality.

Accordingly, we affirm the order of the Superior Court reversing and remanding for further proceedings.

Flaherty, Justice, dissenting.

The majority cites *Cantwell v. Allegheny County*, 506 Pa. 35, 483 A.2d 1350 (1984) for the proposition that a professional may be held liable to a third party under the terms of Restatement of Torts (Second) § 324A if the professional has undertaken to render services to another which he should recognize as necessary for the protection of a third person. In doing so, the majority misstates the rule of *Cantwell*. *Cantwell* was written in the context of its facts, not involving professional services, and close on the heels of *Guy v. Liederbach*, 501 Pa. 47, 459 A.2d 744 (1983), in which this Court clearly set out the requirements for the liability of professionals to third parties on a negligence theory.

In *Guy v. Liederbach*, a beneficiary who was also named executrix under a will brought suit against a Pennsylvania attorney who drafted the will and directed her to witness it, which, under applicable New Jersey law, voided her legacy. In an action brought by the beneficiary against the attorney, this Court held that a legatee of a will may bring an action as an intended third party

beneficiary of the contract between the attorney and the testator, pursuant to § 302 of the Restatement (Second) of Contracts (1979), but that "important policies require privity (an attorney-client or analogous professional relationship, or a specific undertaking) to maintain an action in negligence for professional malpractice . . . ." 501 Pa. 47, 51, 459 A.2d 744, 746 (1983). This holding was consistent with *Lawall v. Groman*, 180 Pa. 532, 37 A. 98 (1897), in which this Court, in dicta, stated that an attorney has a duty to third parties and may be liable for misfeasance if (1) the attorney undertook to perform a specific service for a third party, (2) the third party relied on this service, and (3) the attorney was aware of the reliance. Building on this, we stated in *Guy v. Liederbach*: Thus, we retain the requirement that plaintiff must show an attorney-client relationship or a specific undertaking by the attorney furnishing professional services, as in *Lawall*, as a necessary prerequisite for maintaining such suits in trespass on a theory of negligence.

In this case, as in *Liederbach*, the professional service was not performed for the third party, and the doctor did not even know of the existence of the third party. Thus, there was neither privity nor a specific undertaking in favor of the third party, as is required under Liederbach, and in the absence of privity or specific undertaking, the doctors had no duty of care, and thus no liability, with respect to DiMarco.

As we stated in *Liederbach*, the dangers of adopting a negligence concept of duty analyzed in terms of scope of the risk or foreseeability are considerable and are to be avoided.

These dangers include not only the imposition of liability in favor of third parties in situations which are beyond the control of the professional rendering the service, but also the prospect of inducing professionals to narrow their inquiries into the client or patient situation, to the detriment of the client or patient, so as to avoid possible liability toward third parties which might come from knowing "too much." In failing to apply the rule of Liederbach the majority has not only ignored this Court's own case law, but has done a disservice to plaintiffs of the sort it seeks to protect.

Predicting Dangerousness: Does a physician have a duty to warn third parties of dangerous propensities of a patient? Does a physician have a duty to warn third parties of a patient's HIV infection?

The obligation of a health care provider to persons other than his (or her) patient is an issue of utmost importance to physicians. In the famous California *Tarasoff* case, it was held that a mental health professional could be held liable for his patient's attack upon a third party under certain circumstances. The Pennsylvania case that follows, although similar, ultimately rules in favor of the mental health professional. Note, however, that, unlike the *Tarasoff* case, in *Dunkle*, the assailant did not announce any intent to injure a particular person.

Although most of these types of cases have resolved around the issue of psychotherapy, the theory can be applied to infectious diseases as well. Of particular concern is the issue of transmission of the HIV virus by an infected person engaging in "unsafe" sexual practices. What should be the health care professional's obligation where her (or his) patient states that he does not want his spouse to know of his infection, and he will not use "safe" sex practices?

Pennsylvania's Confidentiality of HIV-Related Information Act, Act 148 of 1990, 75 Pa. C. S. 7601, et. seq. addresses that issue in Section 9, which provides physicians with immunity and an option: (a) breach confidentiality and warn the "significant contact" -- in which case the physician is immune from suit by the patient for such disclosure or (b) maintain confidentiality -- in which case the physician is immune from suit by the significant contact.

Close examination of the statute reveals that even if the physician decides to advise the contact of the risk, only limited disclosure is allowed ("Mrs. Smith, you are at risk of contracting HIV.") Disclosure of the identity is not allowed ("Mrs. Smith you are at risk of contracting HIV from your husband who is my patient.").

Dunkle v. Food Service East Inc., et al.
400 Pa. Super. 58 (1990)

Judge Popovich wrote the opinion for the court.

This controversial appeal involves the strangulation death of Senie Eyer. What began as a simple action in negligence against the store where Eyer was attacked has now escalated into an attempt to hold the perpetrator's treating psychologist, counselor and doctor liable in damages for failing to warn the victim of their patient's propensity towards violence. Our duty is to consider whether the trial court properly determined that the above additional defendants owed no legal duty to protect the plaintiffs' decedent from their patient's hostility.

We are cognizant of the

extreme importance of this complex issue, as well as the public interest in its resolution. Indeed, whether a psychologist or other health professional owes a duty to one other than his patient, and, if so, under what circumstances, has been a question largely unexplored in our legal precedent. Nevertheless, the appeal before us is from the orders entered in the Court of Common of Pleas of Centre County granting summary judgment in favor of the additional defendants, and thus our function is limited to specific determinations. Since we find that no evidence was presented to create a genuine issue of fact as to the claims asserted against the additional defendants in this case, we must affirm the orders of the trial court.

This Court recently reiterated the correct standard of review when considering an appeal from the grant of a motion for summary judgment. In *Vargo v. Hunt*, 398 Pa.Super. 600, 581 A.2d 625 (1990), we stated, "A determination of whether the grant or denial of a motion for summary judgment is to be upheld requires an appellate court to decide whether the pleadings, depositions, answers to interrogatories, admissions and affidavits show that there is no genuine issue as to any material fact, and that the moving party is entitled to judgment as a matter of law. In making such a finding, we must accept as true all properly pleaded facts, as well as all reasonable inferences which might be drawn therefrom. Furthermore, we shall not disturb the trial court's ruling unless there has been an error of law or a manifest abuse of discretion. Summary Judgment is appropriate only in those cases which are clear and free from doubt."); Pa.R.C.P.

1035. With these standards in mind, we will briefly set forth the facts and procedural history of this case, as well as the issue on appeal. On March 6, 1987, the plaintiff Steve Dunkle, administrator of the estate of Senie Eyer, instituted an action for damages against the original defendants (hereinafter "the Cannery"). The plaintiffs alleged that the defendants were negligent in failing to maintain a safe place for business and in failing to stop Bruce Tindal from fatally choking Senie Eyer upon their premises. Eyer, Tindal's live-in girlfriend, died one week after the attack.

Prior to this incident, Tindal had been receiving psychiatric care from Dr. Hylbert. Hylbert had diagnosed Tindal as having schizophreniform disorder. At that time, Tindal was taking medication called Navane to treat his illness. In December, 1983, Hylbert instructed Tindal to discontinue regular use of the drug. After he stopped taking his medication, Tindal's behavior became "nasty" and "violent." As a result, Hylbert re-prescribed the Navane. As both the appellant (the Cannery) and the appellees acknowledge, "[t]here is nothing in the record to indicate that Tindal expressed any specific tendencies vis-a-vis Eyer." In December, 1984, Hylbert discharged Tindal and discontinued his medication, instructing him to take Navane on an as-needed basis. Tindal was still under treatment by Keith A. Berfield, a counselor at The Pennsylvania State University.

In March, 1985, Tindal confessed to the Penn State police that he had been stealing property. The police contacted Berfield, who neither confirmed nor denied his association with Tindal. The following day, Tindal and Eyer went to the Cannery to shop. At that location, Tindal and Eyer entered the men's room and Tindal strangled Eyer, believing her to be a Russian agent.

In June, 1987, the original defendants filed a writ of summons joining the additional defendants. Thereafter, a complaint was filed against the additional defendants. Except for Hylbert and Tindal, the additional defendants filed preliminary objections, contending that the original defendants failed to state a claim upon which relief could be granted. The trial court dismissed the preliminary objections pending Tindal's deposition. The trial court stated that discovery should be effectuated before it would render a decision regarding the legal issues raised in the preceding pleadings. In particular, the trial court found that it was necessary to depose Tindal before it could determine whether Eyer was a "readily identifiable" victim of Tindal's attack. Trial court opinion, March 31, 1989. An amended complaint to join was filed subsequently. Answers were timely filed. Ultimately, discovery was completed.

In the final months of 1989, all of the additional defendants filed their respective motions for summary judgment. Specifically, the additional defendants alleged that they owed no duty to the decedent and hence, could not be held liable for her ensuing death. On January 18, 1990, the trial court granted the various motions and dismissed the original defendants' complaint to join. This appeal followed.

The Cannery raises one issue for our review: Did the additional defendants owe a duty to the plaintiffs' decedent? In its summary of the argument, the Cannery asserts the following: The trial Court erred in two respects. First, it held that a duty of a physician to a third-party, non-patient did not exist in this Commonwealth as set forth in *Tarasoff v. Regents of University of California*, 17 Cal.3d 425 [131 Cal.Rptr. 14], 551 P.2d 334 (1976) and adopted by this Court in *Coath v. Jones*, 277 Pa.Super. 479, 419 A.2d 1249 (1980). In addition, it made an error in deciding that the case in *DiMarco v. Lynch Homes -- Chester County*, [384] Pa.Super. [463], 559 A.2d 530 (1989), was not dispositive of the issues raised by this case. We have read the record in this case. In addition, we have extensively and thoroughly researched the issue raised by the Cannery. After careful consideration, we find that the trial court properly granted summary judgment in favor of the additional defendants.

The trial court correctly concluded that the additional defendants did not owe the plaintiffs' decedent any duty at law to protect her from Tindal's violent act. Although our research has failed to provide us with Pennsylvania caselaw that is directly on point, other jurisdictions have confronted analogous issues.

In *Tarasoff v. Regents of University of California*, 17 Cal.3d 425, 551 P.2d 334, 131 Cal.Rptr. 14 (1976), the California Supreme Court was faced with the question of whether a cause of action could exist for a psychologist's failure to warn a third party of his patient's dangerous propensities. The court concluded that in certain, very limited circumstances, the public's interest in safety must take precedence over the patient's interest in confidentiality and therefore, a psychologist may have a duty to protect identifiable, foreseeable victims from a patient's threats of violence. Notably, in *Tarasoff*, the patient actually confided to his psychologist his intent to commit violent acts against a specified target, Tatiana Tarasoff, before he in fact killed her. The court stated that [a]lthough . . ., under the common law, as a general rule, one person owed no duty to control the conduct of another . . ., nor to warn those endangered by such conduct . . ., the courts have carved out an exception to this rule in cases in which the defendant stands in some special relationship to either the person whose conduct needs to be controlled or in a relationship to the foreseeable victim of that conduct . . . .

In the instant case, it is apparent that the additional defendants did not share with Eyer the type of "special relationship" contemplated by the California Supreme Court that would justify the imposition of a duty to warn. Additionally, the record very clearly indicates that Tindal communicated no resolve, nor manifested any inclination to harm Eyer prior to the date that he strangled her. We recognize the additional defendants' duty to treat Tindal; however, under the factual scenario before us, we decline to extend the duty to protect a non-identifiable (in advance of her death) and arguably non-foreseeable third party victim. The fact that Tindal lived with Eyer did not automatically predispose her to abuse, nor may one infer that by virtue of their cohabitation, Eyer would be the most likely target of Tindal's possibly violent tendencies.

The United States District Court, Middle District of Pennsylvania, previously rejected this argument in *Leedy v. Hartnett*, 510 F.Supp. 1125 (M.D.Pa.1981).

We echo the trial court's observation that [t]he case now before us presents an issue similar to that in *Leedy* rather than in *Tarasoff*. In their Complaint to Join Additional Defendants, Original Defendants allege in relevant part: (1) Senie Eyer attended "one or more counseling sessions" with Bruce Tindal, provided by Additional Defendants; (2) Bruce Tindal "exhibited signs and symptoms of his deteriorating mental condition, indicating that he presented a danger to himself, and specifically to Senie Eyer;" (3) prior to March 16, 1985, Additional Defendants knew or should have known Bruce Tindal "would present and did present a danger to himself and to Senie Eyer;" (4) Additional Defendants were negligent in failing to warn Senie Eyer of, and protect her from, Bruce Tindal's dangerous propensities; and (5) Senie Eyer was the foreseeable victim of violent behaviour on the part of Bruce Tindal. [. . . .] Even taking all these allegations as true, for the purposes of summary judgment, Original Defendants have not alleged enough to hold the moving Additional Defendants in this case under *Leedy*.

The issue in *Leedy v. Hartnett*, 510 F.Supp. 1125 (M.D.Pa.1981) was whether VA hospital personnel had a duty to warn the Leedys that Hartnett, a former patient, exhibited violent inclinations when he drank. The personnel, aware that Hartnett intended to stay with the Leedys when he left the hospital, failed to inform them of any potential danger. Subsequently, Hartnett attacked the

Leedys. In holding for the defendant, the Leedy court concluded that the patient did not pose a threat to the plaintiffs any greater than the danger he posed to the general public. The court did not positively correlate frequent contact among individuals and their victims with the probability of violence as a result of those associations. Conversely, *Leedy* stands for the proposition that a victim may not be deemed "readily identifiable" merely because there exists a statistical possibility that increased contact will yield a higher likelihood of an attack. The court stated: Plaintiffs, recognizing that their case does not fall squarely within the confines of *Tarasoff*, seek to convince the Court that there exists a material issue of fact as to whether they were part of a readily identifiable group of people to whom Hartnett poses a special risk of danger. They seek to define this group as those who had frequent social contact with Hartnett. The Plaintiffs do not contend that Hartnett ever made any threat against them or that he was more likely to become violent toward people in whose presence he was comfortable. Indeed, the past acts of violence relied on by the Plaintiffs to show that Hartnett was dangerous do not fall into any pattern. At most, they demonstrate that Hartnett was prone to violent behavior and that that tendency was aggravated when he drank. There is no evidence from which it can be concluded that even when he drank Hartnett was more likely to become violent toward the people with whom he was drinking rather than others in the area. Plaintiffs appear to be arguing that since Hartnett had a tendency to commit violent acts, people with

whom he had frequent contact would be more likely to be victims of such acts and for that reason a special duty was owed to any such people known to the hospital's personnel. Assuming that Pennsylvania would adopt a theory of liability similar to that in Tarasoff, the Court is of the view that Pennsylvania would not extend that theory to cover the facts of this case. In order for the rule of liability announced in *Tarasoff* to be kept within workable limits, those charged with the care of potentially dangerous people must be able to know to whom to give warnings. When, as in *Tarasoff*, . . . a particular victim can be identified, there is good reason to impose upon psychiatrists or custodians a duty to warn the intended victim of the danger posed by the person under their care. On the facts of this case, however, Hartnett did not pose any danger to the Leedys different from the danger he posed to anyone with whom he might be in contact when he became violent. This is not a case in which it is alleged that the propensity to violence is increased by frequent contacts with the same people; rather, Plaintiffs' claim that they represent a readily identifiable group rests solely on a statistical probability that the more one saw Hartnett the more likely it is that one would be a victim of any violent outbreak by him. This is not the type of readily identifiable victim or group of victims to which the California Supreme Court made reference in *Tarasoff* . . . .

This Commonwealth has never expressly adopted the California opinion in Tarasoff. However, even if we were to accept the *Tarasoff* holding as law in this jurisdiction, we would not find that decision determinative of the instant appeal. Conversely, we find that the *Tarasoff* rationale should be confined to the very limited circumstances presented in that case. We narrowly construe the California court's holding. Contrary to the appellants' position in the instant case, we will not interpret *Tarasoff* to mean that, in effect, strict liability should be imposed upon treating physicians for the wrongful acts of their patients where there is any reason to believe that a third party might be endangered by the patient's possible misconduct and the medical professional fails to inform the third party of same. Such a rule would be unworkable and illogical. More importantly, it would infringe upon other well-established doctrines in our jurisprudence.

We are in agreement with the various appellees' position that a psychologist (or psychiatrist) owes no duty to warn or otherwise protect a non-patient where the patient has not threatened to inflict harm on a particular individual. To hold otherwise would not only hinder the psychologist's relationship with the patient and frustrate the psychologist's ability to properly treat the patient, but additionally, it would infringe upon the psychologist-patient privilege. Moreover, as the *Tarasoff* court well-noted: We realize that the open and confidential character of psychotherapeutic dialogue encourages patients to express threats of violence, few of which are ever executed. Certainly a therapist should not be encouraged routinely to reveal such threats; such disclosures could seriously disrupt the patient's relationship with his therapist and with the persons threatened. To the contrary, the therapist's obligations to

his patient require that he not disclose a confidence unless such disclosure is necessary to avert danger to others, and even then that he do so discreetly, and in a fashion that would preserve the privacy of his patient to the fullest extent compatible with the prevention of the threatened danger.

We find no common law rule that imposes a duty on a psychologist or psychiatrist to warn a non-patient of a patient's dangerous propensities. In Pennsylvania, nor is there a statutory duty to protect a non-patient from similar potential harm. In the absence of legislative directives or reforms that specifically address this problematic issue, we decline to impose such a stringent legal duty on health care professionals under the facts of this case.

Finally, we agree with the trial court that this Court's decision in *DiMarco v. Lynch Homes -- Chester County*, 384 Pa.Super. 463, 559 A.2d 530 (1989) is inapposite to the instant appeal. In *DiMarco*, the plaintiff/appellant (Joseph DiMarco) sued the defendants/appellees (physicians) for, inter alia, negligently advising Janet Viscichini, DiMarco's sexual partner, that she could safely resume sexual activities six weeks after she was exposed to hepatitis. Three months after the fact, Viscichini was diagnosed as having hepatitis. Six months after the fact, DiMarco was informed that he too had contracted the disease. The trial court originally dismissed the complaint, but this Court reversed, stating that the physicians might be liable to DiMarco if he could prove that he knew of the doctors' advice to Viscichini, detrimentally relied upon that advice, and suffered resulting harm.

The original defendants in the instant case cite *DiMarco* for the notion that foreseeability is immaterial; a third party victim does not have to be "readily identifiable" for a patient's treating physician to be liable to the third party who is injured as a result of the physician's wrongful diagnosis to the patient. However, the *DiMarco* case is clearly distinguishable on its facts. In addition, this Court was clear in its directive that *DiMarco* be confined to the circumstances of that case. We stated: "Our decision is limited to the facts of the case presently before us . . . . We do not hold that [the woman's] physicians had a duty to control her conduct, but only that they had a duty to act reasonably in advising her regarding her ability to transmit her communicable disease. This case is one which involves medical advice, given in the context of a physician-patient relationship, concerning precautions to prevent the spread of a communicable disease by the patient. Importantly, in the case at bar, the third party to the physician-patient relationship claims to have been aware of the medical advice concerning the transmittal of the disease, and to have relied and acted upon this medical advice in interacting with the patient . . . . Under these circumstances, we are willing to find that the physicians owed a duty of reasonable care to the non-patient."

As the trial court found in the instant case, "[i]t is nowhere alleged [that] Senie Eyer relied and acted upon advice given by [the] additional defendants to their patient, Bruce Tindal, nor is it alleged [that] she suffered detrimental harm as a result of reliance upon erroneous advice from physician to patient." We agree with the trial court that the *DiMarco* holding should not be extended to encompass "the completely distinct factual circumstances of the case at bar." Here, there was no dispute as to any material facts. Moreover, no evidence was offered to create any genuine issues of fact regarding the claims against the additional defendants. Clearly, the additional defendants owed no duty to the plaintiffs' decedent. Thus, summary judgment was properly entered as a matter of law.

Orders affirmed.

35 P.S. § 7601 (1991)

§ 7605. Consent to HIV-related test

(A) CONSENT.   Except as provided in section 6 with respect to the involuntary testing of a source patient, no HIV-related test shall be performed without first obtaining the informed written consent of the subject. Any consent shall be preceded by an explanation of the test, including its purpose, potential uses, limitations and the meaning of its results.

(B) PRETEST COUNSELING. No HIV-related test may be performed without first making available to the subject information regarding measures for the prevention of, exposure to and transmission of HIV.

(C) CONFIRMATORY TEST. No test result shall be determined as positive, and no positive test result shall be revealed, without confirmatory testing if it is required by generally accepted medical standards.

(D) NOTICE OF TEST RESULT. The physician who ordered the test, the physician's designee or a successor in the same relationship to the subject shall make a good faith effort to inform the subject of the result regardless of whether the result is positive or negative.

(E) POST-TEST COUNSELING.

> (1) No positive or negative test result shall be revealed to the subject without affording the subject the immediate opportunity for individual, face-to-face counseling about:
>
>> (i) The significance of the test results.
>>
>> (ii) Measures for the prevention of the transmission of HIV.
>>
>> (iii) The benefits of locating and counseling any individual by whom the subject may have been exposed to HIV and the availability of any services with respect to locating and counseling such individual.
>
> (2) No positive test result shall be revealed to the subject without, in addition to meeting the requirements of paragraph (1), also affording the subject the immediate opportunity for individual, face-to-face counseling about:
>
>> (i) The availability of any appropriate health care services, including mental health care, and appropriate social and support services.

(ii) The benefits of locating and counseling any individual who the infected subject may have exposed to HIV and the availability of any services with respect to locating and counseling such individual.

§ 7606. Certification of significant exposure and testing procedures

(A) PHYSICIAN'S EVALUATION OF SIGNIFICANT EXPOSURE.

(1) Whenever an individual health care provider or first responder experiences an exposure to a patient's blood or bodily fluids during the course of rendering health care or occupational services, the individual may request an evaluation of the exposure, by a physician, to determine if it is a significant exposure as defined in this act. No physician shall certify his own significant exposure or that of any of his employees. Such requests shall be made within 72 hours of the exposure.

(2) Within 72 hours of the request, the physician shall make written certification of the significance of the exposure.

(3) If the physician determines that the individual health care provider or first responder has experienced a significant exposure, the physician shall offer the exposed individual the opportunity to undergo testing, following the procedure outlined in section 5.

(B) OPPORTUNITY FOR SOURCE PATIENT TO CONSENT.

(1)   In the event that an exposed individual health care provider or first responder is certified to have experienced a significant exposure and has submitted to an HIV-related test, no testing shall be performed on a source patient's available blood unless the certifying physician provides a copy of the written certification of significant exposure to the source patient's physician or institutional health care provider in possession of the available blood and the source patient's physician or institutional health care provider has made a good faith effort to:

(i) Notify the source patient or substitute decisionmaker of the significant exposure.

(ii) Seek the source patient's voluntary informed consent to the HIV-related testing as specified in section 5(a).

(iii) Provide counseling as required under section 5(b).

(2)   The source patient's physician or institutional health care provider that receives a certification of significant exposure shall begin

to comply with the request within 24 hours. If the source patient's physician or institutional health care provider is unable to secure the source patient's consent because the source patient or the source patient's substitute decisionmaker refuses to grant informed consent or the source patient cannot be located, the source patient's physician or institutional health care provider shall arrange for an entry to be placed on the source patient's medical record to that effect. If these procedures are followed and the entry is made on the source patient's medical record, then HIV-related tests shall be performed on the source patient's available blood if requested by the exposed individual health care provider or first responder who has submitted to an HIV-related test.

(3)   The physician ordering the HIV-related test on a source patient's available blood on behalf of the source patient's physician or institutional health care provider shall comply with section 5(c) through (e).

(4)   The health care provider or first responder shall be notified of the results of the HIV-related test on the source patient's blood if the health care provider or first responder's baseline HIV-related test is negative. Further disclosure of the test results is prohibited unless authorized under section 7.

§ 7607. Confidentiality of records

(A) LIMITATIONS ON DISCLOSURE. No person or employee, or agent of such person, who obtains confidential HIV-related information in the course of providing any health or social service or pursuant to a release of confidential HIV-related information under subsection (c) may disclose or be compelled to disclose the information, except to the following persons:

(1)   The subject.

(2)   The physician who ordered the test, or the physician's designee.

(3)   Any person specifically designated in a written consent as provided for in subsection (c).

(4)   An agent, employee or medical staff member of a health care provider, when the health care provider has received confidential HIV-related information during the course of the subject's diagnosis or treatment by the health care provider, provided that the agent, employee or medical staff member is involved in the medical care or treatment of the subject. Nothing in this paragraph shall be construed to require the segregation of confidential HIV-related information from a subject's medical record. . . .

(10) A person allowed access to the information by a court order issued pursuant to section 8. . . .

(C) REQUIRED ELEMENTS OF WRITTEN CONSENT TO DISCLOSURE. A written consent to disclosure of confidential HIV-related information shall include:

(1) The specific name or general designation of the person permitted to make the disclosure.

(2) The name or title of the individual, or the name of the organization to which the disclosure is to be made.

(3) The name of the subject.

(4) The purpose of the disclosure.

(5) How much and what kind of information is to be disclosed.

(6) The signature of the subject.

(7) The date on which the consent is signed.

(8) A statement that the consent is subject to revocation at any time except to the extent that the person who is to make the disclosure has already acted in reliance on it.

(9) The date, event or condition upon which the consent will expire, if not earlier revoked. . . .

§ 7608. Court order

(A) ORDER TO DISCLOSE. No court may issue an order to allow access to confidential HIV-related information unless the court finds, upon application, that one of the following conditions exists:

(1) The person seeking the information has demonstrated a compelling need for that information which cannot be accommodated by other means.

(2) The person seeking to disclose the information has a compelling need to do so.

(B) ORDER TO TEST AND DISCLOSE. No court may order the performance of an HIV-related test and allow access to the test result unless the court finds, upon application, that all of the following conditions exist:

(1)   The individual whose test is sought was afforded informed consent and pretest counseling procedures required by section 5(a) and (b) and the subject refused to give consent or was not capable of providing consent.

(2)   The applicant was exposed to a body fluid of the individual whose test is sought and that exposure presents a significant risk of exposure to HIV infection. A determination that the applicant has incurred a significant risk of exposure to HIV infection must be supported by medical and epidemiologic data regarding the transmission of HIV, including, if available, information about the HIV risk status of the source individual and the circumstances in which the alleged exposure took place.

(3)   The applicant has a compelling need to ascertain the HIV test result of the source individual.

(C) COMPELLING NEED. In assessing compelling need for subsections (a) and (b), the court shall weigh the need for disclosure against the privacy interest of the individual and the public interests which may be harmed by disclosure.

(D) PLEADINGS. Pleadings under this section shall substitute a pseudonym for the true name of the individual whose test result is sought. Disclosure to the parties of the individual's true name shall be communicated confidentially in documents not filed with the court.

(E) NOTICE. Before granting an order for testing or disclosure and as soon as practicable after the filing of a petition under this section, the court shall provide the individual whose test result is sought with notice and a reasonable opportunity to participate in the proceeding if the individual is not already a party.

(F) IN CAMERA PROCEEDINGS. Court proceedings under this section shall be conducted in camera, unless the individual agrees to a hearing in open court or unless the court determines that a public hearing is necessary to the public interest and the proper administration of justice.

(G) EXPEDITED PROCEEDING. The court shall provide for an expedited proceeding if it is requested by the applicant and the application includes verified statements that:

(1)   The applicant has been exposed to a body fluid that poses a risk of HIV infection from the individual whose test result is sought.

(2)   The exposure occurred within six weeks of the filing of the application.

(3)   The exposure involves:

(i) a percutaneous injury to the applicant's skin from a needle stick or other sharp object;

(ii) contact of the applicant's eyes, mouth or other mucous membrane;

(iii) contact of chapped or abraded skin of the applicant; or

(iv) prolonged contact of the applicant's skin.

An expedited proceeding on the application shall be held no later than five days after the court complies with subsection (e), pertaining to notice requirements.

(H) SAFEGUARDS AGAINST DISCLOSURE. Upon the issuance of an order to disclose the information, the court shall impose appropriate safeguards against unauthorized disclosure which shall specify the following:

(1)   The particular information which is essential to accommodate the need of the party seeking disclosure.

(2)   The persons who may have access to the information.

(3)   The purposes for which the information will be used.

(4)   The appropriate prohibitions on future disclosure as provided for in section 7.

§ 7609. Civil immunity for certain physicians

(A) PERMISSIBLE DISCLOSURE. Notwithstanding the provisions of section 7, a physician may disclose confidential HIV-related information if all of the following conditions are met:

(1)   The disclosure is made to a known contact of the subject.

(2)   The physician reasonably believes disclosure is medically appropriate, and there is a significant risk of future infection to the contact.

(3)   The physician has counseled the subject regarding the need to notify the contact, and the physician reasonably believes the subject will not inform the contact or abstain from sexual or needle-sharing behavior which poses a significant risk of infection to the contact.

(4)   The physician has informed the subject of his intent to make such disclosure.

(B) SUBJECT NOT TO BE IDENTIFIED. When making such disclosure to a contact, the physician shall not disclose the identity of the subject or any other contact. Disclosure shall be made in person except where circumstances reasonably prevent doing so.

(C) DUTIES RELATING TO CONTACTS. A physician shall have no duty to identify, locate or notify any contact, and no cause of action shall arise for nondisclosure or for disclosure in conformity with this section.

(D) OTHER IMMUNITY. The physician who certifies that a significant exposure has occurred as provided by section 6 shall not be subject to civil liability for the exposure evaluation if acting in the good faith and reasonable belief that the certification was appropriate and consistent with this act. . . .

Duty to Protect Customers: Is a business liable when customers are injured on the premises by the criminal acts of third parties?

The duty of possessors of land to protect patrons from criminals has become an increasingly important issue as violent crime increases in the 1990's. Under what circumstances should the law permit a crime victim to recover money damages from a parking lot operator, a retail establishment, a motel, or any other possessor of land on whose premises the crime has occurred? In those states which recognize the duty of a possessor of land to protect patrons from criminals, the courts generally ask whether or not such crime was foreseeable and if it was, whether the steps taken to protect patrons were adequate. Pennsylvania courts follow this approach as evidenced in the following case.

It is probably true that the expansion of tort doctrine to include a duty to protect business invitees from the criminal acts of third parties is derived from "the search for deep pockets." After all, the typical criminal is unlikely to be in a financial position to pay damages. As you would imagine, this doctrine is disfavored by businesses who feel they are treated unfairly when found liable for the intentional wrongdoing of persons not in their employ.

Yet, where the business is aware of a particular risk (or should be aware of a particular risk), that would not be patently obvious to a business invitee, most observers agree that it is fair that the business should be obligated to take reasonable measures to protect or warn its invitee. For example, if a business owner is aware that a particular flight of stairs are dangerous because they are wet, he is obligated to warn customers.

Why should there be any difference when the business owner is aware that there is a particular risk of being assaulted because of a history of disturbances at a particular place on his premises?

Moran v. Valley Forge Drive-In Theater
431 Pa. 432 (1968)

Jones, Justice

This appeal challenges the propriety of the refusal of the Court of Common Pleas of Montgomery County to enter a judgment n.o.v. or, in the alternative, grant a new trial in a trespass action for personal injuries instituted by Donald J. Moran against Valley Forge Theater, Inc. and certain individuals, allegedly the owners and operators of a drive-in theater (Theater), wherein a $ 12,000 verdict was entered in Moran's favor.

On May 17, 1963, Moran, with his wife and two minor children, purchased tickets for the evening show at the Theater and entered upon the Theater premises. At the conclusion of the first movie showing, Moran went to the theater rest room and, while approaching the rest room, observed 6 or 8 teenagers acting in a boisterous manner near the rest room. While Moran was in the rest room a lighted firecracker explosion took place therein as a result of which, for a period of time, Moran lost his hearing, and, thereafter, had a loud ringing in his ear accompanied by shock.

The Theater urges that the court below erred in refusing to enter judgment n.o.v. in that Moran failed to carry his burden of proving negligence on the part of the Theater which caused the accident. The thrust of the Theater's argument is that there was no testimony showing that it knew or had reason to know of the likelihood of a firecracker explosion in the rest room as distinguished from other portions of the Theater premises.

The record reveals that, on rather frequent occasions prior to the accident, boisterous and disorderly conduct had taken place on the Theater premises. On approximately twelve occasions each year over the two year period immediately preceding this accident there had been firecracker explosions on the Theater's premises and, on one occasion, a firecracker had been exploded in the men's rest room of the Theater; on one occasion, Theater guardians had been roughly treated and other acts of rowdyism had taken place in the same two year period. The Theater gave no warning, either by prohibiting the lighting of firecrackers or by signs warning patrons of the possibility of firecrackers being exploded on the premises, although on the night of the accident three rampmen, charged with maintaining decorum, were on duty.

After a study of this record, we are convinced that Moran did establish sufficient facts from which the jury reasonably could have inferred negligence on the part of the Theater. We believe the court below adequately disposed of this contention in the following manner: "There is a well established Rule of Law that the liability of a possessor of land who holds that land open to patrons for business purposes has a duty to prevent tortious acts of third parties to his patrons, or to warn his patrons of the possibility of such tortious acts. The law regarding this duty is well set forth in Section 344 of the Restatement 2d, Torts: 'A possessor of land who holds it open to the public for entry for his business purposes is subject to liability to members of the public while they are upon the land for such a purpose, for physical harm caused by the accidental, negligent or intentionally harmful acts of third persons . . . of the possessor to exercise reasonable care to (a) discover that such acts are being done or are likely to be done, or (b) give a warning adequate to enable the visitors to avoid the harm, or otherwise protect them against it.'

"Comment f to Section 344, applies with specific particularity to the present case at bar, and states as follows: 'Since the possessor is not an insurer of the visitor's safety, he is ordinarily under no duty to exercise any care until he knows or has reason to know that the acts of the third person are occurring, or are about to occur. He may, however, know or have reason to know, from past experience, that there is a likelihood of conduct on the part of the third persons in general which is likely to endanger the safety of the visitor, even though he has no reason to expect it on the part of any particular individual. If the place or character of his business, or his past experience, is such that he should reasonably anticipate a careless or criminal conduct on the part of third persons, either generally or at some particular time, he may be under a duty to take precautions against it, and to provide a reasonably sufficient number of servants to afford a reasonable protection.'

"Applying the above law to the evidence in this case, we must conclude that the prior occurrences of rowdiness by teenagers; the multitudinous firecracker explosions; and the inability of rampmen to maintain proper decorum were sufficient to make out a question of fact for the jury. It was also a question of fact for the Jury as to whether or not the [Theater] took adequate measures to either warn patrons of possible danger or to prevent acts on the part of third persons which might injure patrons of the theater. The [Theater] contend[s] in their brief that the record is devoid of testimony which would show that the [Theater] knew an explosion was to take place in the rest room, and further was devoid of testimony that there were any means by which the [Theater] could have discovered that an explosion was to take place. Under Section 344 of the Restatement 2d, Torts, it is not necessary for defendants to be specifically aware of the exact location on their premises where patrons might be injured by the tortious acts of third persons. It is sufficient to establish a jury question of liability if the evidence, as in this case, shows that the defendants had notice, either actual or constructive, of prior acts committed by third persons within their premises which might cause injuries to patrons.

"The second basis of [The Theater's] Motion for Judgment N.O.V. is the contention that there was nothing the defendants could have done which would have prevented the injuries to the plaintiff. The defendants argue that there is no way of preventing someone from throwing a firecracker if that person has such an intent. We feel this argument is not justified under the applicable rule of law. It is not necessary that there be an absolute protection of all persons since the occupant of land for business purposes is not the insurer of the safety of his patrons. It is merely necessary, under the Restatement 2d, Torts, Section 344, that reasonable measures be taken to control the conduct of third persons, or to give adequate warning to enable patrons to avoid possible harm. It then becomes a question of fact for the jury as to whether or not the [Theater] fulfilled [its] responsibility under the law. In this case there was a jury question as to whether adequate measures were taken to control the conduct of third persons, and further, a question for the jury as to whether or not the [Theater was] justified in failing to give sufficient warning which might have enabled the patrons, such as [Moran], to avoid possible danger. The Jury having decided these questions in favor of [Moran] and against the [Theater], this Court sees no reason for entering a Judgment N.O.V."

We agree with the court below in its refusal to enter a judgment n.o.v.

New Trial

It is initially contended that the trial court erred in permitting testimony relating to prior disturbances on the Theater premises which were not restricted to the rest room of the Theater. It is urged that only firecracker incidents which took place within the theater rest room were admissible into evidence. The court below permitted testimony as to firecracker incidents which took place not only in the rest room but in other portions of the premises of the drive-in theater.

The Theater relies upon *Regelski v. F. W. Woolworth Co.*, 423 Pa. 524, 225 A. 2d 561 (1967), and it reads Regelski as mandating that evidence relating to prior incidents of disorder be restricted to the particular portion of the premises wherein the accident occurred and directing that other evidence of prior incidents of rowdyism elsewhere on the premises be excluded. We do not so read Regelski. In our view, *Regelski* did not limit the introduction of testimony of prior incidents to the exact place on the premises where the injury occurred.

Comment f to Section 344 of Restatement 2d, Torts, states: "If the place or character of [the land possessors] business, or his past experience, is such that he should reasonably anticipate careless or criminal conduct on the part of third persons, either generally or at some particular time, he may be under a duty to take precautions against it, and to provide a reasonably sufficient number of servants to afford a reasonable protection."

The Theater invited the public to its entire premises and, in view of the testimony that, prior to the accident, rowdyism and boisterous conduct had occurred, including the explosion of firecrackers, it would be highly unreasonable to limit an injured person to the introduction of testimony solely relating to the actual place where the injury occurred and would, in our opinion, be in conflict with the sound principles of Section 344 of Restatement 2d, Torts. W e find no merit in this contention of the Theater.

Lastly, it is urged that the verdict of $12,000 was grossly excessive because Moran had only $65.00 in medical expenses and his salary has increased since the time of the accident. We believe that the trial court, who heard and saw the witnesses, particularly Moran and his medical witness, Dr. Rex, properly disposed of this contention in the following manner: "We feel that in this case where the hearing of the plaintiff has been so greatly affected, the reasonableness of the verdict cannot be determined on the basis of possible multiples of the special damages. As shown from the plaintiff's testimony, he has a permanent partial loss of hearing and a continual ringing in his ear in addition to experiencing difficulty in hearing what is said in large groups. This loss has also greatly affected the plaintiff's relationship with his family. His temper flares up more when he is talking with his wife and family. Under the circumstances of a permanent partial loss of hearing causing difficulties with his familyand with others, which the plaintiff will have to live with in the future, we cannot see that the verdict of the Jury was so grossly shocking to our sense of justice so as to make necessary a new trial of this case."

Our examination of the instant record leads us to the conclusion that the court below properly refused to enter a judgment n.o.v. or, in the alternative, to grant a new trial.

Judgment affirmed.

Dissenting Opinion by Mr. Chief Justice Bell:

I would grant a Judgment N.O.V., or at least a new trial.

In order to reach its conclusion, the Majority first change, by necessary implication, and in practical effect ignore the principle that a possessor of land is not an insurer. Moreover, the prior disturbances occurred in another part of the theatre, and the theatre had three rampmen to police or attempt to police the theatre. Furthermore, the Majority then let the jury guess (1) what warning should have been given, and (2) how any warning would have prevented this unlawful and criminal act of rowdy, undisciplined children, and (3) what additional protection the defendants should have supplied.

For each and all of these reasons, I dissent.

Comparative Negligence: What is the comparative negligence rule?

The common law rule of contributory negligence meant that an injured plaintiff could not recover against a negligent defendant if the plaintiff had also been partially at fault in causing his own injury. Even if the defendant was 99% at fault and the plaintiff only 1%, the plaintiff was barred from all recovery. This harsh outcome has been rejected in most jurisdictions today and replaced, as in Pennsylvania, with the concept of comparative negligence.

Under the Pennsylvania Comparative Negligence Act, a plaintiff is barred from recovery only when the plaintiff's negligence is greater than the defendant's, i.e., when the plaintiff's negligence is determined to be 51% or more. Note that if both parties have been injured, the defendant who was 49% negligent would prevail in a counterclaim against the plaintiff! Once the apportionment of negligence is determined, the amount of damages awarded to the plaintiff is reduced by the degree of negligence of the plaintiff.

Pennsylvania's rule represents an example of the "modified comparative negligence" model. Under "true comparative negligence" (as found in admiralty cases), every party's own negligence mitigates his liability, but there is no requirement that one party's negligence be less than another's. Thus, a ship that sustained only $10,000 damage, and which was only 10% responsible for the collision which caused $500,000 worth of damage to another vessel (which was 90% negligent), would be liable to the other ship for $50,000 minus the amount owed to it (90% of $10,000) or a total of $49,000! Note that under Pennsylvania's rule there may be situations where a defendant may be less than 50% responsible for the accident, yet be liable to the plaintiff. For example the situation where the plaintiff is 20% responsible, one defendant is 50%, and the other defendant is 30% responsible. In such an event, both defendants are liable to the plaintiff. Obviously there are many combinations of percentages that can result in similar outcomes.

In the following case, where a judge in a non-jury trial found that the plaintiff and defendant were each 50% negligent, the judge incorrectly concluded that neither party could recover.

Lopa v. McGee
373 Pa. Superior Ct. 85 (1988)

President Judge Cirillo wrote the opinion for the court.

This is an appeal from a judgment entered in the Court of Common Pleas of Bucks County in favor of appellees Maureen and Charles McGee and against appellant Kalani J. Lopa.

On September 16, 1983, Mr. Lopa filed a complaint in trespass against Maureen and Charles McGee seeking to recover for personal injuries and property damage which he suffered as a result of a motor vehicle accident on October 17, 1982. Mr. McGee filed a counterclaim to recover property damages arising out of the same incident. The accident occurred at the intersection of Trenton Road and Forsythia Drive South in Levittown, Bucks County. Mr. Lopa and Ms. McGee were approaching the intersection from opposite directions on Trenton Road. As Mr. Lopa proceeded on his motorcycle through the intersection, he was struck by the car driven by Ms. McGee, as it made a left turn. The car was owned by Charles McGee. The accident occurred at dusk.

After a non-jury trial, the Honorable William Hart Rufe, III, found that Mr. Lopa was negligent because his motorcycle headlight was not illuminated so that he was not properly visible. In addition, Judge Rufe found Ms. McGee was negligent because there was sufficient light for her to have seen Mr. Lopa if she had looked carefully and properly. Then, applying the Comparative Negligence Act, 42 Pa.C.S. § 7102, Judge Rufe held that fifty percent of the causal negligence was attributable to Mr. Lopa and fifty percent attributable to Ms. McGee. Having made this assessment, Judge Rufe then found for Maureen and Charles McGee on Mr. Lopa's claim, and for Mr. Lopa on Mr. McGee's claim. Thus, neither party was awarded recovery from the other.

Mr. Lopa filed post-trial motions and amended post-trial motions requesting the trial court to mold the judgment to the findings of fact or to enter a judgment non obstante veredicto. The trial court denied these motions. It is from this denial that Mr. Lopa appeals. Mr. Lopa raises the following issues for our review: (1) should the trial court reapportion liability under the doctrine of comparative negligence where the apportionment of liability does not logically flow from the trier's findings of fact; (2) should the trial court grant a judgment N.O.V. when, under the doctrine of comparative negligence, the apportionment of liability does not logically flow from the trier's findings of fact; and (3) under the Pennsylvania Comparative Negligence Act, 42 Pa.C.S. § 7102, is the appellant entitled to recover from the appellees.

In responding to the first issue Mr. Lopa raises on appeal, we note, as the trial court did, that in *Burns v. City of Philadelphia*, 350 Pa.Super. 615, 504 A.2d 1321 (1986), we enunciated the standard of review to be applied in reviewing a trial court's apportionment of negligence under the Comparative Negligence Act. We stated that "the standard to be applied is not whether the court would have come to a different conclusion, but whether there are 'evidentiary circumstances or incontrovertible facts of such weight as to convince the court that an injustice has been done.'"

Mr. Lopa does not dispute the trial court's findings of fact; rather, he argues that the only logical conclusion that flows from them is that Ms. McGee was more negligent than he was. We disagree with this contention. The facts as found by the trial court can undoubtedly support the trial court's apportionment of negligence between the parties. The trial court stated: "Although [Ms. McGee] did not maintain a careful and proper lookout, had [Mr. Lopa] been driving with his motorcycle headlight illuminated, he would have been more visible to [Ms. McGee]. In short, we find that the negligence of [Mr. Lopa] and [Ms. McGee] were substantial contributing factors to the accident and that [Ms. McGee] established [Mr. Lopa's] contributory negligence to be fifty percent. Thus we see no injustice in finding [Mr. Lopa] fifty percent negligent." We are unable to ascertain any valid reason that would support our overturning the trial court's apportionment of negligence.

Mr. Lopa argues that the trial court improperly denied his motion for judgment N.O.V. since its apportionment of liability under the doctrine of comparative negligence does not logically flow from its findings of fact. In reviewing a trial court's denial of a motion for judgment notwithstanding the verdict, we must view the evidence in the light most favorable to the verdict winner, resolving all doubts in his favor and giving him the benefit of every reasonable inference arising from the evidence. Furthermore, it is well established that a judgment notwithstanding the verdict should be entered only in a clear case, when the facts are such that no two reasonable people could fail to agree that the verdict was improper. Mr. Lopa does not contest the trial court's findings of fact. Therefore, since we find no error in the trial court's apportionment of liability based on its findings of fact, we refuse to overturn the court's denial of Mr. Lopa's motion for judgment N.O.V.

Mr. Lopa also objects to the trial court's determination that because he was fifty-percent negligent, he was barred from recovery. Pennsylvania's Comparative Negligence statute states as follows: a) General rule. -- In all actions brought to recover damages for negligence resulting in death or injury to person or property, the fact that the plaintiff may have been guilty of contributory negligence shall not bar a recovery by the plaintiff or his legal representative where such negligence was not greater than the causal negligence of the defendant or defendants against whom recovery is sought, but any damages sustained by the plaintiff shall be diminished in proportion to the amount of negligence attributed to the plaintiff. 42 Pa.C.S. § 7102. Applying the plain wording of the statute, recovery is barred only when a plaintiff is more negligent than the defendant or defendants. Since Mr. Lopa was fifty percent negligent and Ms. McGee was fifty percent negligent, Mr. Lopa's negligence was not greater than the causalnegligence of Ms. McGee. Accordingly, we find that Mr. Lopa is entitled to recover fifty-percent of his damages. See also *Deitrick v. Karnes*, 329 Pa.Super. 372, 382, 478 A.2d 835, 840 (1984) (actual damages diminished by fifty percent to reflect appellant's causal negligence).

In accordance with the foregoing discussion, we reverse the order of the trial court and remand this case so that damages can be assessed and then properly apportioned between the parties pursuant to the findings of negligence made by the trial court. Jurisdiction is relinquished.

Strict Liability: When is a product "defective?" Does misuse of a product bar recovery?

The initial "revolution" in product liability cases was the expansion of contract principles into tort law. This was brought about by a series of cases that held that there were certain expressed and implied warranties made by the manufacturer to the consumer public. That revolution (flying directly in the face of the long time warning -- "caveat emptor") was soon supplemented by the the promulgation of Section 402(a) of the *Restatement of Torts*, making a manufacturer strictly liable for defects in its products. The elimination of the need to prove negligence of the defendant is an obvious boon to the plaintiff.

The following Pennsylvania case explores what proof must be supplied by the plaintiff, and what types of defenses are available to the manufacturer.

Berkebile v. Brantly Helicopter Corporation
462 Pa. 83 (1975)

Chief Justice Jones wrote the opinion for the court.

This case is before us on a grant of allocatur. The Superior Court reversed a verdict for the defendant-appellant in the trial court. We affirm.

Cloyd Berkebile was killed on July 9, 1962 when the helicopter he was piloting crashed while in climbing flight. The executrix wife brought this wrongful death and survival action against Brantly Helicopter Corporation, the manufacturer of the helicopter. The plaintiff relied upon the theory of strict liability. Restatement (Second) of Torts, § 402A. Several significant issues of importance in the growing area of strict liability recovery are presented in this multifaceted appeal. To avoid further confusion we find it necessary to clarify the concepts of strict liability under Pennsylvania law.

Brantly manufactured the small, two-person, B-2 model helicopter in October of 1961. Addressing itself to the general aviation market, the advertising described the helicopter as "safe, dependable," not "tricky to operate," and one that "beginners and professional pilots alike agree . . . is easy to fly." Brantly had experienced some difficulties in designing its rotor blades and autorotation in the development stage and modified the system to some degree prior to its distribution. In January, 1962, Mr. Berkebile, a businessman, purchased the helicopter from defendant's distributor. Mr. Berkebile flew alone on July 9, and while in climbing flight the seven-foot outboard section of one of the three main rotor blades separated. The helicopter crashed on a wooded hillside, killing Mr. Berkebile.

Plaintiff proposed four grounds for recovery at the second trial: (1) The design of the rotor system of the helicopter was defective because the average pilot had insufficient time to place the helicopter in autorotation in an emergency power failure in climbing flight; (2) The rotor blade was defectively manufactured and designed; (3) The defendant rendered the helicopter defective as a result of the inadequate warnings regarding the possible risks and inherent limitations of one of the systems of the helicopter; and (4) The defendant misrepresented the safety of the helicopter in its advertising brochures.

The defendant, denying the existence of any defective condition in its product, theorized that the helicopter's rotor blade had fractured due to an abnormal use brought about by power failure resulting from fuel exhaustion, followed by a failure on decedent's part to push down the collective pitch in time to go into autorotation and to effect a proper emergency landing.

Plaintiff contends on appeal that the trial court erred in charging the jury on the law to be applied to these facts and erred in several of its evidentiary rulings. A review of the record and of the court's charge in particular, when taken as a whole, demonstrates a basic confusion concerning the principles of strict liability in torts. Despite the diligent efforts of the trial judge to conform his charge to the law, this case has been tried twice and, regretfully, must be tried for the third time. Although we have recognized strict liability recovery since our decision in *Webb v. Zern*, 422 Pa. 424, 220 A.2d 853 (1966), it is apparent that the lack of clearly articulated standards has generated much misinterpretation.

The law of products liability developed in response to changing societal concerns over the relationship between the consumer and the seller of a product. The increasing complexity of the manufacturing and distributional process placed upon the injured plaintiff a nearly impossible burden of proving negligence where, for policy reasons, it was felt that a seller should be responsible for injuries caused by defects in his products. See Restatement (Second) of Torts § 402A, comment, c. We therefore held in *Webb v. Zern*, supra, that the seller of a product would be responsible for injury caused by his defective product even if he had exercised all possible care in its design, manufacture and distribution. We emphasized the principle of liability without fault most recently by stating that the seller is "effectively the guarantor of his product's safety," in *Salvador v. Atlantic Steel Boiler Co.*, 457 Pa. 24, 32, 319 A.2d 903, 907 (1974).

"Our courts have determined that a manufacturer by marketing and advertising his product impliedly represents that it is safe for its intended use. We have decided that no current societal interest is served by permitting the manufacturer to place a defective article in the stream of commerce and then to avoid responsibility for damages caused by the defect."

Strict liability requires, in substance, only two elements of requisite proof: the need to prove that the product was defective, and the need to prove that the defect was a proximate cause of the plaintiff's injuries. Thus, the plaintiff cannot recover if he proves injury from a product absent proof of defect, such as developing diabetic shock from eating sugar or becoming intoxicated from drinking whiskey. Neither can plaintiff recover by proving a defect in the product absent proof of causation, as where plaintiff sustains eye injury while not wearing defective safety glasses. Also, plaintiff must prove that the defect causing the injury existed at the time the product left the seller's hands; the seller is not liable if a safe product is made unsafe by subsequent changes. The trial court correctly identified these as pertinent issues in a strict liability case.

The crucial difference between strict liability and negligence is that the existence of due care, whether on the part of seller or consumer, is irrelevant. The seller is responsible for injury caused by his defective product even if he "has exercised all possible care in the preparation and sale of his product." Restatement (Second) of Torts, § 402A(2)(a). As we declared in *Salvador*, supra, 457 Pa. at 32, 319 A.2d at 907, the seller "may not preclude an injured plaintiff's recovery by forcing him to prove negligence in the manufacturing process." What the seller is not permitted to do directly, we will not allow him to do indirectly by injecting negligence concepts into strict liability theory. In attempting to articulate the definition of "defective condition" and to define the issue of proximate cause, the trial court here unnecessarily and improperly injected negligence principles into this strict liability case.

Section 402A recognizes liability without fault and properly limits such liability to defective products. The seller of a product is not responsible for harm caused by such inherently dangerous products as whiskey or knives that despite perfection in manufacture, design or distribution, can cause injury. See Restatement (Second) of Torts, § 402A, comment i. At first glance, however, it would appear that the section does impose a contradictory burden of proof in that the defect also be "unreasonably dangerous." An examination of comment i indicates that the purpose of the drafters of the clause was to differentiate those products which are by their very nature unsafe but not defective from those which can truly be called defective. The late Dean Prosser, the reporter of the Restatement (Second) of Torts, has suggested that the only purpose for the clause was to foreclose any argument that the seller of a product with inherent possibilities for harm would become "automatically responsible for all the harm that such things do in the world." Prosser, Strict Liability to the Consumer in California, 18 Hast.L.J. 9, 23 (1926). Commentators and courts, attempting to define "defective condition" have suggested tests based upon the negligence-oriented "reasonable man" that have further diluted the strict liability concept. The purpose of the "unreasonably dangerous" clause would appear to be best served by its inclusion in the issue of proximate cause. Those courts in the van-guard of products liability law, in doing away with this distinction, have adopted this analysis. The California Supreme Court, after reviewing the purpose of the "unreasonably dangerous" clause, said: "The result of the limitation . . . has not been merely to prevent the seller from becoming an insurer of his products with respect to all harm generated by their use. Rather, it has burdened the injured plaintiff with proof of an element which rings of negligence. As a result, if, in view of the trier of fact, the 'ordinary consumer' would have expected the defective condition of a product, the seller is not strictly liable, regardless of the expectations of the injured plaintiff. . . ."

"We recognize that the words 'unreasonably dangerous' may . . . serve the beneficial purpose of preventing the seller from being treated as the insurer of its products. However, we think that such protective end is attained by the necessity of proving that there was a defect in the manufacture or design of the product, and that such defect was a proximate cause of the injuries."

We hold today that the "reasonable man" standard in any form has no place in a strict liability case. The salutary purpose of the "unreasonably dangerous" qualification is to preclude the seller's liability where it cannot be said that the product is defective; this purpose can be met by requiring proof of a defect. To charge the jury or permit argument concerning the reasonableness of a consumer's or seller's actions and knowledge, even if merely to define "defective condition" undermines the policy considerations that have led us to hold in *Salvador* that the manufacturer is effectively the guarantor of his product's safety. The plaintiff must still prove that there was a defect in the product and that the defect caused his injury; but if he sustains this burden, he will have proved that as to him the product was unreasonably dangerous. It is therefore unnecessary and improper to charge the jury on "reasonableness."

The trial court further confused the standards of strict liability in its charge on proximate cause. The court charged that, in order for it to be said that a defect caused plaintiff's injury, "such a consequence, under all the surrounding circumstances of the case, must have been foreseeable by the seller." To require foreseeability is to require the manufacturer to use due care in preparing his product. In strict liability, the manufacturer is liable even if he has exercised all due care. Restatement (Second) of Torts, § 402(A)(2)(a). Foreseeability is not a test of proximate cause; it is a test of negligence. Because the seller is liable in strict liability regardless of any negligence, whether he could have foreseen a particular injury is irrelevant in a strict liability case. In either negligence or strict liability, once the negligence or defective product is shown, the actor is responsible for all the unforeseen consequences thereof no matter how remote, which follow in a natural sequence of events.

The trial court further erred in charging the jury separately on the issue of "abnormal use." On this issue the court charged in part: "The defendant is not liable if the product is used in an abnormal manner, or in a way in which it was not designed to be used. . . . If you take a helicopter and use it abnormally . . ., and such improper use was the proximate cause of the accident, that does not make the helicopter defective. . . . It must be used normally and properly in order for it to be defective and dangerous. . . . If you push the collective lever down and go into autorotation within the necessary time, then you are using it normally, but if you do not do it then you are not using it normally." On plaintiff's theory that the helicopter was designed defectively in that there was not enough time for the average pilot to effect autorotation safely, the question of "necessary time" to go into autorotation was the plaintiff's entire case. Under this theory, plaintiff agreed that the decedent did not achieve autorotation but argued that this was because of the defect in that system's design. When the trial judge drew the factual and legal conclusions for the jury that if plaintiff's decedent did not place the helicopter in autorotation there could be no recovery, it was tantamount to his directing a verdict against plaintiff on this theory. Such charge was error.

The evidence such as was introduced by the defense in this case under the guise of "abnormal use" was admissible but for a different purpose. Plaintiff must prove a defect existing in the product at the time the product left the seller's hands and he must prove proximate cause. If the seller can prove the defect arose from use after sale he would not be liable. Plaintiff contended that the blade fractured because of a defect in manufacture; defendant's contention that the blade fractured from impact with the "stops" rebutted the contention of this defect. Plaintiff contended the autorotation system was defective because it gave a pilot insufficient time to activate it. The autorotation system is a safety device existing for the sole purpose of preventing a crash in the event of engine failure for any reason. The reason the engine failed is irrelevant. Even defendant's argument that decedent was flying without gas, would be no "abnormal use." The autorotation system only comes into use in the event of engine failure for whatever reason it may be. Nor can it be said that the failure of decedent to go into autorotation

"within the necessary time" rebuts the contention that the autorotation system was defective in not allowing sufficient time for its activation. What constitutes "necessary time" is the key to the issue of the defect. For example, if defendant showed that an average pilot required one second to achieve autorotation and also showed that this helicopter gave decedent one second to achieve autorotation in climbing flight, he would rebut the contention of this defect. Whether decedent actually attempted autorotation is relevant to the issue of causation. If the jury were to conclude, for example, that a non-defective system would allow two seconds for autorotation and that the decedent did not attempt autorotation for three seconds; even if a defect was shown, it could not have been the proximate cause of the crash. In conclusion, evidence which would be admissible in a negligence case to prove "abnormal use" is admissible in a strict liability case only for the purpose of rebutting the plaintiff's contentions of defect and proximate cause. It is not properly submitted to the jury as a separate defense.

The trial court's charge on "abnormal use" permitted the jury to conclude that an alleged failure on decedent's part to determine the amount of gas available for flight precluded plaintiff's recovery on any theory. A plaintiff cannot be precluded from recovery in a strict liability case because of his own negligence. He is precluded from recovery only if he knows of the specific defect eventually causing his injury and voluntarily proceeds to use the product with knowledge of the danger caused by the defect. Furthermore, a finding of assumption of risk must be based on the individual's own subjective knowledge, not upon the objective knowledge of a "reasonable man." Such a defense can be charged upon by the court only if there is evidence introduced by defendant that the decedent knew of the specific defect causing his death and appreciated the danger it involved before using the aircraft.

A "defective condition" is not limited to defects in design or manufacture. The seller must provide with the product every element necessary to make it safe for use. One such element may be warnings and/or instructions concerning use of the product. A seller must give such warning and instructions as are required to inform the user or consumer of the possible risks and inherent limitations of his product. Restatement (Second) of Torts § 402A, comment h. If the product is defective absent such warnings, and the defect is a proximate cause of the plaintiff's injury, the seller is strictly liable without proof of negligence.

"Comment h to the section [402-A] makes it clear that a product, as to which adequate warning of danger involved in its use is required, sold without such warning is in a 'defective condition.'"

In the instant case, the warnings of the dangers and instructions for flying the B-2 are contained in the Rotorcraft Flight Manual and in the cockpit placard. There is no specific warning as to the time needed to get into autorotation, and there is no direction or warning with respect to "Engine Failure in Climbing Flight." There are, however, directions to the pilot to lower the collective pitch lever in case of engine failure; that autorotation should be implemented at no less than 300 rotor RPM; and, that failure to comply "may result in damage to the outer blades."

The question for the jury concerning warnings was whether the warnings appearing in the flight manual and the cockpit placard were sufficient to make Mr. Berkebile aware of the dangers of power failure and delayed autorotation, and whether said warnings adequately conveyed the urgency of the situation and the need to react almost instantaneously. If the jury determines that the helicopter was in a defective condition by the failure to provide sufficient warnings and directions for use, the seller is liable for all harm caused thereby.

It must be emphasized that the test of the necessity of warnings or instructions is not to be governed by the reasonable man standard. In the strict liability context we reject standards based upon what the "reasonable" consumer could be expected to know, or what the "reasonable" manufacturer could be expected to "foresee" about the consumers who use his product. Compare *Maize v. Atlantic Refining Co.*, 352 Pa. 51, 41 A.2d 850 (1945); *Thomas v. Avron Products Co.*, 424 Pa. 365, 227 A.2d 897 (1967) (negligence actions where we recognize the affirmative duty of a seller to give warnings but base it on the reasonable man standard). Rather, the sole question here is whether the seller accompanied his product with sufficient instructions and warnings so as to make his product safe. This is for the jury to determine. The necessity and adequacy of warnings in determining the existence of a defect can and should be considered with a view to all the evidence. The jury should view the relative degrees of danger associated with use of the product since a greater degree of danger requires a greater degree of protection. E. g., *Thomas v. Avron Products, Inc.*, supra. In this case, plaintiff argued that the most serious emergency in the event of power failure was in climbing flight, since there would be the greatest rotor decay and thus least amount of time available for activating the autorotation system. In cruise flight, rotor decay upon engine failure is the least serious emergency and thus gives the greatest amount of time in which to achieve autorotation. In hovering flight, rotor decay is in an intermediate amount. Defendant's flight manual for the helicopter's operation gives the maximum detailed warnings in regard to the minimum emergency (cruise) and the minimum warnings (none) in the maximum emergency situation (climb). One study done by defendant and specifically excluded by the trial court showed a concern on the part of defendant's chief test pilot regarding rapid rotor decay in climbing flight. If the jury determined this was an insufficient warning, the product would be defective even if the product had been perfectly designed and manufactured. The jury would have to go on to conclude that the defective condition was the proximate cause of decedent's death before there would be recovery. As an example, the failure of a seller of ordinary knives to warn of dangerous propensities can not be considered the proximate cause of a consumer's cutting his finger since the potentiality of its danger is generally known and recognized. It is sometimes necessary to consider whether any warnings are required. Here the only issue was the adequacy of warnings since FAA regulations and the defendant's own inclusion of some warnings in regard to the autorotation system demonstrated the necessity of warnings. The issue of necessity and adequacy of warnings and instructions for use must also be considered in light of any contradictory promotional activities on the part of the seller.

Where warnings or instructions are required to make a product nondefective, it is the duty of the manufacturer to provide such warnings in a form that will reach the ultimate consumer and inform of the risks and inherent limits of the product. The duty to provide a non-defective product is non-delegable.

The trial judge refused to charge the jury separately on the issue of misrepresentation under Restatement (Second) of Torts, § 402B, stating that the advertising claims were part of the warning issue under Section 402A rather than a separate issue under Section 402B. Plaintiff contended that brochures stating that "you are assured of a safe, dependable helicopter" and that the helicopter was "easy to operate" were a misrepresentation of material facts concerning the character or quality of a chattel. Misrepresentation must be distinguished from mere "puffing." We find these statements do not constitute misrepresentations of material fact.

The order of the Superior Court is affirmed.

Social Host Liability I: Are social hosts liable when their adult guests drink too much and harm others in automobile accidents?

Many states, including Pennsylvania, have statutes called Dram Shop Acts which permit plaintiffs who are injured by drunk drivers to recover against defendants who have sold liquor to visibly customers under circumstances where a reasonable person would not have sold that customer any more alcoholic beverages. The Pennsylvania law does not permit a cause of action for the intoxicated customer himself. In any event, Dram Shop statutes apply exclusively to situations in which alcohol is sold in a tavern or restaurant. They do not apply in social situations such as parties at private homes or businesses. But drunk drivers may become just as intoxicated when liquor is not sold, but provided in a social setting.

The question of social host liability, therefore, was left for the courts to address. In *Klein v. Raysinger* the Pennsylvania Supreme Court ruled that social hosts could not be held responsible when their adult guests drank too much and caused harm to others because it was the drinking of the alcohol, not the serving of the alcohol, which caused the harm to the injured plaintiff.

Klein v. Raysinger et al.
504 Pa. 141 (1983)

Justice McDermott wrote the opinion for the court.

. . . Appellant in No. 44, Michael Klein, filed a personal injury action against Mark Raysinger and others, as a result of an automobile accident. Appellants in No. 94, Myron and Phillip Klein, filed personal injury actions against Mark Raysinger and others (including Michael Klein, as the driver of the vehicle in which they were travelling); and Myron Klein as the Administrator of the Estate of Shirley M. Klein, filed a personal injury action, a wrongful death action, and a survivors action against Mark Raysinger and others (including Michael Klein, as the driver of the vehicle in which Shirley M. Klein was travelling). As part of these actions the Kleins instituted suit against Mr. and Mrs. William Gilligan and their son Michael Gilligan, who were charged with negligence in serving one or more alcoholic beverages to Raysinger at a time when the latter was visibly intoxicated.

In each case the Gilligans filed preliminary objections in the nature of a demurrer. In both instances the preliminary objections were sustained by the Court of Common Pleas of Montgomery County. On appeal the Superior Court affirmed. Petitions for allowance of appeal were filed and granted, and the cases were consolidated for our review. Upon demurrer, a reviewing court must regard as true all well pleaded facts and reasonable inferences deducible therefrom. Given this standard we are confronted with the following facts: On or about May 8, 1978, Michael Klein and his family were driving on the Pennsylvania Turnpike when they were struck in the rear by a vehicle which was driven by Mark Raysinger. Prior to the collision Raysinger had been a patron of the Neptune Inn, where he had consumed an undisclosed amount of alcohol. Prior thereto, Mr. Raysinger had been served beer and other alcoholic beverages at the home of the Gilligans. It is alleged that Raysinger was visibly intoxicated at the time he was served by the Gilligans, and that it was known at the time that Raysinger would be driving. As a consequence, appellants' claim that the Gilligans are liable in negligence for the injuries they sustained in the accident.

Although the lower courts relied in part on *Manning v. Andy*, 454 Pa. 237, 310 A.2d 75 (1973), this case is in reality one of first impression in this jurisdiction. Appellants are requesting this Court to recognize a new cause of action in negligence, against a social host who serves alcohol to a visibly intoxicated person, whom the host knows, or should know, intends to drive a motor vehicle. A number of other jurisdictions have considered this issue, and our research, aided by the able briefs of counsel for both appellants and appellees, reveal only two jurisdictions in which a cause of action in negligence has actually been recognized against a social host serving alcoholic beverages to a person past the legal drinking age: California and New Jersey. In

Coulter v. Superior Court of San Mateo, 21 Cal.3rd 144, 145 Cal.Rptr. 534, 577 P.2d 669 (1979) the California Supreme Court held that under modern negligence law "a social host who furnishes alcoholic beverages to an obviously intoxicated person, under circumstances which create a reasonably foreseeable risk of harm to others, may be held legally accountable to those third parties who are injured when that harm occurs." However, this cause of action was very short lived, as the California Legislature expressly abrogated this holding by enacting §1714 of the California Civil Code. In New Jersey, a trial court in ruling on a motion for summary judgment, ignored the California Legislature's actions and relied upon *Coulter*, supra, in holding that a social host was liable for furnishing alcoholic beverages to an obviously intoxicated person. *Figuly v. Knoll*, 185 N.J.Super., 477, 449 A.2d 564 (1982). However, the case was never appealed, and the issue has yet to be addressed by an appellate court in that jurisdiction.

A third jurisdiction, Oregon, has in the past, indicated a willingness to entertain a cause of action in negligence. However, the facts of that case involved the service of a minor, a fact which we find significant. In this regard, we note that there are no reported Oregon cases finding common law social host liability in the situation where an adult guest was the consumer of alcohol. Also, similar to the California Legislature, the Oregon legislative body took the issue out of the hands of the Courts, by legislatively defining the possible cause of actions. While it is true that some other jurisdictions have recognized a common law action against a social host, they have done so only in the limited situations where an adult host has served intoxicants to a minor; or the individual served was under a special disability. But for the above noted exceptions no other jurisdiction has been willing to extend liability to the social host who has served intoxicants to his adult guests.

Thus, the great weight of authority supports the view that in the case of an ordinary able bodied man it is the consumption of the alcohol, rather than the furnishing of the alcohol, which is the proximate cause of any subsequent occurrence. This is in accord with the recognized rule at common law. We agree with this common law view, and consequently hold that there can be no liability on the part of a social host who serves alcoholic beverages to his or her adult guests.

Therefore, we affirm the order of the Superior Court and remand this case to the Court of Common Pleas of Montgomery County for proceedings not inconsistent with this opinion.

ROBERTS, Chief Justice, dissenting.

Section 493(1) of the Liquor Code makes it "unlawful . . . for any licensee or the board, or any employe, servant or agent of such licensee, or the board, or any other person, to sell, furnish or give any liquor . . . or to permit any liquor . . . to be sold, furnished or given, to any person visibly intoxicated . . . ." 47 P.S. § 4-493(1). The use of the language "any other person" clearly manifests a legislative intent to impose an obligation upon all persons to refrain from furnishing alcoholic beverages to

visibly intoxicated persons in circumstances which create a reasonably foreseeable risk of harm to third parties. In light of this legislatively imposed standard of conduct, the complaint in trespass, which seeks recovery for injuries allegedly caused by the serving of liquor by a social host to a visibly intoxicated guest, should be reinstated. Accordingly, I dissent, would reverse the order of the Superior Court, and would allow the case to proceed to trial.

LARSEN, Justice, dissenting.

I dissent and in support thereof quote in full the late Mr. Justice Manderino's dissent. . .in *Manning v. Andy*, 454 Pa. 237, 242-50, 310 A.2d 75, 77-81 (1973): "Dissenting Opinion by Mr. Justice Manderino: I must dissent. The majority establishes a new immunity in tort law previously unheard of in the decisions of this Court. Ironically, the pronouncement of this new immunity takes place at a time when most courts, including this one, have been most diligent in striking down old immunities which deprived citizens of their day in court. Liquor dispensers who act negligently and cause harm should not be given any special privilege of immunity from liability. We do not give such immunity to automobile drivers. We do not give such immunity to drug dispensers. We do not give such immunity to homeowners. Once there was a special immunity for charities -- but no longer. Once there was a special immunity for municipalities -- but no longer. Once there was a special immunity for parents -- but no longer. The creation of a new class and the establishment of a new immunity makes history -- bad history. The combination of an intoxicated person and an automobile causes death and serious harm to many each day. Such victims are entitled to their day in court. That day in court is guaranteed by the declaration of rights in the Pennsylvania Constitution which states that '. . . every man for any injury done him in his lands, goods, person or reputation shall have remedy by due course of law, and right and justice administered without sale, denial or delay.' Pa. Const. art. I, § 11. This case is at an early stage. The appellant has alleged that he was harmed by the negligent conduct of the appellees. He is entitled to an opportunity to prove his allegations according to ancient principles of tort law. We have no right to deprive him of that opportunity.

The trial court erred in reasoning that a trespass action in negligence must state a cause of action under a statute. The courts may -- or may not -- look to a statute for a controlling or guiding standard of due care to be applied in a negligence action. Indeed, in Pennsylvania, the overwhelming number of trespass actions in negligence are unrelated to any statute. Simply stated, negligent conduct is the want of due care which a reasonable man would exercise under the circumstances. If such negligent conduct is the legal cause of harm, a cause of action is stated. A demurrer can only be sustained if it is certain that no recovery is permitted. Any doubt must be resolved against sustaining the demurrer. The factual allegations in the complaint must be examined to determine whether reasonable men might infer a lack of due care by the appellees which legally caused harm to the appellant. It is alleged that the appellees furnished or supplied intoxicating liquors or beverages to Walters and continued to furnish such intoxicating liquors or beverages to Walters when he was in a state of visible intoxication. Might not reasonable men infer that there was a want of due care which the appellees should have exercised under the circumstances? Can we declare as a matter of law that it is reasonable conduct (due care) to serve intoxicating liquors to a person who is in a state of visible intoxication? I think the question answers itself. In acting, a person is assumed to know what the reasonable man in the society knows. The common knowledge of the reasonable man certainly includes information concerning the effects of alcoholic beverages and the consequences of intoxication on human behavior. From the alleged facts, reasonable men could infer negligent conduct by the appellees.

Even though the complaint is sufficient in that reasonable men might conclude that the appellees engaged in negligent conduct, there is a further inquiry which must be made. Would the facts in the complaint permit reasonable men to infer that the appellees' negligent conduct was the legal cause of harm to the plaintiff. Since the facts alleged obviously permit an inference of causation, the only possible question as to legal cause is whether the intervening act of someone, other than the appellee, can be declared, as a matter of law, to be a superseding cause, relieving the appellee of liability. It cannot be said that the intervening act of Walters, the alleged intoxicated employee, was, as a matter of law, a superseding cause of appellant's injuries, relieving the appellees of liability even if the appellees' conduct involved a want of due care which caused harm to the appellant. The intervening negligent act of a third person (Walters) is not a superseding cause of harm to another (the appellant) which the actors' (appellees) negligent conduct is a substantial factor in bringing about, if (a) the (appellees) should have realized that (Walters) might so act or (b) (Walters') act was not highly extraordinary, or (c) the act of (Walters) is a normal consequence of a situation created by the actors' (appellees) conduct and the manner in which it is done is not extraordinarily negligent. It cannot be said as a matter of law that the intervening negligent act of an intoxicated person (a) should not have been anticipated, or (b) was so highly extraordinary, or (c) was not a normal consequence of the intoxication allegedly caused by the appellees' conduct. Thus, the complaint cannot be dismissed on the legal cause issue. During the trial, of course, the parties will have an opportunity to present a complete detailed picture of all of the circumstances under which the parties allegedly acted. Such details are not required at the complaint stage. The appellant is not required to plead his proof.

The Liquor Code aside in this case, I cannot say, as a matter of law, that the complaint fails to state a cause of action. In *Jardine v. Upper Darby Lodge No. 1973, Inc.*, 413 Pa. 626, 631, 198 A.2d 550, 553 (1964), this Court said: 'The first prime requisite to de-intoxicate one who has, [*153] because of alcohol, lost control over his reflexes, judgment and sense of responsibility to others, is to stop pouring alcohol into him. This is a duty which everyone owes to society and to law entirely apart from any statute.' Since the complaint in this case alleges facts from which reasonable men might conclude that the appellees' negligent conduct was the legal cause of harm to the appellant, a cause of action is stated. We look to section 493(1) of the Liquor Code, to consider (1) whether the Code establishes a standard of conduct for persons such as the appellees, and (2) if it does, whether that standard should control on the question of due care in this case.

Section 493(1) of the Liquor Code, does provide a standard of conduct for persons such as the appellees in this case. By its very terms, the statute covers unlawful conduct, not only for licensees (including their employees, servants and agents) but also for any other person. . . The meaning of any other person was accurately explained in *Commonwealth v. Randall*, 183 Pa. Superior Ct. 603, 615-16, 133 A.2d 276, 281-82 (1957), cert. denied, 355 U.S. 954, 2 L.Ed.2d 530, 78 S.Ct. 539 (1958): 'Secs. 491, 492 and 493, 47 P.S. §§ 4-491, 4-492, 4-493, set forth in separate paragraphs the "Unlawful acts relative to liquor alcohol and liquor licensees" the "Unlawful acts relative to malt or brewed beverages and licensees," and the "Unlawful acts relative to liquor, malt and brewed beverages and licensees." We deem it noteworthy that the legislature carefully differentiated between "persons," "licensees," "manufacturers," etc., in its enumeration of prohibited acts. In some instances all "persons" are prohibited from doing certain things; in other instances the prohibition applies only to licensees of various types or their "servants, agents or employees" etc. This is a clear indication that the legislature intended that some of the prohibitions were to apply to all persons while others were to apply only to "licensees", or "their servants, agents or employees". ' It is particularly significant that sec. 403 sets forth 25 prohibited acts relative to liquor, malt and brewed beverages, and that the words "or any other person" are included only in the subparagraph which makes it unlawful to sell, furnish or give any liquor or malt or brewed beverages to minors. It is significant also that minors are not the only class of persons to whom liquor or malt or brewed beverages may not be sold, furnished or given. Visibly intoxicated persons, insane persons, habitual drunkards, and persons of known intemperate habits are similarly protected. 'We think that the legislature in using the words "or any other person" deliberately selected these words in order to prohibit minors, visibly intoxicated persons, insane persons, habitual drunkards, and persons of known intemperate habits, from obtaining liquor, malt or brewed beverages, whether by purchase or gift, from licensees or any other persons . . . . If we were to restrict this section of the Act to "licensees" or their "servants, agents or employees," we would nullify the very purpose of the Act.' The reasoning of Randall, as to the meaning of any other person is indisputable. The Liquor Code defines person as ' . . . a natural person, association or corporation . . . .' Act of April 12, 1951, P.L. 90, art. I, § 102, as amended, 47 P.S. 1-102. Only by a gross distortion of the meaning of language can we interpret any other person to mean some but not all persons. 'When the words of a statute are clear and free from all ambiguity, the letter of it is not to be disregarded under the pretext of pursuing its spirit.' 1 P.S. § 1921(b) (1973). . .

The question remains whether that standard should be adopted as the standard of due care in this case.

'The court may adopt as the standard of conduct of a reasonable man the requirements of a legislative enactment or an administrative regulation whose purpose is found to be exclusively or in part (a) to protect a class of persons which includes the one whose interest is invaded, and (b) to protect the particular interest which is invaded, and (c) to protect that interest against the kind of harm which has resulted, and (d) to protect that interest against the particular hazard from which the harm results.' Restatement (Second) of Torts § 286 (1965).

A statute providing for criminal liability but not civil liability leaves a court free to accept or not accept the legislatively established standard of conduct for purposes of a tort action. '[T]he decision to adopt the standard is purely a judicial one, for the court to make. When the court does adopt the legislative standard, it is acting to further the general purpose which it finds in the legislation . . . .' Restatement (Second) of Torts, Explanatory Notes § 286, comment d at 26 (1965). The purpose of the Liquor Code is stated as follows: 'This act shall be deemed an exercise of the police power of the Commonwealth for the protection of the public welfare, health, peace and morals of the people of the Commonwealth and to prohibit forever the open saloon, and all of the provisions of this act shall be liberally construed for the accomplishment of this purpose.' Act of April 12, 1951, P.L. 90, art. I, § 104(a), 47 P.S. 1-104(a). The purposes of the Liquor Code are broadly stated for the protection of the public and in *Jardine v. Upper Darby Lodge No. 1973, Inc.*, 413 Pa. 626, 198 A.2d 550 (1964), this Court specifically held that one of the purposes of section 493(1) of the Liquor Code was to protect the interest of a third party injured as the result of the conduct of an intoxicated person. In light of the general purpose of the statutory enactment; the legislative standard of conduct is the standard of conduct required of a reasonable man in a negligence action. Violation of this statute is negligent conduct in itself. Section 493(1) of the Liquor Code does not create the cause of action in this case. The ordinary principles of negligence do that. By section 493(1) of the Liquor Code the legislature has established a standard of reasonable conduct from which no one can deviate without criminal liability. That same standard should apply in negligence.

The trial court expressed concern that there would be a flood of litigation in the courts if it were held that any person (as distinguished from licensees, their employees, servants or agents) could be held responsible for negligent conduct that caused harm to another as the result of furnishing liquor to a visibly intoxicated person. We recently answered that argument in *Ayala v. Philadelphia Board of Public Education*, 453 Pa. 584, 595-96, 305 A.2d 877, 882 (1973), by restating what this Court said on other occasions when faced with the flood of litigation argument. "We obviously do not accept the 'too much work to do' rationale. We place the responsibility exactly where it should be: not in denying relief to those who have been injured, but on the judicial machinery of the Commonwealth to fulfill its obligation to make itself available to litigants. Who is to say which class of aggrieved plaintiffs should be denied access to our courts because of speculation that the workload will be a burden? Certainly this Court is unwilling to allow such considerations to influence a determination whether a class of litigants will be denied or permitted to seek adjudication of its claims." The facts alleged in appellant's complaint are sufficient to state a cause of action. The trial court, therefore, erred in dismissing the complaint after sustaining the preliminary objections. The order of the trial court should be reversed and the matter remanded for further proceedings."

Social Host Liability II: Are social hosts liable when their minor guests drink too much and are injured in automobile accidents?

The Pennsylvania Supreme Court took a different approach, however, in the following case where the plaintiff was a minor who was injured in an auto accident after being served alcohol at his employer's Christmas party. Because the Pennsylvania Crimes Code prohibits an adult from serving alcohol to a minor, the Court ruled in favor of the plaintiff.

Note the two major differences between *Klein* and *Congini*: In *Klein*, the plaintiff was a <u>third party</u> who was injured by an <u>adult</u> intoxicated guest; In *Congini*, the plaintiff <u>was</u> the <u>guest</u> and was a <u>minor</u>. Note also that in ruling for Congini, the court emphasized that the social host "knowingly furnished intoxicants" to him.

Congini v. Portersville Valve Company
504 Pa. 157 (1983)

Justice McDermott wrote the opinion for the court.

This appeal arises from an action in trespass for personal injuries sustained by Mark Congini in an automobile accident which occurred on December 22, 1978. His parents instituted suit on his behalf, and on their own behalf, in the Court of Common Pleas of Lawrence County against the Portersville Valve Company (Portersville). The defendant filed preliminary objections in the nature of demurrer. The trial judge, the Honorable William R. Balph, sustained the preliminary objections and the Conginis' complaint was dismissed on August 18, 1980. On appeal the Superior Court affirmed, relying in part on our decision in *Manning v. Andy*, 454 Pa. 237, 310 A.2d 75 (1973). On demurrer we must accept as true all well pleaded facts and the reasonable inference therefrom. Thus for purposes of this appeal we are confronted with the following facts. At the time of the accident in question Mark Congini was eighteen (18) years of age and an employee of Portersville. On December 22, 1978 Portersville held a Christmas party for its employees at which alcoholic beverages were served. Mark attended the party and, as a result of consuming an undisclosed amount of alcohol, became intoxicated.

Mark's car was parked at Portersville plant, which was the scene of the party, and appellee, through one of its agents, had possession and custody of the car keys. Although Portersville's agent was aware of Mark's intoxicated condition, the keys were given to Mark upon his request so that he could drive from the plant to his home.

While Mark was operating the car on the highway, he drove it into the rear of another vehicle which was proceeding in the same direction. As a result of this accident Mark suffered multiple fractures and brain damage which have left him totally and permanently disabled.

In their appeal appellants have alleged several grounds of liability: first, that defendant was negligent in providing Mark with alcoholic beverages to the point that he became intoxicated; second, that defendant was negligent in surrendering the car keys to Mark, knowing that Mark was intoxicated and that he would drive; and third, that appellee, as a landowner, was negligent in breaching a duty owed to Mark as an invitee. Appellants have not alleged that appellee was a licensee of the Pennsylvania Liquor Control Board.

The first issue before us is similar to that raised in *Klein v. Raysinger*, decided this day at 504 Pa. 141, 470 A.2d 507 (1983), i.e., the extent to which a social host can be held liable for injuries sustained by his guest to whom he has served intoxicating liquors. This case, however, differs in two respects: that the guest here was a minor; and that the plaintiff here is the guest to whom the intoxicants were served, rather than a third person injured by a person who was served alcoholic beverages. As we note in *Klein*, our sister state jurisdictions are virtually unanimous in refusing to extend common law liability to an adult social host serving intoxicants to his adult guests. However, there is no such unanimity in cases where an adult host has knowingly served intoxicants to a minor.

In *Klein v. Raysinger*, supra,

we held that there exists no common law liability on the part of a social host for the service of intoxicants to his adult guests. In arriving at this decision we relied upon the common law rule that in the case of an ordinary able bodied man, it is the consumption of alcohol rather than the furnishing thereof, that is the proximate cause of any subsequent damage.

However, our legislature has made a legislative judgment that persons under twenty-one years of age are incompetent to handle alcohol. Under Section 6308 of the Crimes Code 18 Pa.C.S. § 6308, a person "less than 21 years of age" commits a summary offense if he "attempts to purchase, purchases, consumes, possesses or transports any alcohol, liquor or malt or brewed beverages." Furthermore, under Section 306 of the Crimes Code, 18 Pa.C.S.A. § 306, an adult who furnishes liquor to a minor would be liable as an accomplice to the same extent as the offending minor.

This legislative judgment compels a different result than *Klein*, for here we are not dealing with ordinary able bodied men. Rather, we are confronted with persons who are, at least in the eyes of the law, incompetent to handle the affects of alcohol. Section 286 of the Restatement of Torts Second provides: § 286. When Standard of Conduct Defined by Legislation or Regulation Will Be Adopted: The court may adopt as the standard of conduct of a reasonable man the requirements of a legislative enactment or an administrative regulation whose purpose is found to be exclusively or in part (a) to protect a class of persons which includes the one whose interest is invaded, and (b) to protect the particular interest which is invaded, and (c) to protect that interest against the kind of harm which has resulted, and (d) to protect that interest against the particular hazard from which the harm results. We have previously relied upon this Section and accepted it as an accurate statement of the law. Section 6308 of the Crimes Code represents an obvious legislative decision to protect both minors and the public at large from the perceived deleterious effects of serving alcohol to persons under twenty-one years of age. Thus, we find that defendants were negligent per se in serving alcohol to the point of intoxication to a person less than twenty-one years of age, and that they can be held liable for injuries proximately resulting from the minor's intoxication. Our inquiry, however, can not stop here. As noted above the plaintiff here was not an unwitting third party to the actor's negligence, but the person to whom the intoxicants were allegedly served. Nevertheless, for the purpose of deciding whether a cause of action exists, we see no valid distinction which would warrant a limitation on the action to third parties alone. Under our analysis, an actor's negligence exists in furnishing intoxicants to a class of persons legislatively determined to be incompetent to handle its effects. It is the person's service which forms the basis of the cause of action, not whether or not a putative plaintiff is entitled to recover. Resolution of this latter issue requires a fuller record than the one which we have on demurrer. We note, however, that under the scheme set up by this Court in *Kuhns v. Brugger*, 390 Pa. 331, 135 A.2d 395 (1957) an eighteen year old person is "presumptively capable of negligence." We further note that an eighteen year old is liable as an adult for the offenses which he commits, and that by knowingly consuming alcohol an eighteen year old is also guilty of a summary offense. Thus, although we recognize that an eighteen year old minor may state a cause of action against an adult social host who has knowingly served him intoxicants, the social host in turn may assert as a defense the minor's "contributory" negligence. Thereafter, under our Comparative Negligence Act 42 Pa.C.S. § 7102 it will remain for the fact finder to resolve whether the defendant's negligence was such as to allow recovery. Appellants have also asserted two separate issues, neither of which do we find meritorious. The first involves the alleged negligent entrustment of an automobile to one who is intoxicated. However, this cause of action has been recognized only in those situations where the person sought to be held liable was "the owner or other person responsible for its (automobile) use." Appellants have cited no cases which extend this liability to persons who were not the owner or otherwise responsible for the automobile in question. The appellee here had no right of control over Mark Congini's car, and we see no basis upon which to extend liability to the situation posited here. Finally, appellants have argued that the defendants breached a duty as a landowner to Mark Congini. The Superior Court refused to discuss this issue, as they found that it was not fairly raised by the pleadings. Since there was nowhere pleaded that Mark Congini was required by his employer to attend the party in question, it appears at most that he was a gratuitous licensee. To such a person Section 341 of the Restatement of Torts, Second provides: § 341. Activities Dangerous to Licensees A possessor of land is subject to liability to his licensees for physical harm caused to them by his failure to carry on his activities with reasonable care for their safety if, but only if, (a) he should expect that they will not discover or realize the danger, and (b) they do not know or have reason to know of the possessor's activities and of the risk involved. Appellants did not plead that Mark Congini was without knowledge of the possessor's activities, or of the risks involved in consuming alcoholic beverages. Indeed, it would have been impossible to contend that Mark Congini was ignorant of the appellee's activities, since that was the reason for his presence. Furthermore, appellant's injuries at most would seem to have resulted from "existent conditions upon the premises" (i.e., the availability of alcohol), as opposed to "any affirmative or 'active' negligence on [the defendant's] part." In such a case a possessor of land is not liable to a licensee in the absence of willful and wanton injury. Such liability was not pleaded by the appellants. We therefore, agree with the Superior Court that a cause of action under this theory was not stated. In light of appellee's potential liability as a social host, we reverse the order of the Superior Court and remand this case to the court of common pleas for proceeding not inconsistent with our opinion. As to appellants' other contentions, we affirm the order of the Superior Court.

Zappala, Justice, dissenting.

In *Klein v. Raysinger*, 504 Pa. 141, 470 A.2d 507 (1983), we held that no duty exists under the common law which would impose liability upon a social host who serves alcohol to an adult guest for conduct of the guest which results in injury to himself or to a third party. We recognized that it is the consumption of alcohol, rather than the furnishing of alcohol to an individual, which is the proximate cause of any subsequent occurrence. In the instant case, however, the majority opinion concludes that liability of a social host may arise from the act of furnishing alcohol to a minor and that such liability may extend to harm suffered by the minor. By adopting this legal premise, the majority today is effectively overruling *Klein*. The analysis employed by the majority is clearly inconsistent with that enunciated in *Klein*, and for that reason I must dissent.

The majority attempts to reconcile the inconsistency based upon a perceived public policy to protect minors and the public from the potentially harmful effects of alcohol. This public policy is gleaned from § 6308 of the Crimes Code which imposes criminal liability on a person under 21 who attempts to purchase, purchases, consumes, possesses or transports alcohol. Although the legislature may have determined that persons under 21 are incompetent to handle alcohol, as the majority suggests, it is evident that the legislature has defined the offense so as to render the minor culpable for his own conduct which violates the statute. A minor could not defend his conduct by demonstrating that an adult had furnished him with the alcohol.

Thus, the statute which the majority interprets as evincing a policy to protect minors does not shield them from their acts which contravene the statute.

The majority attempts to distinguish underage drinkers from those over 21 years by stating that minors are deemed incompetent to handle the effects of alcohol. This distinction is irrelevant, however, to the issue of whether a social host who furnishes alcohol to a minor may be held liable for injuries sustained by the minor or a third party as the result of the minor's actions. It is not the knowledge of a social host of the ability or inability of a guest to handle the effects of alcohol, or knowledge of a person's condition, which would give rise to a duty not to furnish alcohol to the guest. We declined to impose liability on that basis in *Klein*, when we refused to recognize a cause of action, urged by the Appellants therein, against a social host who serves alcohol to a visibly intoxicated person who the host knows, or should know, intends to drive a motor vehicle. I cannot agree, therefore, that liability should be imposed on a social host serving alcohol to a person under 21 based upon the rationale that minors are incompetent to handle alcohol. If it is consumption by an adult guest, rather than the furnishing of alcohol by a host, which is the proximate cause of subsequent occurrences, then it is not less compelling to conclude that it is a minor's voluntary consumption of alcohol which is the proximate cause of harm which results. I find it inconceivable that a minor or an innocent third party who suffers harm under the factual circumstances alleged in the instant case may assert a cause of action against the social host who has dispensed the alcohol, yet an innocent third party who suffers harm under the factual circumstances set forth in *Klein* would be precluded from asserting a similar cause of action. These inapposite results arise solely from the fortuitous circumstance of the age of the tortfeasor, rather than the conduct of the social host. I would hold, consistent with *Klein*, that no cause of action exists against a social host for providing alcohol to a guest under the facts alleged in this action. This matter is better left to legislative action than to judicial gymnastics.

Social Host Liability III: May a fraternity or university be held responsible when a minor consumes alcohol at a party and damages the property of another?

A slightly different set of facts in the next case involves the liability of a fraternity (national and/or local chapter) or a university where alcoholic beverages are consumed at a fraternity party and intoxicated students damages the property of a third party. Here the court distinguishes the facts from *Congini* primarily on the ground that the defendants did not "knowingly furnish" alcohol to the minor involved in the accident.

In this unfortunately common situation on college campuses, the minors consumed alcoholic beverages at a fraternity party: the Bucknell University chapter of Sigma Chi. The two intoxicated minor students then negligently started a fire which damaged the neighboring Lambda Chia Alpha fraternity The two students attempted to blame the national fraternity, the local chapter, and Bucknell University on the theory that these three were responsible for getting them intoxicated in the first place!

The trial court ruled that the national fraternity and the University were not social hosts under these facts and that while the local chapter may have been a social host, the fire damage to a neighboring property was not a foreseeable harm for which the chapter should be liable. The Superior Court agreed as to the national and the University, but reversed with regard to the local chapter, holding that such harm was a foreseeable risk of serving alcohol to minor students. The students appealed the dismissal of their claims against the national chapter and the University. In the following opinion the Supreme Court reviews its position in *Congini* and refuses to recognize a cause of action against the national fraternity or the University.

Alumni Association v. Sullivan et al.
572 A.2d 1209 (Supreme Court, 1990)

Chief Justice Nix delivered the opinion of the court.

The instant question under consideration in this appeal is whether a cause of action for negligence may be maintained against instant appellees for recovery of damages caused by an intoxicated minor to third parties absent any allegation that appellees served or furnished the alcoholic beverages to the minor. For the reasons that follow we agree that the complaint failed to set forth a valid cause of action against instant appellees and therefore affirm the order of the Superior Court.

On December 7, 1983, appellant Ronald C. Unterberger, an eighteen year old freshman at

Bucknell University, attended a party held in his freshman dormitory, Trax Hall, and a second party hosted by the Kappa Chapter of Sigma Chi Fraternity at their fraternity house. At both parties alcohol was served and was consumed openly by Unterberger. The owner of the neighboring fraternity house, Lambda Chi Alpha Fraternity, subsequently filed a claim against Unterberger and a companion, Van Kingsley Sullivan, alleging that the two had negligently caused or failed to control a fire in the Lambda Chi Alpha house which resulted in over $400,000 in property damage. Unterberger filed a complaint to join Bucknell University, the Kappa Chapter of Sigma Chi, and Sigma Chi Fraternity as additional defendants, alleging that they were negligent in providing him, a minor, with alcoholic beverages at the parties he attended. Appellant alleged that this negligence proximately resulted in the conduct which caused the fire.

The trial court sustained appellees' preliminary objections and dismissed appellant's complaint against all three parties. The trial court found that under our holding in *Congini v. Portersville Valve Co.*, 504 Pa. 157, 470 A.2d 515 (1983), appellees Sigma Chi and Bucknell were not social hosts who knowingly served intoxicants to a minor. The trial court further found that while Kappa Chapter may have been a social host, it was under no duty to protect against the unforeseeable risk of harm to the neighboring Lambda Chi Alpha house.

On appeal, the Superior Court affirmed the dismissal of the complaints against Bucknell and Sigma Chi. The court determined that an allegation that a defendant should have known alcohol was being served on its premises was insufficient to sustain a cause of action under *Congini*, supra, which hinges on the party having "knowingly furnished intoxicants to a [minor]." However, the dismissal of the complaint against Kappa Chapter was reversed; the Superior Court held that although Kappa Chapter was a social host, the risk of damage to a neighboring property as a result of Unterberger's intoxication was a foreseeable risk of Kappa Chapter's having provided him with alcohol. Unterberger sought review by this Court.

In this appeal we are called upon to determine whether, under *Congini v. Portersville*, supra, and *Orner v. Mallick*, 515 Pa. 132, 527 A.2d 521 (1987), authority exists for finding a cause of action against Bucknell University and/or Sigma Chi Fraternity.

Unterberger alleges that the Superior Court erred in refusing to extend the rationale of Congini to the instant case. He contends that the *Congini* requirement that an alleged defendant "knowingly furnished" intoxicants to a minor is to be accorded a broad interpretation. He therefore claims that the court should have sustained his cause of action against parties who allegedly should have known that alcohol was being provided for minors on their premises.

Bucknell and Sigma Chi, on the other hand, claim that the social host doctrine as established in *Congini* is no broader than is indicated by its plain language. They therefore submit that the lower courts were correct in finding no cause of action had been stated in appellant's allegation that appellees "should have known" alcohol was being provided for minors. For the following reasons, we agree with appellees' position, and we affirm the order of the Superior Court.

It is a fundamental principle of tort law there cannot be a valid claim sounding in negligence unless there is a duty upon the defendant in favor of the plaintiff which has been breached. The allegations as they refer to the University simply state appellant resided in a campus dormitory designated for the occupancy of freshmen, and the University employed Resident Advisors and a Resident Director who knew, or should have known, of this activity. The allegations do not contend that any agent, servant, employee or other personnel of Bucknell was in any way responsible for supplying, serving, dispensing or otherwise furnishing alcoholic beverages to appellant. As to the allegations relating to Sigma Chi, it is asserted that the fraternity was the reputed owner of the property where the party was held. There are no allegations the fraternity had actual knowledge of the activities allegedly occurring at the local chapter or of the ability of the national body to control said activities. Appellant herein would have us find Bucknell had a duty to supervise private social functions held on the University campus to ensure no one under the age of twenty-one consumed alcoholic beverages. They also contend the national fraternal organization should have a similar responsibility to monitor the activities of its Chapters.

Full appreciation of the impact of the step we are urged to take in this appeal requires a review of the development of this new cause of action. In *Manning v. Andy*, 454 Pa. 237, 310 A.2d 75 (1973), we expressly declined to use the provisions of the Liquor Code, 47 P.S. § 4-493(1), as creating a duty to support civil liability against a social host. Therein we were requested to find liability against an employee who became intoxicated during a party hosted by his employer for the employees, during which the employer "did furnish or supply intoxicating liquors or beverages which were consumed by . . . [the employee] . . . when he was in a state of visible intoxication." As a result of his state of intoxication, the employee was involved in an automobile accident resulting in injuries to the passenger in the employee's vehicle, a fellow employee. We dismissed this contention stating: We find no error in the trial court's dismissal of appellant's complaint. Only licensed persons engaged in the sale of intoxicants have been held to be civilly liable to injured parties. Appellant asks us to impose civil liability on nonlicensed persons like appellees, who furnish intoxicants for no remuneration. We decline to do so. While appellant's proposal may have merit, we feel that a decision of this monumental nature is best left to the legislature.

Our decision in *Manning* articulated a fundamental policy decision that the Court would not use the provisions of the Liquor Code as a basis for imposing civil liability on nonlicensed persons who furnish intoxicants without remuneration. This position was premised upon the view that such judgments are best left to the General Assembly.

In *Klein v. Raysinger*, 504 Pa. 141, 470 A.2d 507 (1983), this Court refused to recognize a common law social host liability for serving alcohol to a visibly intoxicated person, whom the host knew, or should have known, intends to drive a motor vehicle. Notwithstanding the language of the majority opinion which premised the decision on the common law rule that it was the consumption of alcohol rather than the furnishing of it that is the proximate cause of any subsequent occurrence, the majority declined, in *Klein*, to premise a duty based upon section 493(1) of the Liquor Code, as urged by Chief Justice Roberts in his dissent.

The one exception to the general rule that liability under the Liquor Code will not be applied to the social host was first announced in which was handed down on the same day as *Klein*. The basis for this exception has been explained by the Court in *Orner v. Mallick*, 515 Pa. 132, 527 A.2d 521 (1987). In that decision the Court stated: [I]n *Congini* we held that a social host "was negligent per se in serving alcohol to the point of intoxication to a person less than twenty-one years of age, and that they can be held liable for injuries proximately resulting from the minor's intoxication." In arriving at this conclusion we emphasized that in Pennsylvania "our legislature has made a legislative judgment that persons under twenty-one years of age are incompetent to handle alcohol," and we accepted that legislative judgment as defining a duty of care on the part of adults vis-a-vis their minor guests.

In *Congini*, an employee of Portersville Valve Company, Mark Congini, became intoxicated at the company's Christmas party but was given his car keys by a Portersville

agent despite his inebriated condition. He sustained severe permanent injuries in the resulting car accident, and he sued his employer for providing him with liquor in violation of the Crimes Code. The party was sponsored by the company and the alcohol was served by the agents and/or employees of the company. Under these facts, the Court found the company to be the host and deemed that it was negligent per se to serve alcohol to the point of intoxication to a person less than twenty-one years of age, thus justifying the imposition of liability for injuries proximately resulting from the minor's intoxication. Similarly, in *Orner v. Mallick*, supra, allegations were found to state a cause of action under the social host liability theory where the defendant was aware that minors would ingest the alcoholic beverages she provided at a high school graduation party in her home. In *Congini* and *Orner* the court employed the standard of "knowingly furnishing" intoxicating beverages to minors.

In the instant appeal it is argued that the "knowingly furnished" standard is overly restrictive; that we should adopt the standard "knew or should have known." In support of this contention, appellant points to two decisions by the Third Circuit, *Fassett v. Delta Kappa Epsilon*, 807 F.2d 1150, (3d Cir.1986), and *Macleary v. Hines*, 817 F.2d 1081 (3d Cir.1987), which appellant argues are a more expansive interpretation of our holdings in *Congini* and *Orner*. Appellant insists that the standard of "substantial assistance," as developed by the federal court, supports a finding that appellees can be held liable as social hosts upon the instant facts. However, appellant's reliance on these cases is misplaced. In *Fassett*, supra, the Third Circuit drew from our holding in *Congini* and from the Restatement of Torts, 2d, the requirement that a defendant in this type of case has rendered substantial assistance in the minor's consumption of alcohol. In *Macleary v. Hines*, that court reiterated the reasoning of *Fassett* and developed the rule that the social host must have "intentionally and substantially aided and encouraged the consumption of alcohol by a minor guest . . . ." We believe that that interpretation does not offend our case law but merely restates our position that a social host must have "knowingly furnished" alcoholic beverages to a minor. The "knowingly furnished" standard requires actual knowledge on the part of the social host as opposed to imputed knowledge imposed as a result of the relationship. In both cases the Third Circuit held as potential social hosts individuals who had participated in the planning and the funding of social events where alcohol was consumed by minors. In each instance the social host was aware of the degree of consumption by the minors. The Third Circuit correctly determined in both instances that we would not restrict the application of the social host theory to solely those instances where the defendant was alleged to have physically handed an alcoholic beverage to a minor. Upon the facts presented, we, too, would have found that defendants met the "knowingly furnished" requirement.

To the contrary, the instant facts support no such conclusion. As previously stated, there are no allegations that either the fraternity or the University was involved in the planning of these events or the serving, supplying, or purchasing of liquor. The fact that the functions were held on property which arguably was owned by appellees is of no consequence in light of appellees' detachment from the events in question. Appellees' conduct is insufficient to establish them as social hosts for the purpose of finding potential liability.

Appellant's view would have us impose upon appellees a custodial relationship with University students. Clearly, in modern times, it would be inappropriate to impose an in loco parentis duty upon a university. Instructive on this point are the observations of Judge Aldisert in *Bradshaw v. Rawlings*, 612 F.2d 135 (1979): [T]he statement that there is or is not a duty begs the essential question, which is whether the plaintiff's interests are entitled to legal protection against the defendant's conduct. . . . Thus, we may perceive duty simply as an obligation to which the law will give recognition in order to require one person to conform to a particular standard of conduct with respect to another person.

These abstract descriptions of duty cannot be helpful, however, unless they are directly related to the competing individual, public and social interests implicated in any case . . . .

Our beginning point is a recognition that the modern American college is not an insurer of the safety of its students. Whatever may have been its responsibility in an earlier era, the authoritarian role of today's college administrations has been notably diluted in recent decades. Trustees, administrators, and faculties have been required to yield to the expanding rights and privileges of their students.

It is equally clear appellee Sigma Chi fraternity is an inappropriate body from which to require the duty urged by appellant. By definition such organizations are based upon fraternal, not paternal relationships. National organizations do not have the ability to monitor the activities of their respective chapters which would justify imposing the duty appellant seeks. The national organization in fraternal groups has only the power to discipline an errant chapter after the fact. It does not possess the resources to monitor the activities of its chapters contemporaneously with the event. Fraternal organizations are premised upon a fellowship of equals; it is not a relationship where one group is superior to the other and may be held responsible for the conduct of the other. From this factual matrix, there is no basis in the relationship to expand the liability of the national body to include responsibility for the conduct of one of its chapters.

We thus conclude that the modern perception of the relationships between the University and their students, and the respective units of fraternal organizations is totally antithetical to the heightened duty we are here being importuned to accept. Moreover, the increased cost which would enure to such bodies could seriously impede the mission of these institutions which serve a vital role in the development of our youth. Neither are we persuaded these relatively rare, regrettable incidents require the dramatic response sought here. We empathize with the victims and their families in these tragic situations, but experience does not establish a statistical basis which justifies such a sweeping change of our existing law.

Accordingly, the Order of the Superior Court is affirmed.

Proximate Cause: When does an independent, intervening event break the chain of causation?

Tort liability requires a finding that the defendant's negligence was the proximate cause of the plaintiff's injury. Where an independent force intervenes after the defendant's negligent act and that force is so great as to supercede the negligence of the defendant, the defendant may be relieved of all responsibility for the harm to the plaintiff.

In the following case the plaintiff was killed when the roof of the defendant fell on him. The jury ruled in favor of the plaintiff, and the defendant appealed on the grounds that the trial judge should never have sent the case to the jury because there was evidence that despite possible negligent maintainence of the roof by the defendant, the harm was caused by a "cyclonic wind of an extraordinary intensity." In other words, the defendant argues that the wind constituted an intervening, superceding force which should legally the defendant of liability.

Just as in the field of philosophy, the law spends a great deal of energy dealing with the issue of "causation." Legally there is a tremendous difference between "cause in fact" and "proximate cause." A cause in fact is simply the existence of something that "but for" its existence, the result in question would not have occurred. For example, among the causes in fact for you reading this book may be the fact that you are taking a legal studies class, that you are a college student, that you are interested in such topics, and that the book is required by an instructor. If any one cause in fact had not occurred, you would not be reading the book. Obviously, there are an infinite number of causes in fact. Thus, the law, before finding liability, requires proximate cause, or "the moving cause, that cause which stands next to the effect." In the following Pennsylvania case the Court demonstrates how difficult it is to distinguish between these two types of causes.

Kimble v. Mackintosh Hemphill Company
359 Pa. 461 (1948)

Chief Justice Maxey delivered the opinion of the court.

Virginia M. Kimble, wife of decedent Harry P. Kimble, instituted two actions in trespass to recover damages sustained as a result of her husband's death allegedly caused by the roof of defendant's foundry falling upon him. The first suit was a "death action" brought by plaintiff to recover expenses and for financial loss suffered by her and her children. The second suit was a "survival action" whereby plaintiff as administratrix of decedent's estate sought to recover the present worth of Harry P. Kimble's future earnings. These were cumulative suits. The jury returned a verdict in favor of plaintiff as personal representative of decedent in the sum of $5,823.20 and in favor of plaintiff as administratrix of the estate of Harry P. Kimble in the sum of $10,000. Defendant's motion for judgment n.o.v. was denied. This appeal followed.

Defendant is the owner and operator of a plant in Midland, Pennsylvania, where it manufactures castings and other products. The main part of the plant consists of a foundry building 740 feet long, 150 feet wide, and 64 feet high, with a monitor roof. The framework of the roof consists of steel trusses to which are attached steel purlins extending from the comb of the roof to the eaves. Wooden nailers are bolted to the purlins by carriage bolts. Spiked to the purlins and extending lengthwise of the building is 2 x 6 wooden sheathing. Over this sheathing is 1 x 8 sheathing, laid crosswise of the underlying sheathing. The lower deck was spiked to the nailers in the purlins, and the top deck was nailed to the under deck.

Plaintiff's decedent was employed by the Treadwell Construction Company as a brakeman on a "dinkey" engine used to shift railroad freight cars. On November 14, 1944, the defendant company leased to the Construction Company trackage and operating rights over a railroad siding serving defendant's plant and connecting with the Pennsylvania Railroad Company. The Construction Company agreed to move defendant's freight cars to and from its plant. These cars were moved by the engine owned by the Construction Company and operated by its employees.

Mike Rubino, who operated the engine on which decedent was brakeman, testified that about 12:30 P.M. on March 31, 1945, he heard a "tearing or ripping of boards" as he sat in the cab watching Kimble, who had left the cab, walk the length of the engine in the direction of one Boice, defendant's employee, to receive instructions regarding the movement of defendant's cars. Kimble was struck by boards and timbers falling from the roof of defendant's foundry building. Decedent died an hour later from injuries thus sustained. When the crash came, Rubino was almost struck by a piece of board. He immediately got out of the cab to look for Kimble. He testified: "I didn't spend more than ten or fifteen seconds [looking for Kimble]. I had to run, because that other roof was coming down." The first section hit the engine and the second section "hit about ten or fifteen feet away, towards the east." About three seconds elapsed between the falling of the two sections, which measured 100 feet long, 22 feet wide and weighed 12 tons.

Defendant's liability is predicated upon its failure to maintain the roof in a safe condition and in failing to inspect, discover and correct its faulty condition. Witnesses testified that the lumber in the roof was rotted. James H. Cregar, a shipping helper at Treadwell, when asked "what was the condition of this part of roof lumber, and what not, that you found there on Harry Kimble?" replied: "Well, the roofing, why, it was good, but the other stuff was rotten." He described "the other stuff" as "heavy boards; it was rotten; there wasn't anything to it. That was one reason we didn't have any trouble getting it off of him." Charles O. Baker, another employee in the shipping department at Treadwell testified that "the lumber was in very poor condition. These two by fours that was bolted on to the purlins was very rotten, and the bolts had pulled right though the bolt holes, and the two by fours were rotted, and that is why they ripped loose in the roof. Otherwise, it wouldn't have come off like that; it probably would have busted up in different pieces, and part of it would have stuck to the roof --." When asked: "What was the condition of the two by fours, that you saw on the ground?" he answered: "Why, the bolt holes were rotted out of it."

Arthur Williams, construction superintendent for the Nellis Company, which had the job of repairing the foundry building for defendant company on April 1, 1945, made an examination of that part of the monitor from which the roof was gone and found it "in very bad shape. When questioned as to the condition of the nailers on that date, he said: "They were rotten." The bolts "were rusted away". As for the nailers and the tongue and groove in the part of the blown off roof, he stated "The nailers were not much account, at all." Mr. Williams was asked: "Could the condition of these nailers, and this tongue and groove, nailed to the nailers -- have been disclosed by an inspection from the interior of that building, on March 31st, 1945, or a reasonable length of time ahead of that date?" He replied: "Yes, it could." There was other testimony of the same purport.

Defendant disclaims liability alleging (1) that the proximate cause of the fatality was a cyclonic wind of an extraordinary intensity and that this relieved defendant from liability irrespective of whether or not its claimed antecedent negligence was a substantial factor in bringing about the harm; and (2) at the time of the accident, Kimble was either a licensee, engaged exclusively in the business of his employer, to whom no duty of inspection and repair was owed, or a statutory employee whose sole remedy was an action under the Workman's Compensation Act.

Defendant called a number of witnesses to prove that the winds at the time of decedent's injuries were of an unusually severe velocity such as had never occurred in that vicinity before and could not have been reasonably anticipated by it, and which ordinary skill and foresight could not guard against. An employee of defendant company, Erwin C. St. George, stated: "I heard a ripping and tearing sound, and an awful crash. So, we had been nervous, all morning, about the wind. It was an unusually high wind, to begin with, and the buildings around there had been swaying, and the trees, on the Crucible side were swinging back and forth, and I made everybody get out of there; and, when I got down there, I seen Mike running down." Charles H. Bryan, Chief of the Fire Department of East Liverpool, Ohio; Fred Hilditch, a resident of Midland for forty-one years; Delmar Manning, a fireman in East Liverpool for thirteen years, and Ira W. Cunningham, a policeman from East Liverpool for six years all testified that in their opinion the wind on that day was the strongest they had observed. W. S. Brontzman, employee of the U.S. Weather Bureau in charge of the Pittsburgh office, testified that at 12:28 P.M. the wind in Pittsburgh at the Allegheny County Airport (which is 30 to 35 miles from Midland) was

200

south-south-west a velocity of thirty-eight miles per hour with fifty mile per hour gusts. At 1:00 P.M. the wind was south-southwest velocity of 38 miles per hour. At 1:28 P.M. the wind was west-southwest velocity of forty-three miles per hour. In comparing the East Liverpool record with the Pittsburgh record, it seemed there was about an hour's difference, that is, what occurred in East Liverpool would occur in Pittsburgh about one hour later. Arthur J. LaComb, observer for the U.S. Weather Bureau stationed at the Airport at East Liverpool, Ohio, stated that at twelve-twenty seven the wind was west-southwest with a velocity of thirty-five miles with gusts up to sixty-five miles per hour.

Plaintiff's witnesses contradicted the evidence with regard to the severity of the wind on the date of the accident. Mr. Cregar was asked: "What was the condition of the weather, in Midland, about a quarter to one, or thereabouts, on the 31st day of March, 1945, in the vicinity of those two plants, Treadwell and Mackintosh Hemphill? He answered: "Well, in my judgment -- you are referring to the wind, is that what you are referring to? Q. All right; let's go to the wind. A. To my judgment, the wind wasn't any stronger, at the time I went out there, then it was several times that I have seen it around that vicinity, before." He added: "There was a high wind... I have seen winds just as heavy as that."

Defendant contends that the court erred in submitting the question of negligence to the jury and should have declared as a matter of law that an act of God was responsible for Kimble's death. Whether or not the fatal injury to plaintiff's decedent was due to an act of God or to defendant's negligence was a question of fact for the jury. The condition of the roof, the intensity of the wind on the date of the accident and on previous occasions at the same place were factual questions. The charge of the court was comprehensive and accurate. The trial judge charged: "It is the law that no person is answerable for what is termed an act of Providence, that is, if some visitation of Providence comes along that in our ordinary experience we are not... anticipating, then no one can be held to answer for that act, so that if the wind on this day was of such severity that it could not be reasonably anticipated by the Defendant, and that by reason of that wind, a part of the roof was blown off, then the Defendant would not be liable. However, if the storm were not of that severity, if it were only such a storm as occasionally happens, but is reasonably to be anticipated on occasions of every year or two, then that would not be an act of Providence... if they were such as were reasonably to be expected to occur occasionally, then such storms should be guarded against. An act of Providence as related to cases of injurious negligence is one against which ordinary skill and foresight is not expected to provide. Whether the injury in this case is attributable to such a cause or is the consequence of negligence is a question of fact for you to determine... Even if, with an extraordinary wind or storm there is concurring negligence, the party chargeable with it will be relieved from liability if the wind or storm is so overwhelming in character that it would of itself have produced the injury complained of, independently of negligence if there were negligence."

In *Sakach et ux. v. Antonoplos*, 298 Pa. 130, 148 A. 58, this Court said: "Where there is sufficient evidence upon which a jury may found a verdict, the question should be submitted to them and it is error in such case to grant a non suit: *Lehman v. Kellerman*, 65 Pa. 489. The test of the sufficiency of the evidence is whether the circumstances detailed are such as to satisfy reasonable and well-balanced minds that the accident resulted from the negligence of the defendant: *Ferry v. P.R.T.*, 232 Pa. 403, 406." On review, this Court "may not consider the veracity of the witnesses, the conflict of testimony, or the weight of the evidence. These are matters exclusively for the jury." Although individuals are not required to guard against every risk they conceive to the possible, they are under a legal duty to prevent hazards which they can forecast as possible. There must be antecedent probability. An act which may be prevented by the exercise of ordinary care is not an act of God since the latter is a casualty not due to or in any way contributed to by human agency. In *Pope v. Reading Company*, 304 Pa. 326, 156 A. 106, this Court said: "Negligence has been often and authoritatively defined as 'want of care under the circumstances'. The word 'circumstances' is comprehensive. It embraces the entire sum of the attendant facts, including the operation of the forces of nature so far as they bear upon or relate to the happening of the central event. A person is charged with ordinary knowledge of the workings of these forces, and his conduct, if it is to escape being stigmatized as

wanting in care, must conform to the normal workings of the forces of nature. At common law it was held that every man must have some knowledge 'of the quality of his beast' (1 Hale P.S. 430) and use appropriate means to keep that beast from harming people. Public welfare requires that this same salutary rule apply to the inanimate objects in a man's possession and subject to his intelligent control." In the instant case, defendant by using ordinary diligence and attention could have prevented the serious consequences which resulted from its failure to inspect and correct the faulty condition of the foundry roof. We said in *Fitzpatrick v. Penfield*, 267 Pa. 564, 109 A. 653: "High winds are not of infrequent occurrence, and this particular wind was termed an ordinary wind occurring three or four times in a year. It was not an unusual one and it was for the jury to find under all the evidence whether it was likely to have occurred and should have been provided against. We cannot say that the intervening cause was vis major. One who fails in his duty to remedy a defective or dangerous condition is liable for injuries resulting therefrom although the immediate cause of the injury is the wind. The casual connection is not broken and the original wrongdoer is liable for the injury sustained."

For any owner of a building to permit its roof and the roof's supports to become rotten and its nails or bolts rusted, as was described in this case is an omission of due care which amounts to negligence. In *Bisson v. John B. Kelly, Inc.*, 314 Pa. 99, 110, 170 A. 139, this Court said: "It is a primary social duty of every person to take thought and have a care lest his action result in injuries to others. This social duty the law recognizes and enforces, and for any injury resulting from any person's lack of elementary forethought, the law holds that person accountable. A normal human being is held to foresee those injuries which are the consequence of his acts of omission or commission which he, as a reasonable human being, should have foreseen. The question whether a person charged with negligence or negligent acts of omissions should have foreseen the injuries resulting from those acts or omissions is for the jury, if there is any credible evidence from which a reasonable conclusion can be drawn in support of the claim of neglect of duty." We also said: "All foreseeable dangers are to be considered in the solution of the problem whether the creation of the situation was a negligent act." In *McGlone v. William Angus, Inc.* et al., 248 N.Y. 197, 161 N.E. 469, Judge Crane of the Court of Appeals said: "Negligence is gauged by the ability to anticipate."

We agree with the conclusion of the court below that the decedent was a business visitor on defendant's premises and not a mere licensee or statutory employee. At the moment when the accident occurred, decedent was not engaged in the performance of defendant's business. It was testified that Frank Boice, defendant's shipping clerk, had indicated, by motion or otherwise, that he wanted to talk to decedent; that the engine was stopped and decedent god off for this purpose, but no orders had been given with respect to any work for defendant. Defendant had no authority or control over decedent at that time. Section 332, Restatement of Torts, states: "A business visitor is a person who is invited or permitted to enter or remain on land in the possession of another for a purpose directly or indirectly connected with business dealings between them." As to the duty of care required of the owner of premises to a business visitor, Title E, § 343, comment a, Restatement of Torts states: "Toward the business visitor, the possessor owes the additional duty to exercise reasonable care to make the land safe for the reception of his visitor or, at the least, to ascertain the actual condition of the land so that by warning the visitor thereon, he may give the visitor an opportunity to decide intelligently whether or not to accept the invitation or permission." Decedent does not come within the definition of "employee" as set forth in the Workman's Compensation Act, Act of June 2, 1915, P.L. 736, Art. I, sec. 104; June 4, 1937, P.L. 1552, sec. 1, 77 PS 22. In *McDonald v. Levinson Steel Company*, 302 Pa. 287, 153 A. 424, we said: "Where an owner contracts with another for work on his premises in furtherance of his regular business, the employment is an independent one, establishing the relation of contractee and contractor and not that of master and servant or statutory employer and employee, and a workman injured on that work is not entitled to compensation from the owner as statutory employer or master unless the relation of master and servant is established by the contract reserving control over the means of accomplishing the work as well as over the result to the accomplished:" (Citing cases) Treadwell agreed to shift defendant's railroad cars whenever desired by the latter. Frank J. Boice testified: "The boxcars were always placed, practically, by the Pennsylvania, on the outside, and, inside --." He was asked: "Now, when any cars were placed over on the siding, or in the Mackintosh Hemphill plant, how would they be placed, by whom?" "A. The Treadwell 'dinkey'…. Q. When you had a boxcar to be placed, how did you go about getting it placed? A. Well, sometimes they would come past, and I would stop them and ask them." When asked: "Whenever there was occasion to place a car inside the plant, and the 'dinkey' went by, once you had given the direction to place the car in the plant, did you have anything more to do with that shift?", he answered: "No, I just told them, and they would come in and take the car out and place it on the main line, or bring it from the main line in." Nowhere does the evidence establish the relationship of statutory employer-employee.

The judgment is affirmed.

Dissenting opinion by Mr. Justice Patterson.

The majority holds that appellant company was under a duty to anticipate, as within the realm of reasonable probability, a wind of such intensity and velocity as would tear loose a 12-ton section of roof, break it in half, and carry it over 100 feet. There is no proof of any similar occurrence and the judgment of the court below should be reversed for the reason the appellee has failed to prove a violation of duty owed to the decedent.

A section of a roof weighing 12 tons being ripped loose and carried through the air more than 100 feet is a possibility but certainly not a reasonable probability where there is no proof of a similar occurrence in or about the immediate vicinity. The event was not within the foreseeable risk of harm. The orbit of duty is determined by the reasonable foreseeable risk of harm. In *Irwin Savings & Trust Company v. Penna. R.R. Company*, 349 Pa. 278, 284, 37 A. 2d 432, Mr. Justice Drew, quoting from *South-Side Pass. Ry. Co. v. Trich*, 117 Pa. 390, 399, 11 A. 627, said: "'To impose such a standard of care as requires, in the ordinary affairs of life, precaution on the part of individuals against all the possibilities which may occur, is establishing a degree of responsibility quite beyond any legal limitations which have yet been declared.'"

Negligence does not of itself create liability. Back of the negligent act or failure to act must be sought and found a duty to the person injured, the observance of which would have averted or avoided the injury. Even though it be assumed that the roof was negligently maintained, the unusually high wind was an independent intervening force effecting an unforeseeable event for which appellant should not be held responsible. The duty extended only to reasonably foreseeable circumstances and injury which appellant could reasonably anticipate as a result of such negligence. The event which is the basis for the instant suit was clearly beyond the periphery of the duty.

The judgment of the court below should be reversed and here entered for appellant.

Credit Cards and Privacy: May a business ask a customer to provide any personal information when processing a credit card transaction?

For many years retail merchants have insisted that consumers provide them with a telephone number or other personal information when using a credit card. While collecting such information was never part of the contractual arrangements between merchants and the banks issuing the credit cards, merchants nonetheless often refused to honor credit cards without it. In 1992, the legislature explicitly prohibited this practice in most situations. The law also protects consumers by prohibiting merchants from writing credit card numbers on personal checks as a means of identification.

ACT NO. 1992 - 36

Prohibiting persons who accept credit cards for the transaction of business from requiring certain additional information from the credit cardholder; providing for enforcement of the act; and imposing civil penalties.

TEXT: The General Assembly of the Commonwealth of Pennsylvania hereby enacts as follows:

Section 1. Definitions.

The following words and phrases when used in this act shall have the meanings given to them in this section unless the context clearly indicates otherwise:

"Credit card." A device or instrument which entitles the holder to obtain money, goods, services or anything of value on credit.

"Person." An individual, corporation, trust, partnership, limited partnership, incorporated or unincorporated association or other entity.

Section 2. Requirement of information prohibited.

(a) General rule. No person who accepts credit cards for the transaction of business shall require the credit cardholder to write on the credit card transaction form, nor shall the person write or cause to be written on the form, any personal identification information, including, but not limited to, the credit cardholder's address or telephone number, that is not required by the credit card issuer to complete the credit card transaction: Provided, however, That the credit cardholder's address and telephone number may be required on the form where:

(1) the information is necessary for shipping, delivery or installation of purchased merchandise, warranties or service maintenance agreements, or for special orders;

(2) the person processes credit card transactions by mailing transaction forms to a designated bankcard center for settlement; or

(3) the information is necessary to comply with Federal or State law or regulations adopted pursuant thereto.

(b) Checks. No person shall, as a condition of acceptance of a check for the purchase of goods or services, as a means of identification or for any other purpose, require that a person presenting a check produce a credit card number for recordation. No person shall record a credit card number in connection with:

(1) a sale of goods or services in which a purchaser pays by check; or

(2) the acceptance of a check.

(c) Guaranteed checks. A credit card number may be requested and recorded as a condition for cashing a check where payment of the check is being guaranteed by the credit card issuer and all of the following conditions are met:

(1) the person requesting the card has agreed with the issuer to cash checks as a service to the issuer's cardholders;

(2) the issuer has agreed to guarantee cardholder checks cashed by that person; and

(3) the cardholder has given actual, apparent or implied authority for use of his card number in this manner and for this purpose.

(d) Construction of section. This section shall not be construed to prohibit a person from requesting a purchaser to display a credit card as identification. The only information concerning a credit card which may be recorded when a credit card is being used as identification and the creditcard issuer is not guaranteeing payment is the type, the issuer and the expiration date of the credit card. A credit card number may be requested and recorded as a condition for cashing a check where the credit card was issued by the person accepting the check. This section does not require acceptance of a check whether or not a credit card is presented.

Section 3. Injunctive relief.

Whenever the Attorney General or a district attorney has reason to believe that any person is violating or is about to violate section 2 and that proceedings would be in the public interest, the Attorney General or a district attorney may bring an action in the name of the Commonwealth against the person to restrain, by temporary or permanent injunction, violations of section 2.

Section 4. Assurances of voluntary compliance.

In the administration of this act, the Attorney General may accept an assurance of voluntary compliance with respect to any method, act or practice deemed to be violative of this act from any person who has engaged or was about to engage in the method, act or practice. Any assurance shall be in writing and be filed with the court. The assurance of voluntary compliance shall not be considered an admission of violation for any purpose. Matters thus closed may at any time be reopened by the Attorney General for further proceedings in the public interest, pursuant to section 3.

Section 5. Civil penalties.

(a) Violation of injunction. Any person who violates the terms of an injunction issued under section 3 or any of the terms of an assurance of voluntary compliance duly filed in court under section 4 shall forfeit and pay to the Commonwealth a civil penalty of not more than $250 for the first offense and $ 1,000 for the second or any subsequent offense. For the purpose of this section, the court issuing an injunction or in which an assurance of voluntary compliance is filed shall retain jurisdiction and the cause shall be continued, and, in such cases, the Attorney General or the appropriate district attorney, acting in the name of the Commonwealth, may petition for recovery of civil penalties and any other equitable relief deemed needed or proper.

(b) Willful violations of act. In any action brought under section 3, if the court finds that a person is willfully using or has willfully used a method, act or practice declared unlawful by section 2, the Attorney General or the appropriate district attorney, acting in the name of the Commonwealth, may recover, on behalf of the Commonwealth, a civil penalty not exceeding $ 200 per violation, which civil penalty shall be in addition to other relief which may be granted under this act.

Section 6. Effective date.

This act shall take effect in 60 days.